Seeing Dark Things

Seeing Dark Things

The Philosophy of Shadows

Roy Sorensen

OXFORD
UNIVERSITY PRESS

OXFORD
UNIVERSITY PRESS

Oxford University Press, Inc., publishes works that further
Oxford University's objective of excellence
in research, scholarship, and education.

Oxford   New York
Auckland   Cape Town   Dar es Salaam   Hong Kong   Karachi
Kuala Lumpur   Madrid   Melbourne   Mexico City   Nairobi
New Delhi   Shanghai   Taipei   Toronto

With offices in
Argentina   Austria   Brazil   Chile   Czech Republic   France   Greece
Guatemala   Hungary   Italy   Japan   Poland   Portugal   Singapore
South Korea   Switzerland   Thailand   Turkey   Ukraine   Vietnam

Copyright © 2008 by Oxford University Press, Inc.

Published by Oxford University Press, Inc.
198 Madison Avenue, New York, New York 10016
www.oup.com

First issued as an Oxford University Press paperback, 2011

Oxford is a registered trademark of Oxford University Press

Library of Congress Cataloging-in-Publication Data
Sorensen, Roy A.
Seeing dark things : the philosophy of shadows / Roy Sorensen.
    p. cm.
Includes bibliographical references and index.
ISBN 978-0-19-979713-4
1. Perception (Philosophy). 2. Shades and shadows.
3. Causation. I. Title.
B828.45.S66 2007
121'.34—dc22   2007001267

Printed in the United States of America
on acid-free paper

To
my youngest son,
Zachary Nicholas Sorensen,
who brightens my mornings
and warms my days.

But mark, madam, we live amongst riddles and mysteries—the
most obvious things, which come in our way, have dark sides,
which the quickest sight cannot penetrate into; and even the
clearest and most exalted understandings amongst us find ourselves
puzzled and at a loss in almost every cranny of nature's works.
—Laurence Sterne (1713–68)

Acknowledgments

This book was made possible, indeed actual, by the absence of teaching obligations funded by the National Endowment for the Humanities.

The first incarnation of this book was a seminar on perception I taught at MIT in 2003. I thank the participants for their comments and suggestions. I also thank two referees from Oxford University Press. The book changed significantly after their helpful remarks.

Six of the fourteen chapters incorporate previously published material. Chapters 1 and 2 include parts of "Seeing Intersecting Eclipses," *Journal of Philosophy* 96 (1999): 25–49. Chapter 3 contains most of "The Disappearing Act," *Analysis* 66/4 (2006): 319–25. Chapter 4 is based on "Spinning Shadows," *Philosophy and Phenomenological Research* 72/2 (2006): 345–65. Chapter 6 contains much of "Para-reflections," *British Journal for the Philosophy of Science* 54 (2003): 93–101, and chapter 13 is based on "We See in the Dark," *Nous* 38/3 (2004): 456–80. I thank the respective journals and publishers for permission to republish this material.

Contents

Illustrations

Seeing Dark Things

Introduction

Magicians have a mind-reading trick. Pick a triplet of letters from the following list:

    EQG   OBH   EBO   BQH   EBQ   QRC

Now look at the list at the end of this introduction on page 19. Your triplet is missing!

You saw the absence of your triplet. What you overlooked were five other absent triplets. The magician conjured the absence of your triplet by conjuring the absence of all the triplets (and then masking their absence by substituting look-alike triplets).

Seeing the absence of a triplet is not the failure to see the triplet. You failed to see the other triplets but did not see their absences. These overlooked absences are not creatures of your expectations. They were there before you opened this book.

When the nearly blind cartoonist James Thurber consulted an eye doctor, he was told that he had lost the "apparatus of vision." Based on the received wisdom of eye specialists, Thurber should be completely blind. Yet with the help of glasses, Thurber could discern enough to sketch pictures for *The New Yorker*. What was going on? The doctor replied, "You can call it God or extra sensory perception. . . . Seriously though, I can't believe God wanted you to do those drawings."

Like Thurber's eye specialist, my training makes me surprised about how much is seen. I have been taught that only physical objects are seen. This explains why no one has seen the equator. I have also been taught the causal theory of perception: something is seen only by virtue of being a cause of what is seen. This explains why you see the front of this page but not its back.

The ancient Greeks extracted classical optics from these modest principles. If you draw straight lines between your eye and the surfaces of the nearest physical objects, you get Euclid's comprehensive answer to the question of what you see. The causal theory of perception delivers the architecture of your visual field.

One objection to the causal theory is that we seem to see things that are not physical objects: shadows, holes, the sky, and so on. These are common in everyday life. Many are in your home. You can photograph them. A second difficulty for the causal theory of perception is that some visible physical objects do not seem to cause our visual experience of them. Indeed, they appear to be rendered visible by an *absence* of a causal connection. Consider the black letters on this page. You see them in virtue of the light they absorb, not the light they reflect. The more light they absorb, the better you see them!

Or consider the shadow your hand casts on this page. Shadows do not even absorb light. Shadows are absences of light. They cannot owe their visibility to any positive action on their part.

Despite the very different ways they become visible, the shadow and the letters on this page have the same color: black. Black seems to be the most opaque of colors. Yet you *see through* the shadow to the page. So there are two things in your line of sight: you see both the front "thing" *and* the back thing. But how can something be transparent black? You can see through a black mesh screen because of the gaps. A homogeneous shadow has no holes; a shadow is itself a hole in the light.

Since the shadow is in front of the page, you are seeing an absence of light in front of you. Yet you still manage to see the page by virtue of the light it reflects into your eyes. Moreover, you manage to see the letters on the page by virtue of the light they prevent from reaching your eyes. How can these letters stop what has already been blocked by the shadow caster?

My focus is on things that are literally dark: crows, silhouettes, shadows, and some esoteric dark phenomena such as the destructive interference of light waves. Nevertheless, the perception of absences is a phenomenon general to all the senses. For instance, chapter 5 has a section on *touching* holes. And I think the most profound perception of an absence is hearing silence (which is the subject of chapter 14).

So some of the phenomena discussed in this book are merely negative. The hole in a doughnut need not be dark. Other negative phenomena, such as silence and the cold, are invisible. Negative phenomena present difficulties that are continuous with literally dark things.

The puzzle of seeing dark things crystallized in the seventeenth century. Isaac Newton settled the issue of whether darkness is a separate force on a par with light. He demonstrated that darkness is the absence of light.

John Locke got busy reconciling the privational nature of dark things with the causal aspect of his theory of perception. According to Locke, we see things indirectly by means of the ideas that those objects cause. Your experience of Westminster Abbey is a representation of Westminster Abbey by virtue of it being caused by Westminster Abbey. Anything that fails to act on our minds through our eyes is invisible to us. But then, how can we see things that do not reflect light? Locke answers:

> The idea of black is no less positive to [one's] Mind, than that of White, however the cause of that Colour in the external Object, may be only a privation. . . . And thus one may truly be said to see Darkness. For supposing a hole perfectly black, from whence no light is reflect, 'tis certain one may see the Figure of it, or it may be painted. (1690, bk. 2, chap. 8, sec. 3, 6)

Ordinary talk of preventions and omissions supports Locke's beliefs that some absences are causes. Scientists also make such remarks as "Tay-Sachs disease is caused by the absence of the enzyme hexosaminidase A." Engineers publishing in *The International Journal of Fracture* even study absences caused by other absences, as when the spread of a crack is halted by a hole at its leading edge.

Absences do not transmit energy or do anything else positive, so many philosophers reject causation by absences. This metaphysical suspicion partly explains why many causal theorists disagree with Locke. To pick a recent representative, Gerald Vision (1997, 256 fn. 1) agrees that it is tempting to say you can see a doorway to a dark room by virtue of its contrast with its surroundings. But suppose you approach the doorway and then pass through the threshold. Do you stop seeing once you lose the contrast? Gerald Vision thinks you *infer* that it is dark from your inability to see. Likewise, you make out the location of the doorway from your inability to see it. You see *that* there is an unilluminated doorway but do not see the unilluminated doorway. Or so says the well-named Professor Vision.

Blindingly bright light shows that we do not always infer darkness from an inability to see. The *Krak Des Chevaliers* (Castle of Knights) in Syria has a covered passageway. When visitors travel through the long stretch of darkness, they emerge suddenly into daylight. The passageway was designed to dazzle invaders.

When a theory of perception predicts that you cannot see something that you do see, then you ought not to believe the theory. But I think friends and foes of the causal theory are too hasty in their assessment of what the theory implies. Recent work on privations and causation by omission supports John Locke's original response. Indeed, I think the causal theory of perception, when unencumbered by a metaphysical outlook skewed in favor of positive things, makes bold, correct predictions about our perception of dark things. Whereas most causal theorists avoid the dark, I am drawn to it.

I disagree with theorists who wish to sidestep the anomalies of darkness by dropping the causal requirement for perception. They think the causal requirement is motivated only by representative realism—the theory that we see physical objects by means of intermediate entities: sense data. Everybody agrees that the causal requirement is useful in explaining which sense data represent which objects. However, theories that dispense with sense data are thought to have no need for the causal condition. I think these acausal theories exchange a penetrating, empirical picture of perception for paper-thin conceptual cartography. This becomes evident when "conceptual truths" about vision are refuted by surprising consequences welling up from the causal theory of perception.

Different dark things pose different challenges. A yellow stork silhouetted in the dawn light looks black but not in virtue of its pigment (fig. I.1). The bird watcher sees the stork by virtue of the light it *blocks*. He may not be in a position to *assert* that he saw a stork. Storks and cranes look alike. The bird watcher would like to enter the stork on his Life's List of observed birds. But the Audubon Society requires perceptual knowledge of the bird. The disappointed bird watcher does have the consolation of knowing that he is either seeing a stork or seeing a crane. He can see a bird without knowing which kind of bird it is.

Normally, we get the best views of objects when they are illuminated from the front. We tend to model vision in terms of these good lighting

Figure I.1 Stork silhouette

conditions. Indeed, our visual system operates under the assumption that the light is coming from above—as if the sun were shining down on the observer's head. This is evident in our perception of objects as being concave or convex. Figure I.2 bulges out like a hill. If the light is coming from above, then the dark area must be a shadow cast by a peak. When you turn the picture upside down, the figure looks like a crater. If the light is coming from above, the darkened region must be a shadow of the surface facing closest to the sun.

Curiously, this convex–concave gestalt switch can also be triggered by standing on your head—even when outdoors and the sun is obviously *below* your inverted head (Ramachandran 1990). The visual system proceeds indirectly, tracking the light source orientation by retinal orientation. Deciduous trees practice similar indirection. They are designed to shed leaves with the approach of cold weather. But they actually shed leaves in accordance with the declining length of the days. Consequently, the trees drop leaves even in an unseasonably warm autumn and do not adjust their schedule to the early onset of cold weather. Just as it is easier for the tree to measure daylight than temperature, it is easier for the relevant module of the visual system to measure the orientation of an object relative to the retina. The visual system is a bag of tricks, individually crude but collectively reliable in the types of environments they evolved.

The principles that work well for frontlit conditions are turned around by the backward case of silhouettes. In addition to exposing a weakness in the brain's heuristics for object identification, silhouettes force a correction of Euclid's optics. A complete geometry of the visual

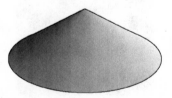

Figure I.2 Convex/concave cone

field must include backlit objects. In chapter 1, these issues are broached by means of a riddle about a double eclipse. Indeed, most of the issues in this book spring from *visual* riddles; this book is philosophy for the eye.

Chapter 2, "Seeing Surfaces," develops my solution. I treat silhouettes as *positive* features of reality. In particular, the silhouette of an opaque object is its *back* surface. This absorption layer becomes visible only in backlit conditions. Given this analysis, Euclid was right to emphasize the primacy of surfaces in vision. He was just too inflexible in his choice of which surface is involved.

Chapters 3, 4, and 5 leave silhouettes behind and concentrate on shadows. Whereas the surface involved in silhouetted seeing is a physical thing, the surfaces of shadows are not material things. The counterintuitive consequences of their lack of materiality are showcased in chapter 3 via a riddle called the "Disappearing Act."

Shadows are far stranger than silhouettes. Shadows are not parts of their material casters. They must be caused by material things but can (briefly) survive the destruction of their casters. Although generally relegated to a supporting role in constructing the visual scene, shadows can step into the spotlight of attention. Shadows are what we look for on a hot summer day.

Fascination with shadows begins in infancy. We innately gravitate toward principles for understanding objects and often extrapolate them to shadows. Shadows are treated as honorary physical objects.

Developmental psychologists regard these overextensions as clues to "folk physics." Just as linguists figure out the innate grammar of tense constructions from the child's use of "runned" and "goed," psychologists hope to figure out the scheme for objecthood and causality from mistakes children make about shadows. Shadows are the irregular verbs of object perception.

Children rapidly acquire a folk physics that allows them to predict the behavior of middle-size objects fairly accurately. (Otherwise, toddlers would not be intrigued by magic tricks.) Children are much slower to acquire a comparable understanding of shadows—even though the shadows almost always accompany objects. Surprisingly, many children younger than nine cannot predict on which side of an object a shadow will fall when told where the light source will be. This ignorance survives the attention children lavish on shadows. Children are opinionated about shadows and emotionally involved with them. They commonly believe shadows emanate from their bodies. (When asked to make their shadows move around a room, six-year-old children rotate their bodies.) Children believe that shadows persist in the dark and are made up of a smoky substance. Shadows give a black eye to the empiricist.

Adults have a better operational grasp of shadows. But their performance still varies with the task. When reaching for an object, they exploit its shadow to perfect their grasp. Yet in many other circumstances, adults ignore shadows as noise. One explanation of this on-again/off-again sensitivity is that shadow information is like scaffolding that builders must eventually remove (Rensink and Cavanagh 2004). More specifically, the observer first processes shadows at a preattentive level to ascertain his spatial relationship with objects, their shapes and color, plus the object's relationship to other objects. After this information is used to construct the visual scene of *objects*, facts about the shadow become an unsightly nuisance. Shadow facts could be confused as facts about the caster. Patients with right posterior lesions have difficulty recognizing ordinary objects containing shadows (Warrington 1982). One possible explanation is a breakdown of censorship.

Object–shadow confusion is demonstrable in two-tone pictures (Moore and Cavanagh 1998). We use continuity of texture to distinguish illumination changes from changes in albedo. (Albedo is the ratio of the light reflected by an object to amount of light that reaches its surface. A perfect reflector has an albedo of 1. A perfectly black object has an albedo of 0. Venus has a high albedo of 0.6, while the moon has a surprisingly low albedo of 0.07.) Blurry vision also undermines the cue of texture continuity. This explains why some visual searches are easiest at noon when there are no shadows.

To prevent object–shadow conflation and to reduce clutter, the visual system cleans up the site. Skeletal frameworks are disassembled, the blueprints discarded, and the detritus of creation are swept away. In short, shadow information is dumped before becoming available to consciousness—use it, then lose it!

The destruction of this unconscious analysis of shadows does not destroy the shadows. They are still out there available to *conscious* inspection. For instance, we notice that sometimes it is easier to measure an object by measuring its shadow. That is how Thales is said to have measured the height of the pyramids. Surveyors develop the trigonometry to perfect this substitution. But conscious analysis of shadows is slow, effortful, and error prone. For accessible, middle-sized objects, it is usually more efficient to exploit other clues. Convenience is king.

Painting a shadow across distinct color borders is very difficult. Artists prefer to provide information about objects through perceptual cues that are easier to render. The geometry of shadows is known in principle but challenging to put into practice. Most paintings that include shadows are not optically realistic (Casati 2003, 159–66). Why bother if your audience is likely not to notice? (The story is different for movie shadows: viewers rely heavily on shadow *movement* to assess object movement. Since inconsistencies pop out in a glaring way, movie editing is meticulous.)

The doctoring of photographs is commonly exposed by impossible shadows and by impossible absences of shadows. All objects are natural sundials, so outdoor shadows contain clues about the time (given the place) and the place (given the time). If Robert Perry had really reached the North Pole, the shadows in the commemorative photograph would have been much longer.

Our scatterbrain processing of shadows is not limited to our failures to exploit information contained in shadows. There are also errors of commission in which we make erroneous inferences from shadows and the absence of shadows. Consider the conspiracy theorists who argue that the Apollo moon landings were a hoax. They point out "impossible shadows" in NASA's own photographs. Their accusations often articulate much common sense about how shadows behave (though not enough astronomy).

Our unsteadiness with shadows does not prevent shadows from being well understood at the mathematical level. Alexius Mobius perfected the geometry of shadow appearances in the nineteenth century. He treats shadows as entities in their own right. Mobius describes the movement of each shadow by appealing to changes in its geometrical center of gravity.

Chapter 4 concerns the movements of shadows. By Mobius's account, the prisoners in Plato's cave should be experts in shadow movements because they have all the data they need. However, I maintain that the movement of shadows must be understood relationally in terms of the movements of their casters. Perceptually, their movements are linked. Shadow motion strongly influences attributions of motion to their casters. This has been demonstrated with computer graphics that, ironically, rely on the geometry of shadows that Mobius developed. His geometrical approach does not cede enough movement to shadows.

I highlight my disagreement with Mobius with a riddle: if a spinning sphere casts a shadow, does the shadow also spin? Most people answer no. Mobius's theory offers a principle to back their answer: rotation does not involve change in the geometrical center of gravity. I disagree; round shadows *can* spin. The causal themes of the first three chapters commit me to a blocking theory of shadows. Shadows are followers of the objects that cast them. Parts of the follower correspond to parts of the leader; consequently, motion of the caster's parts accounts for motions of the shadow's parts. Thus, the riddle about spinning shadows serves as the point of departure for a general investigation into the nature of shadow movement. A comprehensive theory of motion will encompass all moving things, not just physical objects. I conclude with a discussion of how the dynamic aspects of shadows impose subtle constraints on other puzzles about shadows.

The final chapter on shadows focuses on their untouchability. George Berkeley traced the spatiality of sight to our sense of touch. His idea is that we learn to translate the mosaic of colors as signs of distance, shape, size, and orientation. We do not directly perceive distance. I argue that shadows are counterexamples to the hegemony of the hand. Shadows are in the landscape but are available only to the eye.

Next come four short chapters devoted to phenomena that are confused with shadows: para-reflections, para-refractions (which include shadowgrams, shadow bands, and the astronomer's "black drop"), filtows, Mach bands, and sundry holes in the light that form by means other than light blockage. For instance, if you fold an overhead transparency, the crease seems to produce a dark line. But this cannot be a shadow because nothing is blocking the light. Instead, the crease redirects light waves into each other so that they cancel out.

Physics textbooks rarely correct overgeneralizations about shadows. Indeed, the authors use "shadow" as loosely as laymen. They extend "shadow" to any pocket of darkness. For instance, the Fresnel ring is called a shadow even though it arises from diffraction.

This sloppiness about "shadow" spills over into sloppiness about other terminology. Physics textbooks describe the undulating dark lines seen at the bottom of shadow tanks as waves—even though the undulating dark bands are not caused by light blockage and even though these "waves" do not carry energy.

Sloppy usage is usually harmless. How often does it matter whether refraction is called reflection? Rarely. But this loose usage did handicap Aristotle's explanation of the rainbow. The distinction between reflection and refraction does matter if you are interested in describing or manufacturing lenses. And it matters much if you are stating the principles of optics.

How often does it matter whether a dark mark on a surface is called a shadow? Not often. Indeed, physics is sometimes helped by the loose usage. Science museums feature phosphor screens that capture the visitor's shadow for about ten seconds (after a bright flash). Calling the temporary image a shadow makes the phenomenon wondrous. Marvels increase public support for science.

Since I am developing a theory of shadows, I distinguish shadows from a variety of phenomena that physicists are content to lump together as shadows. I think their broad usage leads them to neglect dark phenomena common in daily life. For instance, the image of your pupil in a mirror is not a *reflection* of your pupil. I call these "para-reflections" and examine their significance in chapter 6.

The visual system distinguishes among types of shadows. For instance, figure I.3 is ambiguous between a shadow attached to a cube or a shadow cast by a flat black square.

There is practical importance in distinguishing shadows from other negative phenomena. Large animals must be especially mindful where they tread. Cattle are inclined to interpret shadows as holes—better safe than sorry! This reluctance to move across shadows is magnified by their superior contrast sensitivity. Cattle can see shadows that are invisible to ranchers (Grandin and Johnson 2005, 43).

Lessons about shadows are sometimes best learned through the eyes of animals. The practical value of perceptual empathy is a theme of Plutarch's anecdotes. King Philip of Macedon refused to buy a beautiful horse named Bucephalus. None of his grooms could control the beast. His ten-year-old son Alexander then asked to try his skill. Although fearing for his son's safety, King Philip reluctantly agreed. The prince turned the agitated horse to face the sun—Alexander had noticed that Bucephalus was frightened by his shadow. Calmed, the horse obediently showed off his paces, to the loud applause of the court. Philip kissed his son and said, "Seek another kingdom that may be worthy of your abilities, for Macedonia is too small for you."

There is a statue of Alexander riding Bucephalus in Thessaloniki, Macedonia. The statue looks bottom-lit because we construe the topside grit as attached shadows. Matter can pass as shadow.

Figure I.3 Attached shadow versus cast shadow

And shadow may pass as matter. Consider a hostess who tries to sponge up a stain on her dress. She is relieved that the "stain" jumps up on the napkin.

Surprisingly, many thinkers regard shadows as positive phenomena. In chapter 9, I focus on the belief that bodies of filtered light are shadows. Johann Wolfgang von Goethe invited his readers to observe "colored shadows" by candlelight at dawn. As the sunlight begins to compete with the candlelight, there will be double-shadows formed from the two sources of illumination. One of the shadows will be bluish. Goethe took this to be evidence that colors are composed of mixtures of Light and Darkness. I review Goethe's campaign against Isaac Newton's theory that darkness is merely the privation of light. After all, if shadows are absences of light, then all shadows should be black.

Colored shadows had a persisting influence on impressionist painters such as Claude Monet. But in vision science, colored shadows were buried in the footnotes along with Goethe. Edwin Land, founder of the Polaroid Corporation, inadvertently disinterred colored shadows. He produced spectacular colored shadows of virtually every hue. He used these stunning demonstrations to support his Retinex theory of vision. After reviewing some of the classic demonstrations of red, green, and blue shadows, I explain why Goethe thought colored shadows refuted Isaac Newton's theory of color. Because much of Newton's account of shadows continues to be held by contemporary physicists and color scientists, I shall argue that their talk of "colored shadows" concedes too much to Goethe. To be consistent, color scientists should characterize shadows in the guarded way that physicists ascribe properties to vacuums, cold spots, and other privational phenomena. Just as flying foxes are not foxes (they are big bats), colored shadows are not shadows; they are bodies of filtered light.

Philosophers and physicists often assume that they can reduce shadows to patterns of illumination. However, we use shadows to establish illumination levels—and to establish shapes, and movement, and relationships between objects and the rest of the environment. Talk of shadows is not used to summarize the scene before us; shadows are used to construct the visual field. Efforts to paraphrase away shadows are circular. What is metaphysically secondary can be perceptually primary.

Just as there is ideological pressure to discount the contributions that illegal immigrants make to the American economy, there is metaphysical pressure to keep the contributions of shadows "off the books." Philosophers and physicists alike have a strong conviction that reality is positive. They think a negative statement such as "There is a permanent absence of light in the Shackleton crater" is really about where the light is rather than where it is not. This intuition has many manifestations. One is the doctrine that negative truths are reducible to positive truths. Hence, negative truths are redundant: reality can be described with a long conjunction of positive statements. After the positive truths are accounted for, nothing further needs to be added. Additionally, it is widely felt that negative statements are subjective; there are negative states of affairs only when there are expectations. A student can be absent only when school authorities presume that the student will be present. The subjectivity of the absence is underscored by its egocentricity; the student is not *here* (but has not vanished from the universe). We infer that the student is absent from positive features of the classroom. Talk of absences is disguised talk of presences.

I am a reluctant apostle of negative metaphysics. In a splintery slide against the natural grain of human thought, I conclude all of the above claims are false. The irreducibility of the negative truths to positive truths was eventually conceded by those who were most invested in the reducibility. When the founder of logical atomism, Bertrand Russell, admitted at Harvard that negative facts exist, he claims that a riot nearly ensued. If there is any reduction to be achieved, it will run from positive truths to negative truths. (From a logical point of view, it is more promising to analyze positive truths as the negations of negative truths.)

Aversion to negative things lies behind the anomalies of the color black. Other colors are seen by virtue of light stimulation. The light itself can be colored but cannot be black. Many are tempted to deny that black is a color. At any rate, most color scientists and philosophical commentators on color deny that shadows are black. At best, say they, shadows are *dark*. I defend the blackness of shadows in chapter 11 and argue that blackness is due to many different causes beyond the indiscriminate absorption of light.

Chapter 12 deals the role of negative information in perception. Do people who see in black and white see black and white? Most people assume that totally color-blind people see the whiteness of their shirts, the grayness of their trousers, and the blackness of their shoes. My thesis is that only those who see in color see black and white. Only they can perceive the absence of hues essential to the achromatic colors. My main premise is that some positively equivalent representations have unequal amounts of negative information.

Do we need light to see? In chapter 10, I argue that the black experience of a man in a perfectly dark cave is a representation of an absence of light, not an absence of representation. There is certainly a difference between his perceptual knowledge and that of his blind companion. Only the sighted man can tell whether the cave is dark just by looking. But perhaps he is merely inferring darkness from his failure to see. To avoid ambiguity, we need to focus on cases in which belief plays no role. After this and other safeguards are in place, I make my case that we do see the darkness. (So I am siding with *general* versions of the causal theory—e.g., Michael Tye's [1982; 2002, 157, 168 fn. 11]—that do not restrict the type of causal relation to that light transmission.) In terms of basic information, we see about as much as we do when the lights are on. Depending on what has been seen before and after, we may even see ordinary objects. I conclude that we do see in total darkness.

Not only do we see the absence of light, we see absences within that absence. In 1719, Giovanni Battista Morgagni conducted an experiment to verify that phosphenes are subjective phenomena. While in complete darkness he pressed his eye to create "pressure figures" under the supervision of an assistant. Although a very bright light appeared to Morgagni, his assistant saw no light (Grusser and Hagner 1990, 72–73).

Chapter 14, "Hearing Silence," widens the role of absences in experience. Much of what I say about the perception of total darkness applies to the perception of silence. However, hearing silence does not involve a sensation of silence. Whereas there is a color of darkness (black), there is no sound of silence. Nevertheless, there is a qualitative aspect of hearing silence. When someone is enjoying the silence of an anechoic chamber, he is both perceiving an absence of sound and introspecting an absence of auditory sensations.

The last chapter is conservative in that I defend the prevailing view that sound is a wave in a medium. Recent critics concede that the wave theory conforms to both common sense and acoustics. But they complain that the wave theory conflicts with the fact that sounds have specific locations; the voice I hear is down the hall rather than all around me in the air. The sound waves are heading toward me but the voice is not. Robert Pasnau says the sound is the vibration of an object. The sound is a property of the object like the object's color. I defend common sense and acoustics by the traditional method of semantic ascent. I diagnose the appearance of inconsistency as a misunderstanding of how we talk about the locations of wave phenomena.

This book is, on the whole, conservative because I defend a simple, fairly well entrenched theory of perception—the causal theory. However, I use novel means to defend the status quo against objections. I appeal to absences. Although familiar, the problematic features of absences have bedeviled philosophers since Parmenides. Philosophers have been justified in their efforts to avoid them—as long as there was hope of avoiding them. Since absences now strike me and many other philosophers as here to stay, I have quit the business of expelling them and gone into the business of employing them.

Jean Paul Sartre thinks of absences as mind-dependent constructions of pure nothingness. The absence of Pierre at the café depends on Sartre's disappointment at not seeing him. Without human beings, there would be no nothingness. I am more sympathetic to C. B. Martin (1996) and Boris Kukso (2006). They are naturalistic philosophers who think absences are objective, causally relevant, and perceptible and have locations in space and time. However, they are still top-down thinkers:

> Non-being or absence is not in the usual case meant to be pure noth-
> ing. It is the absence or non-existence of some entity or entities that is
> quite compatible with the presence of existence of other entities at the
> same place and time. Non-being is not a form of being any more than
> being is a form of non-being. Yet the fittings, the warp and woof of
> the presence and absence of something are essential and complemen-
> tary for one another. Indeed, the concept of an edge is concept of the
> limit of where something is and where something isn't. Presences and
> absences are correlative and both are involved in destroying, removing
> and being at a distance from things. (Martin 1996, 64)

I feel an impulse to agree. But what would I be agreeing to? On the
one hand, I believe that my hand casts a shadow, that there is a crack
in the Liberty Bell, and that one of the biggest holes on Earth is an
open pit copper mine in Bingham Canyon, Utah. On the other hand,
it feels paradoxical to say that absences exist—but no better to say that
absences do not exist.

This is a common philosophical predicament. St. Augustine remarks that he knows what time is—except when someone asks him
to explain what time is. On reflection, it seems paradoxical to say time
exists—but no better to say that time does not exist. The same can
be said for space and numbers and ideas.

Do material objects exist? George Berkeley agreed that tables and
trees and squirrels exist. But he argued that "material object" is an
incoherent term invented by philosophers. I have learned good replies
to some of his objections. But Berkeley would discover many faults in
my efforts to explain the general nature of material objects.

I do not attempt a general account of absences. My approach is
bottom-up. Just as fruit flies are instructive research subjects for geneti-
cists, shadows are instructive research subjects for metaphysicians. Shadows are easy to observe, easy to create, and easy to manipulate. Other
absences are invisible, abstract, and cognitively demanding. Before we run
with the likes of Sartre and Martin Heidegger, let us walk with shadows.

EQC   OBA   ERO   BOH   QRG

I

The Eclipse Riddle

I am viewing a double eclipse of the sun (which looks exactly like the single eclipse depicted in fig. 1.1). Traveling east is the heavenly body Far. Traveling west and nearer to me is the smaller body Near. Near is close enough to exactly compensate for its smaller size with respect to shadow formation. Near and Far look the same size from my vantage point. (Note how Near and Far have the same apparent diameter in fig. 1.2.) When Near falls exactly under the shadow of Far, it is as if one of these heavenly bodies has disappeared. Do I see Near or Far? Common sense answers that I see Near rather than Far: Near is an opaque body that completely blocks my view of Far. Since I see something, I see Near.

Jupiter, which has at least sixteen moons, has double eclipses twice a year. On November 10, 1998, astronomers photographed a triple eclipse. That only occurs once in a millennium for Jupiter. But since there are about 10^{21} stars, a significant percentage of which have planets with moons, intersecting eclipses probably occur somewhere every day.

The causal theory precludes near

According to the causal theory of perception, S sees object O just when there is an appropriate causal connection between S and O.

Figure 1.1 Solar eclipse

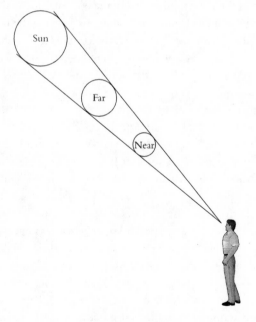

Figure 1.2 Double-eclipse scenario

Michael Tye (1982) and Gerald Vision (1997) have tried to spell out what "appropriate causal connection" amounts to. Regardless of the details, the causal theory entails a necessary condition that decisively precludes the possibility that I see Near: S sees O only if O is a cause of what I see. Near is totally within the shadow cast by Far. An object that is completely enveloped in a perfectly dark shadow cannot be seen. A cat silhouetted against the moon can be seen by virtue of the light it blocks. But because Far is preventing any light from striking Near, Near is not casting a shadow. Near is causally idle and therefore invisible. If light were being reflected by Near into my eyes, Near would preempt Far. And I would see Near. But because I am actually seeing by virtue of partial light blockage, it is Far that preempts Near.

H. P. Grice (1961, 141) motivated the causal theory of perception with a thought experiment. Suppose I believe I am facing an unoccluded pillar. Unbeknownst to me, there is a mirror that is reflecting the image of the pillar to my rear. On the opposite side of the mirror there is a pillar, indeed, one that would look just like the one in the mirror. If the mirror were removed, there would be no discernible difference. Under these conditions, common sense correctly tells me that I see the mirror and not the occluded pillar. The reason is that the occluded pillar plays no causal role in what I see.

Or suppose that there are two identical coins in my line of sight, one behind the other. If the front coin is rolled away, the scene will look the same. Nevertheless, I do not see the rear coin because it makes no actual difference to what I see. I see only the objects facing me because only they are in a position to transmit light into my eyes. More generally, the perceiver's field of vision is widely agreed to comprise the *front* surfaces of those opaque bodies lying within a conical region radiating outward from the perceiver's open eyes. The causal theory of perception provides a natural explanation of why my field of vision is structured as it is.

Alvin Goldman (1977) uses satisfaction of this environmental relation between perceiver and perceived as one of three defeasible factors in determining whether an object is seen. His second factor is the existence of a physical mechanism. By this Goldman means a causal pathway by which the object transfers energy to the perceiver. Goldman's last factor is counterfactual dependency: would the scene have looked different had the object not been there? Each of these factors has some say, but none has a veto. Consequently, there will be hard cases.

Goldman considers Jaegwon Kim's example of an astronomer looking at a black hole. Kim is picturing the scene as in figure 1.3. The astronomer sees the black hole by virtue of its contrast with the background field of shining stars. According to Goldman, the black hole is in the perceiver's field of vision and satisfies the counterfactual dependency condition but violates the physical mechanism condition.

To save the causal theory, Goldman claims that "cause" is ambiguous between a counterfactual dependency sense and a physical mechanism sense. Since parallelism and occasionalism deliver counterfactual dependency without causation, this ambiguity defense fails. For good or ill, the causal theory unequivocally condemns idle objects to invisibility. If Lucifer made an astronomer have hallucinations of a black hole that reliably tracks the black hole, the astronomer would not see the black hole.

Since black holes violate just one of Goldman's conditions, he (correctly) acquiesces to the intuition that the astronomer sees the black hole. It is striking that Far violates all three of Goldman's conditions.

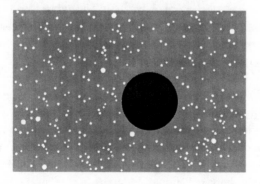

Figure 1.3 Black hole

The environmental relation is unsatisfied because Near is in front of Far. The counterfactual dependency condition is violated because I would notice no change in the scene if Far were not present. And the physical mechanism condition is violated because Goldman requires that the physical mechanism involve an energy transfer from the object to its perceiver.

Although Near satisfies the environmental condition, Near violates Goldman's other two conditions. Near transfers no energy to me. And if Near were absent, the scene would be indistinguishable. Hence, Goldman is committed to saying that I see neither Near nor Far.

Chapter 2 has comments on each of Goldman's factors of perception. But here is an immediate remark about the environmental relation. The relativity of "occlude" forces a corresponding relativization of our field of vision. Consider two dark nebulae that exactly overlap in the manner of Near and Far. A dark nebula is a dense cloud of interstellar dust. Dark nebulae do not transmit light in the optical region of the spectrum. Yet they are conspicuous in any photograph of the Milky Way because of their contrast with ambient starlight. The twist is that "dark" nebulae glow brightly in the infrared because interstellar dust efficiently absorbs optical and ultraviolet radiation. An astronomer peering through an infrared telescope can see the near nebula. But an astronomer using an optical telescope cannot. Relative to infrared observation, the near nebula occludes the far nebula. But the reverse holds for optical observation. The infrared astronomer has a classical field of vision in which he sees the fronts of objects. The optical astronomer has a backlit field of vision in which one of the objects is visible by its backside.

The correct solution to the eclipse riddle is that I see Far. This answer follows as a bold consequence of the causal theory of perception given natural background assumptions. "I see Far" will seem bizarre as long as we persist in modeling all vision on seeing objects that transmit light (by reflection, refraction, or emission). We must be careful not to prejudice the explanation of our field of vision by overlooking alternate lighting conditions. In particular, when objects are backlit and are seen by virtue of their silhouettes, the principles of occlusion are reversed. In backlit conditions, I can hide a small suitcase by placing a large suitcase *behind* it. The reversal runs deeper: we see the backs of backlit objects. Although this thesis seems like parapsychology, my premises are drawn from the reigning orthodoxy. I am a conservative rather than a radical.

Backlighting reverses optical relationships

When objects are frontlit, the darkness of an object correlates with its distance from the viewer. But in backlit conditions, darker objects are seen as closer to the viewer (as in fig. 1.4). Brightness diminishes at a geometric rate with square of distance, so the light nearest you is brighter. Since the blackness of an object is a contrastive phenomenon, near silhouettes are blacker than far silhouettes.

Figure 1.4 Backlit goats

Backlight also reverses depth cues for translucent objects (ones that allow light to pass through but disorganize the information conveyed by the light). When lit from the front, a thicker cloud will be brighter than its thin neighbor, for the thick cloud scatters back more light. But if the two clouds are lit from behind, the thin cloud will let more light shine through, and so it will be brighter than the thick cloud.

Under terrestrial conditions, a Near–Far type of scenario makes it more evident that Far is being viewed. Suppose Near is only a hundred meters away while Far is a kilometer away. They have same apparent diameter, but Far is so big that it reduces the amount of ambient light. Were it not for Far, Near would have a silhouette darker than the one we are now viewing, for the extra brightness of the background would make Near's silhouette darker by comparison. But the silhouette we in fact see is less dark. Removing Near would not affect the appearance of the silhouette. Removing Far would affect the appearance of the silhouette. Therefore, the silhouette is of Far, not Near.

The architecture of shadows

The representational sense of "silhouette" is etymologically prior to the mereological sense. The notorious French controller general of finance Etienne de Silhouette (1709–67) had a hobby of cutting shadow portraits out of black paper. "Silhouette" came to be applied to depictions of this sort and then later became applied to the causal basis of those depictions. Compare "silhouette" with "pinup," which at first denoted only poster depictions of sexy women and then came to denote the subjects of those depictions.

My remarks are confined to what is denoted by the mereological sense of "silhouette." In this sense, the silhouette of an opaque object is the surface of the object that blocks the light. This absorption layer of the object is distinct from any shadow that is cast or attached to the object.

Shadows are not mere absences of light. Shadows require light sources plus transparent or translucent regions where light would have entered were it not for objects that block the source. If I lift the red rock, it casts a shadow. But I have not discovered a preexisting shadow.

Shadows can extend into solid transparent media such as a block of ice. But shadows are excluded from media that are incompatible with light, such as very thick smoke.

Hidden regions of light also curtail shadows. Consider a silhouetted safe that contains a flare. Given this hidden light source, the wall nearest the shadow blocks light.

The distinction between an object's silhouette and its shadow is easiest to see when both are present (fig. 1.5). Architects call the shade lying between the object and its cast shadow "the invisible shadow" (though they admit it can be seen when the air is dusty).

The cast shadow is a surface of a three-dimensional volume. The two dimensionality of the cast shadow is due to its status as a *surface* rather than to its status as a shadowy thing.

Figure 1.5 Silhouetted pyramid

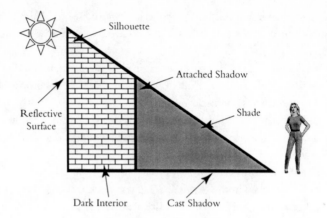

Figure 1.6 Architecture of shadows

To consolidate the above distinctions, consider a solid brick tower casting a shadow (fig. 1.6). It is natural to identify the silhouette with the shadow attached to the shorter side of the tower. But that cannot be what we see when viewing the silhouette of the tower because the short side of the tower is causally idle. The observer must be seeing the long side of the tower. The darkness begins with the layer of brick that absorbs the light. But the shade begins only where the brick ends, for only at that point do we reach an appropriate medium for a shadow (in this case, air).

We normally see through shade in the way we see through the glass cover of an instrument panel. We do not even notice what we are seeing through.

My claim that the subject is seeing the long side of the tower seems like it attributes a kind of X-ray vision. But the image of the silhouette does not need to travel through the wall to reach the observer. The darkness lying between the long side of the wall and the observer is there by default.

It may be less distracting to consider the silhouette of an object that has negligible depth. The silhouette of a sheet of aluminum foil cannot be the side facing the observer. The front side is neither blocking nor reflecting light. So although there is an attached shadow on the front side of the foil, the silhouette is *behind* that shadow.

Since silhouettes block light, they look black to normal observers in normal viewing conditions. They look black and are black. In special circumstances, silhouettes may appear to take on the color of intervening objects. During an annular eclipse at sunset (in which the apparent diameter of the moon is smaller than the apparent diameter of the sun), the silhouette of the moon appears to be beautifully multicolored— even miraculously continuous with its surroundings. But we are then mistaking the colors of intervening clouds and sky with that of the moon. The real color is black and would be seen that way by an observer above the atmosphere.

Depictions of silhouettes are often doctored to increase their recognizability or just for aesthetic interest. In this spirit, artists present us with a wide range on nonblack "silhouettes." Photographic negatives reverse the gray scale, and so silhouettes look white.

Photographic negatives suggest another argument for the thesis that we see dark things: anything that is visible in a photograph is visible in the negative of the photograph. Dark things are visible as light things in a photographic negative. Therefore, dark things are visible in photographs. Anything that is visible in a photograph can be seen directly. Therefore, we can directly see dark things.

This argument survives the footnote that people more easily recognize a face in a photograph than in a negative of that photograph. They also more easily recognize a face in a photograph that is right side up rather than upside down. Turning a photograph upside down alters how easily we process the information, not the information itself.

However, as the role of inference becomes pronounced, we start seeing signs of things rather than the things themselves. The appeal to photographic negatives needs to be tempered by this slippery slope into invisibility.

Ludwig Wittgenstein asks, "Would it be conceivable for someone to see as black everything that we see as white, and *vice versa*?" (1951/1977, sect. III, 84). Justin Broackes (2007) uses our preference for photographs over their negatives to answer no. White and black have a fundamental physical asymmetry; white objects reflect much of their incident light while black objects absorb most of it. Consequently, white objects will vary in appearance as the light varies. Since a black room absorbs more light than a white room, less light is needed to see in a white room. As the light dims in a black room we have more trouble seeing the shadows cast by objects. Often such shadows play a critical role in defining the object. Consequently, that which no longer makes light disappear . . . disappears.

Shadows that survive their casters

The parasitic nature of shadows makes it natural to infer that "a shadow is sustained in existence by the continued existence of its originating source" (Todes 1975, 96). However, shadows (like other holes) can survive the destruction of their originators. Consider a tree that is constantly illuminated as it petrifies into stone. The stone continues the shadow begun by the tree.

There is a legend that after Buddha died, his shadow lingered in a cave. It actually is possible for a shadow to persist without any sustaining object. Light travels at 299,792,458 meters per second in a vacuum. The moon is about 384,400,000 meters away from Earth. Hence, if the moon were instantly obliterated during a solar eclipse, its shadow would linger for more than a second on the surface of Earth. If the moon were farther away, its shadow could last several minutes. We can extrapolate to posthumous shadows that postdate their objects by millions of years. We can also speculate about an infinite past in which a shadow is sustained by a beginningless sequence of objects. As one object is destroyed, an object of the same shape and size seamlessly replaces it. This shadow antedates any object in the sequence and so refutes the principle that every shadow is caused by an object. Shadows are not dedicated dependents. Although slaves to some object or other, they can switch masters.

We can also ask: do we see silhouetted objects that no longer exist? The answer is the same as the solution to the riddle prompted by starlight that survives its star: can we see stars that no longer exist? Yes, but we see them as they were, not as they are. For instance, background light lets astronomers see silhouetted disks of interstellar dust surrounding distant stars. These protoplanetary disks have by now developed into planets and so no longer exist.

Since the silhouette of an object is part of the object, there can be cast shadows without silhouettes. Thus, the leading edge of a shadow need not be a silhouette. (Since an uninterrupted shadow ends at a region of space instead of at the surface, it follows that some shadows have neither a silhouette nor a shadow cast on a surface.) When the object is destroyed, the leading edge of the dark three-dimensional volume races toward its opposite edge at the speed of light. Small volumes of shade appear to be destroyed at exactly the time that the object is destroyed. But, strictly speaking, shadows last longer than their destroyed casters.

L. A. Paul notes that the speed of light compels a surprising qualification to my answer to the eclipse riddle. Initially, Near blocks light because there will be photons trapped between Far and Near. Once Near absorbs these intermediate photons, it will no longer block any light and, consequently, will become invisible. Only at that stage do we see Far. (The qualification is not needed if Far is stationary.)

Whereas cast shadows are displaced and usually distorted, silhouettes provide a visual match that is comparable to that achieved with transmitted light. Seeing a silhouette of an object counts as seeing the object itself. This principle is prehistoric and culturally universal. Silhouette portraits are the earliest and most universal genre of representational art. Some are found in prehistoric caves. There are ancient specimens from Egypt, China, and Greece. Intricate eighteenth-century silhouette portraits are housed in London's National Portrait Gallery (Gombrich 1995).

This simplest form of portraiture was a stepping-stone to early photography. Instead of tracing a shadow by hand, Sir John Herschel had nature fix the image with potassium ferricynanide in 1839. Botanists would place a plant directly on the photosensitive paper and shine a strong light on it. The blue and white image, a precursor

of the blueprint, was sensitive to the varying opacity of the plant—
unlike simple silhouettes. Cyanotype photographers were aware that
the images were of the backsides of the plants, for they warn novices
to turn the intricate features face down. Further piecemeal improvements in photochemistry and optics allowed the object's image to be
taken without direct contact with the photosensitive paper. Further
improvements decreased exposure time, increased the durability of
the photograph, and formed a continuous developmental sequence
leading up to modern photography.

Night photography harkens back to these roots. German naval
archives contain ominous silhouette photographs of targeted ships.
Although New York City was out of range of Nazi bombers, cargo
ships using New York Harbor were in range of Nazi submarines. The
cargo ships turned off their sea lights but were backlit by the bright
lights of Manhattan. (This explains why New York City had to be
blacked out during World War II.) The German archives also include
silhouette photographs of the effects of cargo ships—their wakes,
smoke, debris, and so on. These photographs of ship effects can be
distinguished from the photographs of the ships themselves. Consider
a submarine captain who first spots traces of a ship against the moonlight. Since the captain *sees* that a ship is in the vicinity, he follows its
trail until, finally, he *sees* the ship itself profiled against the moonlight.

When I see smoke rising above a forest, I see an effect of the fire
but do not see the fire. Seeing the silhouette of an object is not like
seeing the smoke from the fire, for one is seeing the object itself when
seeing its silhouette. Consider a scene (fig. 1.7) featuring two balls
separated by a divider. The left ball is made of black velvet and is
frontlit. The right ball is made of red velvet but is backlit and so looks
black. A naive subject is presented with the scene. He does not know
about the special lighting conditions, so he is making no more inference about the left ball than the right ball. Therefore, he is either seeing both balls or neither of the balls. Because he is seeing the left ball,
the subject is also seeing the right ball. Subjects can see silhouetted
objects even if they do not realize that they are seeing them in silhouette, so no extra inference is needed. Nor is there any special need for

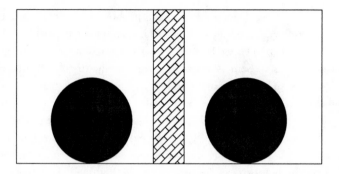

Figure 1.7 Two black balls

memory. The same experiment could be carried out with a pair of highly irregular shapes that the subject has never seen before.

If you bend a coat hanger into an irregular shape and attach it to a spindle of a turntable, then the silhouette of the hanger (as viewed through a translucent screen) will look like a flat scribble. When the spindle rotates, the shadow looks three dimensional. Indeed, you can discern the shape of the coat hanger (Wallach and O'Connell, 1953). Subsequent experiments on the "kinetic depth effect" have extended it to natural, curved shapes such as that of vegetables (Norman et al. 2000).

One might assume that object recognition would require internal contours, texture, and shading. They help. But W. G. Hayward (1998) has shown that even static silhouettes convey most of what human observers need to recognize the sort of objects an experimentalist can present in a laboratory display: simple volumetric primitives ("geons"), aggregates of volumetric primitives, plus animals.

Animals see silhouetted objects

If seeing silhouetted objects were cognitively demanding, brutes would not be able to see silhouetted objects. But purely contrastive seeing is not an ability peculiar to *Homo sapiens*. Aquatic predators frequently hunt from below. Light enters water from above, so prey are backlit. A shark that approaches a school of anchovies from the side will be dazzled by the light reflected by the anchovies' scales as the school sharply pivots in unison. Some sharks counter by driving the school toward the surface and then lunging from below. The sharks see the anchovy silhouettes. They also see the anchovies.

The most extensive evidence that animals see silhouettes comes from their camouflage. Most animals, both predators and prey, are countershaded to weaken their silhouettes. By being darker on top (where the light strikes) and lighter on the bottom (where there is less light), the animal makes less of a contrast with its environment (Ramachandran 1990).

Silhouettes are also masked actively. The pony fish emits a continuous glow that matches the level of background light (Hastings and Mitchell 1971). This camouflages its silhouette. Other bioluminescent fish use irregular lighting to break up their outlines.

Yet other animals exploit gratings. The zebra's stripes make its outline difficult to discern in low light levels. Admittedly, the zebra's dazzle markings make zebras more visible in daytime. But zebras see well in daytime. Their problem is twilight, when predators become most active. The common use of camouflage techniques such as countershading, bioluminescence, and gratings provides strong evidence that creatures other than human beings see silhouettes. Why would they conceal their silhouettes if their silhouettes were already invisible?

Fear of some silhouettes is innate. In *The Study of Instinct* (1951), Niko Tinbergen suggests that ducks and geese have a special mechanism for discriminating hawks from more harmless birds. The "tell" for a hawk is its short neck. Tinbergen tested this hypothesis by constructing a model that looks like the silhouette of a hawk when pulled in one direction and looks like the silhouette of a goose when pulled in the opposite direction (fig. 1.8). Pulling the model in the hawk direction alarmed his stock of ducks and geese. Pulling the model in the goose direction did not alarm them.

Unfortunately, Tinbergen did not control for the novelty of the stimulus. Tinbergen's ducks and geese had seen many geese but few

Figure 1.8 Ambiguous bird silhouette

hawks and so might have been frightened by the unusualness of the hawk shape rather than the hawk shape itself. Robert Hinde (1954) has provided more rigorous evidence of innately feared silhouettes. When he would introduce a silhouette of an owl, chaffinchs would mob the figure. (Mobbing is a conflict behavior in which the bird repeatedly advances and retreats from a threatening object.)

The arguments from improvement and novelty

Reducing light often *improves* vision. In the daylight, beachgoers cannot see islands off shore because of the glare. The islands become visible when silhouetted against the setting sun. The jazzy colors of a fabric conceal runs and wear that become visible when the fabric is silhouetted against a strong light. If we are seeing *better* in silhouette, we are seeing the silhouetted objects.

The observational ingenuity of astronomers provides another argument for the principle that seeing the silhouette of an object counts as seeing the object. Mercury is so close to the sun that it is usually lost in the glare. Diligent observers can see it at sunrise and sunset when its orbit is elongated. Even so, its small size and distance and persistent problems with glare made sightings very rare even among skilled astronomers. After Johannes Kepler worked out Mercury's orbit, he realized that there was a hitherto overlooked opportunity to view Mercury: when it traveled across the sun. Then, Mercury can be seen directly in silhouette (or seen indirectly by observing the shadow it made—the safer alternative). In 1629, Kepler predicted a transit of Mercury for November 7, 1631. Although he died the next year, Pierre Gassendi made the observation. His observation showed that Mercury was much smaller than previously assumed.

Since Kepler discovered a new opportunity to observe Mercury and that opportunity involved seeing a silhouette of Mercury, seeing the silhouette of an object suffices for seeing the object.

A rationale for the silhouette rule

We do not want to require that seen objects be seen in color. Monochromats are not blind.

Nor do we want to insist that the visual presentation involve a tight correspondence to the shape of an object. Euclid's geometry of visual rays predicts that edges of distant rectangular objects will appear rounded. He points out that the corners are the first parts of the object that exceed the range of vision. The eye confuses this absence of representation with the representation of an absence. The eye rounds off the sharp edges. Euclid was also aware of how refraction creates mirages. For instance, we see the sun as it sets even though its image is flattened by the bending of the light. Instead of construing these distortions as presenting a skeptical objection to the claim that the object is seen, he sets himself the technical task of measuring and explaining the mismatch. Euclid rejects a perfectionist criterion for seeing; successfully perceived objects need not appear exactly as they are.

A good rationale for counting the sighting of a silhouette as a sighting of the object is that the visual match is good enough—or as good as obtained during nocturnal conditions when we only see in black and white. This fidelity explains why silhouettes are so widely used as iconographic symbols.

As in the case of seeing frontlit objects, the good visual match holds only as a general tendency. The silhouette of a pile of junk does not look much like a pile of junk. But if I see a silhouette of a pile of junk, I see a pile of junk. Interviewers preserve the anonymity of informants by televising them in silhouette. Viewers see the informants but cannot identify them on the basis of what they see.

Under some conditions, a cast shadow provides just as strong a visual match as the silhouette. Early silhouette portraitists traced the sitter's shadow as it was cast against white paper. Casting a shadow on a cloud with a powerful searchlight makes it seem as if one is seeing an object backlit from the sky above. Hence, the "bat signal" from the *Batman* series is called a silhouette.

A shadow is no more part of a man than his footprint. Only Mohammed can make his footprint, but tourists do not see Mohammed by seeing his footprint at the Topkapi Palace in Istanbul. Mohammed's shadow is a hole that he has made in the light. Mohammed's footprint is a hole that Mohammed has made in plaster. Objects cannot be seen by seeing their holes. The holes made by objects are never parts of those objects.

You can see the shadow of an object that is outside your visual field. You cannot see the silhouette of an object that is outside your visual field.

We can *visualize* objects by looking at their shadows. Visualization is just the development of visual analogies, not literal seeing. For instance, in *Flatland* (1884), Reverend Edwin Abbott depicts a two-dimensional being, A. Square, who learns about three-dimensional objects by seeing their two-dimensional cross sections. This corresponds to the shadows that three-dimensional objects cast on flat surfaces. For instance, A. Square could visualize a cube by viewing the shadow it casts; the shadow would look like a square within a square (fig. 1.9).

The mathematician Charles Howard Hinton developed Abbott's hint. He rationalized the beliefs of spiritualists by positing a fourth dimension. The hyperobjects in this realm are too small to see (if they were bigger

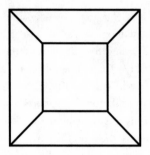

Figure 1.9 Shadow of a cube

than atoms we could detect them much as physicists can detect particles of cigarette smoke). Hinton visualized four-dimensional objects as casting three-dimensional shadows. For instance, he visualized a hypercube by its shadow—which would look like a cube within a cube.

An object's genuine silhouette has a more robust resemblance to the object than does the object's cast shadow. The cast shadow is comparable to the corresponding silhouette only under a narrow set of conditions—and only if we ignore the spatial displacement. Causal theorists reject the hypothesis that seeing is a matter of having experiences that resemble the scene. Resemblance is neither a necessary nor a sufficient condition for seeing. Causal theorists agree that there is generally a good visual match but seek to explain that fidelity in terms of causal connections between visual experience and the scene. *Why* do silhouettes generally provide a better match than do cast shadows? Why do I see an object by seeing its silhouette but not by seeing its cast shadow?

Note that I am using "see" in Fred Dretske's sense of nonepistemic seeing. Whereas seeing *that a* is F entails belief that *a* is F, nonepistemic seeing lacks commitment to a belief content (1969, 88). When cavemen witnessed a solar eclipse, they saw the moon even if they had no beliefs about what they were seeing.

Or consider the original situation in which I am in doubt about whether I am seeing Near or Far. Given my lack of belief, I cannot be said to see *that* the silhouetted object is Near or see *that* the silhouetted object is Far, for I lack the belief that the object is Near and lack the belief that the object is Far.

Nonepistemic seeing is compatible with belief; the caveman can nonepistemically see a distant bird and epistemically see it (by virtue of his belief that the observed creature is a bird). The point of the distinction is partly to focus on the most basic sort of seeing—the type of seeing we comfortably attribute to squirrels. Like Dretske, I reject intellectualist views of seeing. When astronomers go to mountaintops to get a better view of heavenly bodies, they realize that the thin air impairs their judgment more severely than their observations. They go up to see and come back down to think.

Dretske thinks that a seer must have some beliefs or other—but need not have any beliefs in particular. If we assume beliefs require brains, then only animals with brains see. But there appears to be some brainless vision:

> Even more surprising is the occurrence of eyes in creatures without a brain: box jellyfish have camera type eyes feeding information into a simple ring-shaped nervous system, and some dinoflagellates (unicellular algae) have a lens and a retina-like structure all in one cell. (Land and Nilsson 2002, 15)

The six eyes of the box jellyfish vary in structure. Some of the eyes dilate in darkness and form excellent images—but the retina is positioned only to catch blurry, large-scale images. The eyes help the jellyfish answer basic questions: Light or dark? Which way is the surface? The specialization of the eyes invites the suggestion that our own visual system may have modules governed by jellyfish-like neuronal rings.

Shadows as pseudoprocesses

Wesley Salmon (1984) draws a distinction that helps the causal theorist explain why seeing the silhouette of an object is seeing the object but seeing its cast shadow is merely seeing an effect of the object. When a blimp casts a shadow that races along the ground, the moving shadow has persistence conditions that are entirely parasitic on the blimp and the sun. I can predict where the shadow will move by keeping my eyes on the ground and tracking the shadow's speed and direction. But the stages of the shadow's movements are not related as cause and effect. Rather, they relate to the stages of the blimp's movements. Elliott Sober (1985, 303) diagrams the causal structure by using arrows to represent causal connections and broken arrows as the absence of a causal connection (fig. 1.10). If I watch the moving shadow cast by the blimp, then I see a pseudoprocess governed by the blimp's movement. But if I watch the silhouette of the blimp, I see a causal process. The same point holds if the blimp is stationary.

If the blimp collides with a skyscraper and is destroyed, the shadow is terminated. If only the shadow meets the skyscraper, the shadow is momentarily deformed but then, after passing the skyscraper, continues on exactly as before, carrying no trace of its encounter with skyscraper. I can enlarge the cast shadow by inserting a flag into the perimeter of the invisible shadow as the cast shadow passes in front of me. But this alteration does not persist after the shadow passes the flag. Putting a flag on the blimp does result in a lasting change. I can mark the blimp but cannot mark the shadow.

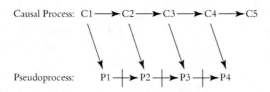

Figure 1.10 Sober's pseudoprocess

A given process, whether it is causal or pseudo, has a certain degree of uniformity—we may say, somewhat loosely, that it exhibits a certain structure. The difference between a causal process and a pseudo-process, I am suggesting, is that the causal process transmits its own structure, while the pseudo-process does not. The distinction between processes that do and those that do not transmit their own structure is revealed by the mark criterion. If a process—a causal process—is transmitting its own structure, then it will be capable of transmitting certain modifications in that structure. (Salmon 1984, 144)

The silhouette of the blimp is a causal process because it satisfies the mark criterion. A change of the silhouette is inherited by future stages of the silhouette.

Because an intrinsic change in the silhouette constitutes an intrinsic change in the object, the silhouette is part of the object. A silhouette, in this mereological sense, is not a depiction because it exists independently of any intention to represent the object.

The moon is like the blimp during a solar eclipse. The silhouette of the moon is a causal process. If the silhouette is changed by a meteor collision, then the silhouette retains that disfigurement. However, the shadow cast by the moon is a pseudoprocess. As it races along the surface of Earth, local interventions have no effect on future stages.

The shadow moves as quickly as Earth spins. In principle, a shadow can move faster than the speed of light. Suppose I hold my thumb over a flashlight that can transmit light across vast distances. I wave the flashlight, sending the shadow of my thumb coursing through the heavens. The rate at which the cast shadow moves increases geometrically with distance. At a large enough distance, my thumb's shadow is moving faster than the speed of light.

This is compatible with the special theory of relativity (Rothman 1960). The theory only says that no *signal* can travel faster than the speed of light. The shadow is not a signal because it cannot transmit information. My thumb's shadow when cast on surface A does not pass on any information from A to any subsequent location B. The shadow's features at B instead depend on the flashlight and my thumb.

The silhouette of my thumb can only move as fast as my thumb. For the silhouette of my thumb is where my thumb is. The persistence conditions of a silhouette make it a causal process. A process is a persistence of something such as a wave or a table (Salmon 1984, 140). Both the object and its silhouette are genuine causal processes.

Plato's allegory of the cave was inspired by the shadow plays of puppeteers. In the allegory, men are shackled together in a way that keeps them facing a cave wall. Behind and above them is a fire and a walled walkway. The barrier conceals servants who stroll by with figurines above their heads. These figurines cast shadows on the cave wall. This shadow play is the only reality for the prisoners who have never seen things under normal conditions. The prisoners consider the shadows as objects in their own right. They do not view them as signs of other objects. They do not know that the shadows are cast by figurines and so do not use the shadows to make inferences about those figurines. When the prisoners view the shadows in this fashion, they do not see the figurines. My explanation is that one can only see an object via a causal process emanating from that object. The prisoners do not see any objects even though they can predict the patterns of shadow play.

If a prisoner is turned toward the silhouettes of the figurines, then he sees the figurines—whether he recognizes them or not. Suppose the prisoner comes to have normal knowledge of the world but resumes his original station in front of the shadows. This prisoner knows that the figurines are casting the shadows. He can see *that* the horse figurine is casting the present shadow. Yet he no more sees the figurine than his ignorant companions. He sees exactly what his ignorant cavemates see. Since nonepistemic seeing has no belief content, learning cannot increase what one sees.

Our resolution to distinguish seeing an object from seeing its shadow is also marked by our willingness to describe an object as invisible even though it is in the scene before us and we are viewing its shadow. For instance, when Io passes between the sun and Jupiter,

Io cannot be seen from the sunward side because Io blends in with Jupiter. However, the shadow of Io is plainly visible because its darkness contrasts sharply with Jupiter. So, although Io and its shadow are in the astronomer's field of vision, only Io's shadow is visible.

We draw the distinction between seeing an object and seeing its shadow even when the observer believes he is seeing the object. In 1656, Christian Huygens saw a dark band across Saturn. He believed that the band was Saturn's ring, but he was actually seeing the shadow of the ring. Huygens did not realize that the ring of Saturn is like a thin sheet. The ring is too flat to be seen edgewise.

Astronomy teachers warn that staring at an eclipse causes irreversible eye damage. Galileo's telescope magnified this destructive power and contributed to his blindness. Hence, teachers encourage students to view eclipses by means of pinhole cameras. The students can safely watch the shadow cast on the ground by the moon as it crosses in front of the sun. Teachers assure the students that they are seeing the moon eclipse the sun. But the students are actually like the enlightened cave prisoner who knows the shadow is cast by an object that is, sadly, out of view. Only a student who steals a glance at the silhouette in the sky sees the moon eclipsing the sun.

2

Seeing Surfaces

O Moon, when I gaze on thy beautiful face,
Careering along through the boundaries of space,
The thought has often come into my mind
If I ever shall see thy glorious behind.

—Quatrain attributed by Edmund
Grosse to his housekeeper

Chapter 1 dawned with the eclipse riddle: do I see Near or Far?
In allegiance with the causal theory of perception, I answered that
I see Far even though Near is closer to me. This follow-up chapter
develops the most paradoxical implication of this solution: we see the
back surfaces of silhouetted objects.

Silhouettes as absorption surfaces

In the case of opaque objects, the silhouette is the *surface* of the object that
makes the object visible by virtue of the light that it blocks. Therefore,
to see a silhouette of an object is to see a *part* of it. Seeing a relevant
attached part of an object suffices for seeing the object. We count seeing
the silhouette of an object as seeing the object (and seeing its shadow
does not count) because we are seeing a surface of the object.

Leonardo da Vinci propounds a whittling objection to the assumption that the surface of an object is the outermost *material* part of an

object (Stroll 1988, 40–46). If the surface is the *outermost* part of the object, then how can it have any thickness? If it were one millimeter thick, then only the outermost half millimeter could be the outermost part of the object. That half millimeter could not be the outermost part because only *its* outer half could qualify as the outermost part of the object. That outer quarter millimeter can itself be halved. And so on. Consequently, surfaces have o thickness and thus cannot be a material part of the object.

Leonardo's whittling argument illicitly privileges immaterial surfaces. He manipulates the domain of discourse for the quantifier "outermost." What counts as the parts of an object varies with purposes. Sometimes the parts include a coat of paint, the enamel, the peel, and so on; sometimes not. The domain is nondissective: parts of the parts need not be in the domain of discourse. If I say that the surface of my couch is plaid, I am not refuted by the observation that none of the small parts of the surface is plaid. Leonardo da Vinci's whittling argument can proceed only by shifts of context to smaller and smaller parts. Thus, the argument that material objects lack material surfaces is much like Peter Unger's (1975) argument that no material object is flat. Both of these arguments are refuted by the kind of contextual analysis David Lewis proposes in "Scorekeeping in a Language Game" (1979).

A surveyor is free to concentrate on the abstract surfaces of objects; he is interested in geometrical relations. A vision scientist must concentrate on concrete surfaces because only they satisfy the causal requirement for seeing. Consequently, most psychologists and philosophers agree that we see opaque objects only by seeing their surfaces. J. J. Gibson writes:

> The surface is where most of the action is. The surface is where light is reflected or absorbed, not the interior of the substance. The surface is what touches the animal, not the interior. The surface is where chemical reaction mostly takes place. The surface is where vaporization or diffusion of substances into the medium occurs. And the surface is where vibrations of the substances are transmitted into the medium. (1979, 23)

The scientist will go to whatever depth is necessary for the action. But he will go no further. For opaque objects, this means he stops early. Rigid objects can be almost entirely hollowed out without disturbing their appearance. Architects and set designers exploit this superficiality of vision.

When objects are covered, we become ambivalent about whether we see them. If we count the cover as part of the object, we say we see the object. But it is often a stretch to count clothes and tarpaulins as outermost parts. So if challenged, we will retract the claim to see the object and only claim to see the covering. This flexibility is predicted by the causal theory of perception (Firth 1966). Causal descriptions are highly sensitive to shifting purposes. The standard example is the description of what caused an automobile accident. The police officer blames the excessive speed of the driver, the mechanic blames the worn brakes, and the road engineer blames the steep grade of the road. There is no disagreement because the causal attributions focus on different aspects of the same causal chain. People tend to focus on whichever links in the causal chain they can best manipulate.

Covers are less troubling to silhouetted seeing. In frontlit circumstances, a ski mask greatly decreases the detail of a head. There is little loss for backlit viewing.

The loose hood of a Ku Klux Klan wizard prevents us from seeing his face. But if he stands in front of a blazing cross, we can see through the cloth to his silhouetted profile. Thanks to our excellent face recognition, this simple shape provides enough information to accurately judge race, gender, age, attractiveness, and to cross identify with front view photographs (Davidenko 2007).

The flexibility of causal attributions helps us deflect counterexamples to the doctrine that we see by seeing surfaces. Consider Avrum Stroll's putative counterexample of Venus: we see Venus even though the surface of Venus is completely covered with clouds (Stroll 1988, 75–76). I say that we see Venus only if we count the clouds of Venus as part of Venus. If we count Venusian clouds as not part of Venus, then we do not see Venus.

Stroll denies that Jupiter has any surface at all because it is gaseous. Here, I concede that "surface of Jupiter" is vague. But the vagueness of the location is compatible with Jupiter having a genuine surface. Microphysicists regard the surfaces of all objects as vague.

Stroll (1988, 175) also has us consider a tomato that is suspended on a string. We can see the surface of the tomato while it is stationary but cannot see its surface when the tomato is spinning. I agree that one cannot make out important features of the surface (bruises, discolorations, etc.). But that is compatible with still seeing the surface. If I see a distant tomato as a red dot, I see the surface of the tomato even though I cannot make out its surface features. My seeing the surface of the tomato explains why the tomato looks red. When I truly stop seeing the surface of an opaque object, I lose sight of the object.

A batter can detect a "slider" by the appearance of a red dot in the upper-right quadrant of a baseball thrown by a right-handed pitcher (Byhill et al. 2005). The red stitches of the ball are rotating at the critical fusion frequency. Baseball coaches mark balls with red dots as a training aid. But the surface of a normal baseball lacks the mark. The batter is seeing an effect of spinning a surface rather than a feature of the surface itself.

When riding an elevator, we see the elevator by seeing the *interior* surfaces of the elevator. The situation is more confusing when we are inside of something that is diffuse. A balloonist approaching a cloud first sees it by virtue of the light its outer portion reflects. As he enters the cloud, he sees the cloud from the inside—but not because any neatly delimited surface is available to him. Light is being scattered into his eyes by an undifferentiated collection of water particles.

As the balloonist exits the cloud, he can see the sky, but not because he sees the surface of the sky. The sky is boundless, extending indefinitely into space. The sky is no more material than a hole. (I return to the sky in chapter 5.) Happily, our sky contains something material, air, which can count as part of the sky. The air constitutes the atmosphere, which is a gradually layered "object." In the daylight, we see the sky by virtue of the lower portions of atmosphere that are made visible by the light it refracts and scatters. You cannot make out which is the last part of the sky you can see. You are akin to a diver who can see the ocean around him even when not looking at the surface or the bottom. At night, you can see much farther because the sun's light no longer washes out much in your field of vision.

Most of these complexities are irrelevant to silhouetted objects. The observer is viewing these light blockers from the outside and can often see the precise boundaries of the object. I assimilate purely contrastive seeing to the case of seeing objects that transmit light.

Surfaces have physical properties. In frontlit conditions, we see an object by virtue of the light transmitted by its front layer. In backlit conditions, we see the object by virtue of light blocked by its back layer. A layer blocks by a different mechanism than it reflects. Consequently, the surface of a backlit object consists of the portion of the object that is just enough to block the light. This absorptive surface must be distinguished from the reflective surface. We can represent the two surfaces of the far side of the moon like so:)). The outer parenthesis is the surface relative to light reflection. The inner parenthesis is the surface relative to light absorption. An astronaut in orbit over the far side of the moon during a solar eclipse does not see the silhouette of the moon even though he sees the reflective surface of the far side of the moon. Viewers from Earth are seeing the absorption surface.

More precisely, the viewers from Earth are looking into a concave, bowl-shaped surface. It is indistinguishable from a dark disk just as the silhouette of a skeletal cube (viewed corner on) is indistinguishable from the silhouette of a flat hexagram. However, we are more apt to interpret the silhouette of the moon three dimensionally as a *convex* surface, in particular, the near side of the moon. This accounts for the temptation to infer that the moon or sun has turned black. Most objects *are* convex rather than concave. Our strong preference for convexity is probably due to the incorporation of this empirical regularity into our visual system.

Familiar seeing by transmitted light is surprisingly interpretative. The image of a square could be produced by an infinite variety of trapezoids or tilted rectangles. But silhouettes are much more interpretive because much less information is conveyed. Perceptual psychologists are impressed by how many of these physically possible interpretations never occur to the viewer. Usually, we promptly commit to a single interpretation. David Marr concludes that we disambiguate by hard-wired guidelines:

> Somewhere, buried in the perceptual machinery that can interpret sil-houettes as three-dimensional shapes, there must lie some source of additional information that constrains us to see silhouettes as we do. Probably, . . . these constraints are general rather than particular and do not require a priori knowledge of the viewed shape. (1982, 219)

Marr articulates these assumptions as if the lines of sight emanate from an illumined object. If each point on the silhouette corresponds to one point on the viewed surface, we obtain a curve that serves as a contour generator. The three-dimensional shape of the object can be inferred given Marr's further pair of assumptions that nearby points on the contour of the image correspond to nearby points on the object and that all points on the contour generator lie in a single plane.

Thus, Marr underwrites our tendency to view the silhouette of the moon as *convex* with this rational reconstruction. If Marr is correct, our visual system violates the causal theory of perception. The system assumes, in effect, that we are seeing a part of the object that is causally idle, namely, the front surface of a silhouetted object. This hard-wired heresy might contribute to the counterintuitiveness of my thesis that we see the backs of silhouetted objects.

Regardless of whether I am laboring against a neurological illusion, my thesis that we see the (inner) far side of the moon during an eclipse is paradoxical. The general reason is that we tend to model vision on cases where we see objects by means of the light they transmit. This makes it seem like we are seeing through the 3,600 kilometers of solid rock between the far side and us.

To lessen the appearance of a miracle, some people suggest that I am only seeing the edge of the moon during a solar eclipse. However, the edge can only block light if it is a physical object rather than an abstract mathematical limit. To be visible from Earth, that edge would have to be many meters wide. If I can see the backside of this giant ring of matter, then I would still be seeing a surface that is behind many kilometers of solid rock! Reducing the quantitative scale of a miracle secures no advantage: "Don't be so incredulous; Jesus only restored sight to *one* eye of the blind man." Half a miracle is still a miracle.

Suppose a florescent balloon meanders in front of a solar eclipse. First, the glowing balloon blocks our view of the bottom edge of the moon, and then the middle of the moon. But if the balloon *blocks* our view of the middle of the moon, then we must have previously seen the middle of the moon. Therefore, we were not just seeing the edge of the moon during the solar eclipse.

A snake has crawled on the skylight above your bed (fig. 2.1). You watch the snake coil more tightly until most of its silhouette resembles a ball. In the process, you saw the spiral gap narrow until the snake's body was contiguous with itself. That required seeing the center of the snake coil.

Here is a summary of the basic argument for the thesis that I see the entire backside of silhouetted objects: When I see the silhouette of an object, I see the object. I see an object only if I see part of it. That part must cause my perception in an appropriate way. In the case of naked, opaque, silhouetted objects, the only part that can play

Figure 2.1 Snake on skylight

this causal role is the object's absorption layer. Therefore, when I see a silhouetted object, I see its back surface.

Implications for transparency

Ludwig Wittgenstein asked why nothing can be transparent white. Nelson Goodman challenged the riddle by claiming that "the glass in a white light bulb is as transparent as that in a red one" (1978, 504). Jonathan Westphal defended Wittgenstein's presupposition: just as two jockeys can be equally tall without either being tall, two surfaces can be equally transparent without either being transparent. The *Oxford English Dictionary* defines translucent as "allowing the passage of light yet diffusing it so as not to render bodies lying beyond it clearly visible."

> A white bulb can have the same degree of translucency as a red one, but for it to be as transparent as the red what lies behind it must be as clearly visible as it is through the red. (The bodies lying beyond or behind a transparent glass must be visible as normal, so that the fact that bodies flush against a white glass are somewhat visible is not enough to make the glass transparent. What is actually seen in such a case is a shadow on the glass. The OED definition requires objects lying *beyond* the transparent medium, not merely behind it, must be completely visible.) (1991, 16)

The distinction between shadows and silhouettes undermines Westphal's defense. True, one cannot see an object by virtue of seeing its shadow. But one can see an object by virtue of seeing its silhouette. Some black objects look the same when backlit as when frontlit. Consider a black phonograph record that hangs behind a pearl-white glass. Because the light emitted from behind the disk is strong, you can see the disk silhouetted (fig. 2.2). You can accurately see how big the disk is, see the hole in the middle, and see that it is swinging back and forth like a pendulum. You are a marksman. You shoot a bullet right through the hole!

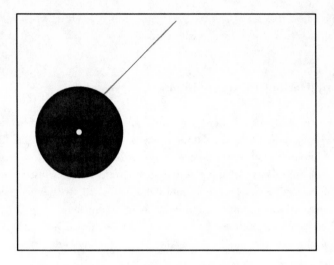

Figure 2.2   Swinging phonograph record

White is transparent with respect to silhouetted objects. That is one normal way in which we see objects. Wittgenstein presupposed that all objects are seen in frontlit circumstances—by light bouncing off them. Since white diffuses light, a white screen does occlude objects relative to that mode of seeing. But there are two sides to occlusion.

Confusion about occlusion

Objects that are seen at least partially in virtue of the light they transmit can be blocked from view by interrupting their transmission of light. But a perfectly dark object does not owe its visibility to the light it transmits. Hence, these nontransmitters are exceptions to the principle that one can always conceal an object by interposing an opaque body. We do not need to see through the "blocking" object.

This point solves a puzzle about cast shadows. The first version was devised by Robert Fogelin around 1967 or 1968. It became a topic of lunchtime conversations with his colleagues at Yale University: Charles Daniels, Robert Stalnaker, Richmond Thomason, Samuel Todes, and Bas van Fraassen. Fogelin reports that he had been dissatisfied with a colleague's analogy between "Only I can feel my pain" and "Only I can cast my shadow." Fogelin devised a complicated enigma involving infinitely many shadow casters. He is not sure whether the simplification to two shadow casters was his doing, the doing of another individual, or the product of the Yale collective consciousness. In any case, the Yale puzzle and its solution were presented in detail by Todes and Daniels (1975) in a format that I discuss in chapter 4 (see fig. 4.9). But I present a more natural version that Bas van Fraassen mentions in *Laws and Symmetry* (1989). Although "shadow" is often used as a count noun, it should be read below as a mass noun (as in "How much shadow is there in the photograph?"):

1.   If X casts any shadow, then some light is falling directly on X.
2.   X cannot cast shadow through an opaque object.
3.   All shadow is shadow of something. (1989, 217)

Imagine a barn casting shadow on a sunny day. A bird flies between the barn and the shadow cast on the ground. The shadow directly beneath the bird cannot be cast by the bird (by virtue of I). Nor can it be cast by the barn (by virtue of II). But no third thing can cast the shadow. Hence, III is violated.

Principle II is true but insinuates that the only way that a shadow can appear on the far side of an intervening object is by penetration. It discourages us from considering the alternative that the shadow appears on the far side by default. Nothing aside from the original blockage of light is needed to place shadow there.

Opaque bodies do not block shadows, nor do they let shadows pass through. It is also a mistake to picture a transparent pane of glass as letting a shadow pass through. The glass lets only light pass through. But this does not mean that glass blocks darkness. Talk of blocking or transmitting shadows is a symptom of the fallacy of reification.

A linguistic philosopher might be tempted to trace the reification to the fact that "shadow" is a mass noun even though it has no mass. However, I suspect a stronger influence is the representational economy of treating shade as if it were colored light. This fiction lets us effortlessly extend the projective geometry that is used to depict illumined objects to the depiction of shadows. Artists sometimes draw with white chalk on dark paper. They represent shadows with undrawn regions. This omissive method of representing shadows echoes scientific reality. However, we normally use light paper. To depict a dark area, we must shade in with a pencil or some dark substance. This practice abets the reification of shadows.

Darkness is an absence of light, not a substantive force that can be stopped with shields. Once the light has been stopped, nothing further needs to be done to ensure darkness. This asymmetry of manipulation is a general difference between properties and their privations. A homeowner who insulates his house can keep the cold out only by keeping the heat in. Cold is the privation of heat and hence is not a substance that can be directly manipulated.

Dark objects must effect contrasts

Lord Brain (1965) regards perception of perfectly dark objects as a counterexample to the causal theory of perception. But a dark object can have appropriate causal connections. Sometimes it is enough that light be transmitted by the object's immediate surroundings.

Consider the trick of hiding a small suitcase in front of a back-lit large suitcase. The main reason for saying that the overshadowed smaller suitcase is invisible is that the smaller suitcase does not causally contribute to what is seen. The overshadowed suitcase also violates the requirement that S nonepistemically sees O only if O "is visually differentiated from its immediate environment by S" (Dretske 1969, 20). Consider a white moth on a white tree trunk. The white moth causes part of what I see although not in a way that enables me to discern its outline. I am looking at the moth but I am not seeing it.

Now consider a perfectly dark moth on a perfectly dark tree trunk. This case differs from the cases involving backlit occlusions. The dark moth does not have a silhouette. The scene is frontlit. Indeed, I am shining a strong light right on the moth. The moth is absorbing virtually all the photons that land on it and hence is playing a causal role in what I am seeing. For instance, if the dark moth is atop a white spot, the moth prevents me from seeing that white spot. Thus, the dark moth satisfies the causal theorist's necessary condition for seeing. The moth is not an idler like Near.

When the dark moth is on a white tree trunk, the moth is seen by the contrast it creates via its light absorption. Absorption is a well-understood physical mechanism. The first step in this understanding is to challenge the question, "Why do black objects absorb energy so well?" Objects are black because they are good absorbers, not the other way around. Good absorbers are also good emitters of energy. That is why radiators are commonly painted black. Whether the surface absorbs or emits depends on the background level of energy. If it is higher, the black object absorbs energy. If the background is lower, then the black object emits energy.

Transmission of light is not a sufficient condition for being seen. The stars shine as brightly during the day as at night. Transmitters of light rely just as much on contrast as dark objects. Human beings have exquisite contrast sensitivity that strains the capabilities of electronic display devices such as television and computer graphics displays. People can detect a change of modulation of less than 1% across a border (Shapley and Lam 1993, xii). This extreme sensitivity to differences in light intensity explains how the "darkness" of an object can itself be a pure contrast effect. Sunspots look dark solely because they are relatively cool spots on the sun. They would shine brightly if they could be removed from the even hotter photosphere of the sun. The universality of this reliance on contrast explains why any object can be camouflaged by muting its contrast with its surroundings. Seen objects normally make a *holistic* contribution to the scene. They are visible by virtue of the differences that they make with their surroundings. The differences can be achieved by going up or down the scale of light intensity—including all the way down to zero.

The contrast between the silhouette and its background is muted by incompletely opaque intermediates such as window curtains. Since our eyelids allow some light to penetrate to the retina, it is possible to see some objects with our eyes closed. Close your eyes and position a bright light bulb so close to them that you can feel the bulb's heat. Now wave a pen just in front of your eyelids. (Contrast sensitivity is enhanced by movement.) Seeing the pen's diffuse silhouette may make you receptive to the hypothesis that purely contrast seeing is biologically prior (phylogenetically and perhaps ontogenetically) to seeing objects by their transmitted light.

All evolutionary accounts start with a proto-eye that is merely sensitive to the presence of light and then develops into a detector of passing shadows. The first seen objects should have been silhouetted figures. Only later would we expect objects to be seen by virtue of the light they transmit. Instead of being a marginal form of vision, purely contrastive seeing is the primal form of seeing. Stereotypical seeing is an elaboration of this more basic ability.

Black holes amass the immediate surroundings that make themselves discernible. The textbook scenario features a black hole that develops from a large star in a binary star system. The larger star has been pulling matter from the smaller star. After the large star accumulates a critical amount of matter, it collapses into a black hole. Since the black hole has the same mass as it had when a large star, it continues to pull matter from its partner star. Since this new matter conserves angular momentum, it forms an accretion disk that revolves around the black hole. The matter from the inner part of the disk accelerates up to nearly the speed of light. The friction creates tremendous heat that in turn emits X-rays. Hence, the black hole makes itself visible by piecing together an environment for itself.

Alvin Goldman (1977, 282) rightly denies that there is a "transfer of energy or force" from the black hole to the observer. But he wrongly denies that there is a physical mechanism by which the black hole makes itself seen. The black hole causes other things to transfer energy to observers. During World War II bombing raids, high-flying bombers could see the silhouettes of low-flying bombers below. The low bombers were bottom-lit from enemy searchlights. The low-flying bombers were not directly transferring energy into the eyes of highflying observers. But the low-flying bombers were still causing themselves to be visible by rousing the enemy below.

Dark objects are a varied lot. Nevertheless, neither the overshadowed suitcase nor the overshadowed heavenly body, Near, satisfy the causal requirement. True, I would see Near if Far vanished. But I see in virtue of actual causation, not hypothetical causation. Consider Harry Frankfurt's (1969) counterexample to the principle that I am responsible only if I could have done otherwise. An evil scientist has rigged up a device that will make me do an evil deed if and only if I fail to do it by my own accord. I do the evil deed, so the device does nothing. I am responsible for the evil deed even though I could not have done otherwise.

Compare Frankfurt's case with David Lewis's (1986, 285) censor. The censor is a device that will make me have the visual experience of a scene if and only if I do not have the visual experience in another way. I am having a visual experience of the scene by opening my eyes and receiving reflected light waves in the normal way. Am I seeing the scene?

Lewis says I see if and only if "the scene before my eyes causes matching visual experience as part of a suitable pattern of counterfactual dependence" (1986, 285). The censor illustrates a lack of suitable dependence:

> The case is one of causal preemption. The scene before my eyes is the actual cause of my visual experience: the censor is an alternative potential cause of the same effect. The actual cause preempts the potential cause, stopping the alternative causal chain that would have otherwise gone to completion. (1986, 285–86)

Substitute "Near" for "the censor." Although the censor is idle, its "idleness is an essential factor in the causal process by which matching visual experience is produced. . . . We cannot uniformly ignore or hold fixed those causal factors which are absences of intervention" (1986, 286). Lewis concludes that I do not see the scene.

Lewis's verdict has been unpopular. His alter ego, "Bruce Le Catt," has tinkered with the counterfactual dependency theory to illuminate the possibility of securing a better match with intuition (Le Catt 1982). But these changes do not address the main problem: underweighting the importance of physical mechanisms. As Brian McLaughlin (1996) stresses, I see because the censor is an external fail-safe device that does not prevent me from exercising my capacity to see.

Let me turn the topic temporarily from nonepistemic seeing to perceptual knowledge. The eclipse riddle does not fit into the tradition of skeptical counterpossibilities. It is not like cases involving dreams, brains in vats, or fake barns (Goldman 1976). I have access to all the relevant facts. When I observe Near and Far approach and then intersect, I know they are behaving just as astronomers predicted many years ago. My situation differs from that of a passerby who had only heard of Near and just happens to look up at the moment of intersection. He might be surprised to learn that the dark shape might be caused by Far. Not me. I have been preparing the observation for years and know all the empirically relevant facts.

The only threat to my perceptual knowledge of Far is conceptual unclarity. If I fail to believe that I am seeing Far, then I do not know that I am seeing Far. Astronomers saw dark nebulae long before they had perceptual knowledge that dark nebulae are clouds of interstellar dust. They had difficulty relinquishing the wonderful possibility that the dark regions in the sky are tunnels through which we look out beyond the stars of the Milky Way into intergalactic space.

We see more than the outlines of silhouetted objects

We are tempted to say we see Near because we seem to see its outline (and so appear to satisfy Dretske's condition of visual differentiation). The influence of the outline can be gauged by considering a scenario that increases the relative size of Far. The huge shadow would make Near invisible. Those tracking the movement of Near would say that they had lost sight of Near as it is submerged into the massive umbra of Far.

When Near and Far have their original dimensions, the trackers of Near would be able to see that Near is aligned with Far even though they cannot see Near. To see an object, the object must be causally responsible for the visual information. This requirement explains why I don't see Mary-Kate Olsen when looking at her identical twin Ashley Olsen. (As child actresses, they played Michelle Tanner in the television series *Full House*.) A photograph of Ashley is not a photograph of Mary-Kate even if their resemblance is exact. In the case of the double eclipse, the astronomers are seeing an object that has the same look as Near. This resemblance ensures that what they see gives them all the visual information about Near that would have been available had Near caused the image itself. Hence, the astronomers tracking Near are reliably guided by the resemblance just as a reporter tracking Mary-Kate Olsen is reliably guided by a photograph of her identical twin, Ashley Olsen.

Visual detection does not suffice for seeing. Astronomers first visually detected planets outside our solar system by observing perturbations of stars through ground telescopes. Only later, with the help of space-based telescopes, will they see a planet outside our solar system.

Is there any advantage in saying we see the *fusion* of near and far?

The Far answer is unaffected by the third possibility that I am seeing a composite object whose parts are Near and Far. This mereological sum, Near + Far, is arbitrary but no more arbitrary than scattered objects such as constellations. We do speak of seeing the moon even when we do not see the far side of the moon. Seeing a relevant, properly attached part of an object counts as seeing the object *simpliciter* (McLaughlin 1984, 580–85). "See" behaves just like most transitive verbs in this respect; to scratch a relevant attached part of an object is to scratch the object itself. Near is the front of Near + Far, and Far is its back. If I see the front of Near + Far, then I see Near. But then the simple answer, that I see Near, would also be correct. The appeal to mereological sums would also be otiose if the simple "I see Far" answer is correct. For if I see the back of Near + Far, I see Far. The composite answer is correct only if one of the simple answers is correct.

A polarizing light filter casts no shadow. But if a second filter of opposite polarity is placed beneath, then the pair jointly cast a shadow. Someone viewing an eclipse involving two such filters might qualify as seeing their mereological sum. Both the near filter and the far filter would each contribute to what is seen. In contrast, the heavenly body Near is completely idle. The same phenomenon arises for some objects that reflect light. Glass mirrors also polarize light. Hence, glass mirrors darken when viewed through a polarizing filter even though everything else in the scene looks perfectly ordinary. The dark mirrors are visible by virtue of their contrast with their surroundings. But unlike Near, the mirrors causally contribute to the scene.

Why we see the *backs* of silhouetted objects

Picture Near and Far coming closer together until they fuse. I still see Far. This reinforces the point that we see the *backs* of backlit dark objects. When the moon eclipses the sun, only the far side of the moon blocks the light. The front half is in the shade. Thus, we see the far side of the moon during a solar eclipse.

True, little of the far side can be differentiated by purely contrastive seeing. Only the outer rim offers positive detail. The middle supplies only the negative information that there are no huge tunnels running straight through the moon. The silhouette of a net has a much higher proportion of positively detailed surface.

We distinguish between observing an effect of an object and seeing the object. The star Algol, in the constellation Perseus, has a companion star that is too dim to be seen. Since the plane on which these two stars revolve is oriented nearly edge on to our line of sight, each star is eclipsed by the other during every revolution. Although the effect of Algol's companion can be discerned by how it periodically dims Algol's light, astronomers describe Algol's companion as invisible. Astronomers cannot even discern its outline. The object must look some way to the perceiver (Dretske 1969, 20).

The analogy with Algol's companion raises the challenge that during a solar eclipse we see an effect of the moon but not the moon. The distinction between seeing and seeing effects can also be drawn in another way that appears to yield the commonsense answer that we see the moon but not the far side of moon. "Seeing the search beam of a lighthouse may count as seeing the lighthouse and not as seeing the bulb inside the searchlight" (McLaughlin 1984, 584). The suggestion is that the moon stands to its far side as the lighthouse stands to its bulb.

However, the far side is not as obscured as the bulb. Aristotle argued that Earth must be round because it always casts a round shadow on the moon during lunar eclipses. We have doubts about whether we see Earth this way because its shadow is displaced; Earth's shadow is on the surface of the moon but Earth is not. Similar reservations affect seeing objects by mirror reflection. But during a solar eclipse, the silhouette of the moon is not displaced. The information we get from the moon's silhouette is normally "discounted" by our ample background knowledge of the moon. However, the empirical content of the silhouetted moon is salient when the observers have unusual background beliefs. Suppose we are worried that a giant meteor struck the moon during the daytime when it is invisible. Instead of waiting until night to find out, we fortunately have the opportunity to check the moon's condition by observing an afternoon eclipse: "What a relief! There the moon is, right on schedule, just where it belongs, entirely intact. The meteor must have missed!"

Seeing a surface does not require seeing much detail. Just before a rocket passes out of view, we see the rocket as a glint or speck in the sky. What chiefly matters is our ability to track its position. We do not even require movement. The arctic anthropologist Gontran de Poncins recalls the excitement of spotting a human being in the distance:

Suddenly I saw a black dot against the white background.

"Inuuk!" (A man!) I called out.

"Na-oo?" Shongli had not seen it.

I pointed, we moved towards it, and there was no doubt about it: that black dot was a man. In this land of one million square miles inhabited by six thousand men, the sight of a human being is overwhelming; it creates an emotion that is like a seizure, difficult to describe. (1941/1988, 232)

Since the man is ice fishing and oblivious to de Poncins, he remains completely motionless. Despite the poverty of shape information, the man is seen.

The distinction between seeing an object and seeing the effect of an object is sensitive to a standard of detail. As a boy, I fed lightning bugs to my pet toad. To my delight, the bugs would continue to light up after being consumed. I could see the toad's *belly* light up periodically. In the dim light of a porch lamp, I was seeing only an effect of the consumed lightning bug. I let my toad hop into the darkness because I could track him by seeing the flashes of the lightning bug. The hitch was that other lightning bugs would alight near the toad. I could not see which was the lightning bug inside the toad and which was the lightning bug outside the toad. From a distance, I was seeing both lightning bugs. Thus, what formerly counted as seeing only an effect of the lightning bug (seeing its flashes through the translucent body of a toad) now qualified as seeing the lightning bug.

The detail from the far side during an eclipse can be greater than that offered by the moon's reflected light during a hazy evening. In an 1836 eclipse, Francis Baily noticed some beadlike features along one side of the moon. "Baily's beads" are the peaks of mountains that lie along the profile of the moon. If the moon revolved with respect to Baily and if the eclipse lasted long enough to complete one revolution, Baily could have surveyed all of the moon's peaks. However, the moon always presents the same side to us. Why? Because the near side bulges about half a kilometer and so is pulled more strongly by Earth's gravity. If a meteor had knocked off this bulgy excess, the moon might have been sent spinning fast enough to make silhouette astronomy informative.

Granted, even Baily's hypothetical survey hardly compares to the rich visual information relayed by the spacecraft *Luna III* in 1959. But even the proud Soviet astronomers granted that, under certain conditions, we very dimly see a portion of the "dark" side of the moon by earthlight (a phenomenon popularly known as "the old moon in the new moon's arms").

When I see the moon in normal conditions at night, I see the moon by virtue of seeing its front. Sticklers deny that I see the moon; I see only the front surface. The same sticklers would say that, on my account, we do not see the moon when it eclipses the sun; we see only the back surface. I admire the insight and attention to detail that motivates the stickler. But I am not a stickler. I say we see the moon during normal conditions at night and that we see the moon during an eclipse. But I need only insist that the stickler's standards be applied uniformly to both cases.

Suppose Near and Far have the same size. Since Far is farther away, it then only prevents light from striking the middle of Near. The stickler will say that I see a "doughnut" composed of an outer ring of Near and an inner core of Far. However, it is doubtful that I see Far in this circumstance. I cannot differentiate Far from its immediate environment. Do I see a little star if it is stationed in front of the sun? If the two are equally luminescent, I cannot differentiate the little star from its immediate environment. Suppose a wall has beige wallpaper. If someone neatly pastes a patch of leftover beige wallpaper on the wall, do I see it? Following Dretske (1969, 23), I answer no.

If I am standing with my nose against a concrete wall, then I see the wall or at least a portion of it. Yet I am not visually differentiating the wall from its immediate environment. Dretske treats this anomaly as a limiting case (1969, 26). He reasons that since there is no *immediate* environment, the requirement of visual differentiation does not apply.

Visual phenomenology is an important factor in first person reports of seeing—especially when the task is to break camouflage. Bird watchers have a vivid "Aha!" experience when they make out a willow ptarmigan in the tall grass. Random-dot stereograms involve camouflage that can be broken only by stereoscopically fusing two individually meaningless images. This conjuring effect is nearly magical. Random-dot stereograms are spectacular illustrations for philosophers who think there are phenomenological constraints on what it is to see an object (Siegel 2006).

One of my astronomer friends, John Thorstensen, discovered that he could see Venus in the daytime. He had assumed that Venus was invisible during the daytime because its light is swamped by the sun's light. But in the course of aligning some equipment, he saw a bright spot that he realized must be Venus. The only visual aid needed is a straight stick to mark the exact line of sight.

The slight difference in brightness is enough to make Venus visible in the daytime. The observation conditions for seeing Near are more generous. I can clearly discern the outline of Near. True, I do not see its center because it is blocked by Far. But the block is not the sort that makes a difference to the visual match with the scene; if Far were absent, the scene would look the same. Since I am a nonstickler, I say that in that circumstance, I see Near because I see a relevant, attached part of it.

Parallel, duplicate blockers are unexpectedly common in our carpentered world of rectangular volumes. Consider a silhouetted box. Although its front side has the same dimensions as its backside, the front side is farther from the light source. Hence, the shadow generated by the backside fails to include the outermost edge of the front. Consequently, the perimeter of the silhouette is actually caused by the front side of the box. The stickler concludes we see a rectangular doughnut. But since the outline of the backside is invisible, the backside fails to satisfy the visual differentiation condition. I conclude we see the front of the silhouetted box. (More precisely, the relevant absorption layer starts from the inside of the front side.) Boxy shapes are rare in nature. Nevertheless, they constitute an important exception to the rule that we see the backs of silhouetted objects.

The causal theory's recovery of primal vision

I now summarize my main theses. Instead of adjusting principles to fit the intuition that I see Near, we ought to disown this piece of common sense as the effect of an overgeneralization. The causal theory of perception unexpectedly but correctly rules out the possibility that we see Near. Its support for Far forces us to recognize that, typically, we see the backs of dark, backlit objects, not their fronts. Thus, "occlude" must be relativized. This forces a corresponding relativization of "field of vision." Thus, the causal theory of perception stirs an ancient species of seeing to the surface. Purely contrastive seeing is a living fossil that has everyday seeing as a descendent. Some minor adjustments are needed to accommodate this recovered form of seeing. Our conception of the physical mechanisms that support vision must be broadened to encompass the various kinds of visible dark objects. To include backlit objects, we must allow partial light blockage to count. Objects are *not* seen simply by virtue of a contrast with their environment. They must cause the contrast. That is the difference between Near and Far.

Intersecting eclipses can form from a fortuitous convergence of heavenly bodies. But they also form in a cyclical fashion. As the moon orbits Earth, Earth eclipses the sun. The scene would be reminiscent of the famous photograph "Earthrise" taken from the vantage point of the moon. Now take a giant step back from the moon by imagining how the scene looks to an astronaut in a high orbit around the moon. Earth is then aligned with the moon, and the astronaut has both of them in his line of sight. Near is the moon. Far is the earth.

3

The Disappearing Act

A conceptual artist suspends a solid cone beneath a lamp to cast a shadow (fig. 3.1). He has duplicated the shadow by molding a brick of black clay (the truncated cone on the left). The artist has treated the brick's surface to make it look like the shadow on the right. It is a perfect match. Indeed, when the brick is slid into the exact spot of the shadow, there is no discernible difference.

The artist has made the brick disappear! He has done so without changing the appearance of the brick and without disturbing your knowledge of its presence. Prior to being parked in the place of the shadow, you saw the brick by virtue of the contrast it made with the environment. But now, no part of brick is exposed to the light, so the brick is no longer absorbing light.

While parked, the brick could grow yellow spots and spin. That would not affect what you see. The brick could contract into the shape of a bowling pin, wobble, and then further shrink into nonexistence. Once again, what you see would not change. This low degree of functional dependence is due to the fact that the brick is causally idle. To be seen, an object must be a cause of what is seen. Therefore, the brick cannot be seen.

The artist has also made the *shadow* disappear—by destroying it. Once the brick moves in, there is no room for the shadow. A shadow

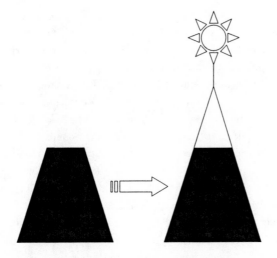

Figure 3.1 Sliding brick

cannot exist wholly within an opaque, solid object. This principle explains why a brick on the ground does not cast a shadow into the earth below it.

Yet you do see something. It has the exact same color and shape as the brick and the shadow.

Occlusion and surfaces:
more against the shadow

Even if you think the shadow survives the parking, you should regard the shadow as blocked from view. This is vivid from the perspective of an observer who witnesses the parking maneuver from behind the brick. He never saw the shadow because the brick always blocked his view: observer → brick → shadow. Viewers from other perspectives saw the shadow. But after the brick is parked, any shadow that remains is blocked from all perspectives.

One might reply that once the brick is fully parked, the shadow comes into view because there is no brick in front of the shadow. Only the part below the surface of the shadow is blocked by the brick. And all that is necessary to see something is to see its surface.

But a visible surface must be a physical surface rather than an abstraction. The physical surface of a brick is composed of the topmost layer of atoms. It can sustain the causal relations needed to be visible. The abstract surface of an object is its outmost boundary: "We arrive at such a conception by a process that consists of the progressive thinning out of a physical surface until we are left with a kind of logical limit or conceptual limit to the object" (Stroll 1988, 46). This type of surface is like the equator. It cannot sustain the causal relations needed for visibility. Which type of surface would the engulfed shadow have? Not a physical surface. The brick takes up all the volume of the shadow. There is not a thin layer of shadow hovering above the brick. Therefore, the surface of the shadow would be abstract.

The cover of darkness: objections to a third entity

Some dark phenomena are quite different from shadows. Sunspots look dark only because they are less luminous than the surface of the sun. If the sunspot were somehow moved off into space, it would be brighter than an electric arc. Diffraction creates dark patches through destructive interference between light waves. Perhaps we are seeing a third type of dark thing, which is neither a shadow nor the brick.

Perhaps. But the darkness is clearly due to same mechanism that produces shadows; the cone is *blocking* the light. If there is no shadow, then the darkness is something quite similar to a shadow.

Postulating a novel type of absence violates a principle of qualitative parsimony: Do not multiply absences beyond necessity. (Admittedly, if one is going to be profligate, be profligate about absences!) The third entity belongs to the cone in the way a shadow does. It shadows shadowhood too closely to be anything but a shadow!

In any case, the distinction between abstract surfaces and physical surfaces also militates against the visibility of the dark thing—whatever it is. The only part of this thing that would not be blocked by the brick would be its boundary with the environment. This abstract surface cannot sustain the causal relations needed for visibility.

You can see a book by seeing its cover (as long as it envelops the book in the normal way). The brick is, as it were, under the cover of darkness. Do you see the brick by seeing this cover? No. The first reason is that this cover of darkness is an abstract boundary. The second reason is the low degree of functional dependence of the cover on what it covers. When you see an Arab woman covered in a burqa, you see her because her shape and movements are responsible for the shape and movements of the burqa. If she were to spin or shrink, the burqa would reflect that movement or shrinkage.

Looking and memory:
more against the brick

The preceding section could be viewed as supporting the brick with an argument by elimination: What we are seeing cannot be a shadow because there is no shadow. What we are seeing cannot be a third type of thing because the brick would entirely block it from view. Nothing causally relevant would remain. (Nothing can be seen solely by virtue of having an unblocked *abstract* surface.)

But this argument for elimination is incomplete. The causal requirement eliminates the brick as readily as it eliminates the other alternatives.

Are there any positive arguments in favor of the brick? It is tempting to appeal to the counterfactual: if the top, full cone hanging below the light source were removed, the observer would still see a black truncated cone, that is, the brick. The counterfactual is true but only because the brick operates as a backup cause for the dark volume. We do not actually see an object by virtue of the fact that it *would* cause us to have the same type of experience (McLaughlin 1996).

It is tempting to argue that the observer sees the brick because he knows, by observation, that the brick is under the cone. But the observer is relying partly on memory. If a newcomer looks at the same scene, he will assume that he is seeing a shadow rather than a brick. What is seen cannot depend so heavily on memory. And remember that the issue is about *seeing* (not seeing that something is the case).

It is also tempting to argue from the premise that the observer is looking at the brick. If looking at *x* entails seeing *x*, the brick is seen.

Certainly the observer's eyes are pointed in the right direction. Onlookers will feel no temptation to adjust their heads or point elsewhere. If the brick were available for viewing, then observers would be locked on target. The problem is that the brick is unavailable. A police officer can know that the fugitive is hiding in the shadow in front of him. Yet the best the police officer can honestly say is "I know you are in there! Step out so that I can see you."

The brick is like a Russian doll that is placed inside another (nearly identical) Russian doll. You saw the inner doll inserted into the outer doll. You know where the inner doll is because of what you saw and what you continue to see. Yet you no longer see the inner doll.

The disanalogy is that, in the case of the Russian doll, there is an unproblematic object of your perception; obviously, you see the outer doll. It has a physical surface. You have trouble finding a counterpart to the outer doll in the "Disappearing Act."

A visual gap?

An alternate solution: Very well, given that you see neither the brick nor the shadow nor a third type of thing, you are not seeing anything. There is just a gap in your visual field that you mistake as the perception of an object.

There are precedents for solving perceptual problems by reigning in our first impressions about how much we see. Consider the resistance most philosophers now mount to the postulation of sense data. While in acute withdrawal, an alcoholic may hallucinate flies. But the opponents of sense data deny that the alcoholic is seeing anything, not even mental "flies."

Consider the simpler case of an actress's afterimage caused by the flash from a camera. If the actress *sees* the afterimage, then she must see more than physical objects. To avoid this proliferation of visual objects, some philosophers deny that the actress is seeing an afterimage. For instance, Austen Clark (2000, 96–97) emphasizes that the afterimage is the effect of a disabling change in eye. The flood of photons bleaches out photopigments. The photographed actress is simply suffering from temporary, partial blindness.

Similarly, when a pilot suffers from tunnel vision, the impoverished blood supply to his brain reduces his peripheral vision. He is not seeing the walls of anything, not even images of walls.

Or consider the blind spot. If you are using only one eye, then you are blind at the point where the optic nerve connects to the retina. This is so even if you "fill in" the missing part of the visual field on the basis of its surroundings.

However, you seem to view the dark volume in much the same way that you view black bricks and shadows. They are visible by virtue of their contrast with their surroundings. Interposing an object can block your view. Once the obstruction is removed, you see the dark volume again. The dark volume can be photographed. It can be detected with a light meter. It is a *public* phenomenon unlike an afterimage or the blind spot in your subjective visual field.

You are designed to see dark things. Natural selection has favored the perception of shadows since the inception of vision 500 million years ago (about when the Cambrian explosion of life forms commenced). Your eye has the normal allotment of photopigments, your brain has the normal supply of blood, and you are looking in a way that does not expose any weakness of your visual system. In short, there is nothing wrong with you. The artist has not contrived external conditions to promote an illusion like the trapezoidal Ames Room (which the eye assumes to be rectangular—triggering a distortion of the perceived sizes of the occupants). He is not playing tricks on you. The artist is willing to let you inspect his display. The puzzle survives and is even enhanced by greater knowledge of how the display works.

Is the scenario possible?

We might use our trouble in arriving at an answer as grounds to doubt the question. If the physical setup is impossible, then there is no need to provide any answer.

The sketch I provided of the disappearing act leaves out details. First, the sketch does not depict the penumbra of the shadow. The umbra of a shadow is an area in which the light is entirely blocked. The penumbra is the gray zone in which the caster only partially blocks the light. If the lamp were a point source of light, then there would be no penumbra (given we ignore a marginal contribution from diffraction). But the artist's lamp is, inevitably, an extended light source, so there will be a penumbra.

The artist considers the penumbra to be an irrelevant distraction. He has used a small, focused beam of light. The artist applies collateral lessons from vision science to make the penumbra visually insignificant.

Arguably, "shadow" really means the umbra because a shadow is an absence of light. The penumbra is merely a region of low illumination. Penumbras are positive entities (bodies of light). Shadows are absences of light. Any light that strays into the umbra *pollutes* the umbra. Light that strays into a penumbra *constitutes* the penumbra. But if you think that a shadow is composed of both the umbra and penumbra, we can recast the puzzle using "umbra" instead of "shadow."

My sketch of the Disappearing Act also fails to explain how the shadow is visible as a three-dimensional volume. In clean air, much of the shadow is invisible. People notice only the shadow cast on the ground. Many of them infer that the shadow is just a two-dimensional patch. But the ground serves only to make one slice of the shadow volume salient. To make the entire shadow visible, the artist needs to make the surrounding light visible. Light is visible when the air is dusty or misty or smoky. For the light is then reflected off the particles.

This makes the shadow visible by contrast. Accordingly, the artist circulates smoke into the display chamber.

Another danger is that reflected light could make the brick visible as a silhouette. To prevent this, the artist lines the walls with black velvet to soak up the light. Observers peer through a peephole.

Some ask whether the artist could achieve the same effect by simply illuminating the brick and dispensing with the cone. The answer is that the observer may then qualify as seeing the brick because he is seeing a part of the object (though much less than he might think). The top of the brick would be absorbing light. You would be seeing something akin to a silhouette—except the business end is at the top instead of the back. (Normally, the light source for a silhouetted object is opposite the observer instead of at a right angle to her.) The hanging cone is designed to decisively disqualify the parked brick as something that is seen.

And the artist appears to have been successful. For he has left us suspended between unacceptable alternatives.

Hollow shadows

My solution to the riddle of the Disappearing Act is that the shadow was hollowed out, not destroyed.

The surface of an object is what remains after we set aside irrelevant inner parts. Suppose our project is to build a brick wall. The mason is interested in the hidden sides of the bricks because they interact with mortar. The decorator is interested only in exposed surfaces. A surveyor cares only about the dimensions of the brick (perhaps to predict whether the wall would cross a property line). Since the surveyor is interested only in the geometrical properties of the brick, this surface is abstract. The abstract surface of a brick encloses a space but does not occupy any space.

Because material things are seen only by virtue of their physical properties, the surveyor's degree of abstraction does not yield a visible surface. Material things cannot be seen by virtue of surfaces that are not material.

The criteria for seeing shadows are broader. Shadows cannot have material surfaces, so they never owe their visibility to the reflective or absorptive properties of their surfaces. The shadow prevails over the brick because the standards for seeing absences are lower than the standards for seeing objects. We thought there was a tie because we mismodeled an object–shadow competition as an object–object competition.

Shadows do have abstract surfaces. Urban architectural codes require architects to report where the shadows of buildings will land. Between the two world wars, skyscrapers in Manhattan were tapered to avoid litigation. Photographs of the skyline from 1940 show districts that look like groups of Mayan pyramids (Casati 2003, 16).

Unlike a material thing, a shadow can be absolutely hollow. There is a limit on how hollow a brick can be. The surface of the brick needs to be strong enough to support its own weight. A shadow does not face this stress. A shadow can be hollowed out until only its abstract surface remains.

The artist's brick perfectly hollows out the shadow. Only the shadow's abstract surface remains. But that is enough for the shadow to persist. The shadow never owed its visibility to an internal part. Shadows look black but not because they absorb light (like crows) or because they block light (like a cat silhouetted against the moon).

Shadows are visible by virtue of their lack of light (and the consequent contrast with their environment). The shadow, even when completely hollowed out, still lacks light. Recall from chapter 2 how James Gibson emphasized that the surface is where the action is. This generalization works well for material objects. But no part of a shadow acts. Shadows are creatures of omission. Shadows are where the inaction is.

One might doubt that anything could be all surface and no content. Can anything be that superficial? David Sanford (1967, 330–34) answers that it is just a contingent fact that material things cannot be hollowed out with the same completeness. He imagines a cubical box composed of material planes. These are two-dimensional physical surfaces that are pressure resistant. Although material planes have no thickness, they can be touched and felt. They might be opaque.

They might come in various colors. When assembled into a cubical box, the planes enclose a volume even though they are themselves without volume. (When you pile the planes on top of each other, the collection does not take up any more space.)

Sanford's box is a material object, but, as he grants, it is precluded by contemporary physics. Shadow shells are not material things and are compatible with physics. Indeed, the artist has brought one into existence.

4

Spinning Shadows

*And Isaiah the prophet cried unto the Lord; and he brought
the shadow ten degrees backward, by which it had gone down
in the sundial of Ahaz.*

—2 Kings 20:9

On January 8, 2004, the rover *Spirit* transmitted the first picture of a
Martian sundial. The children who helped design the sundial can visit
a Web site that features time-lapse photography of the shadow rotating around the gnomon.

Or so says NASA. If textbook laws of motion are exhaustive, then
shadows do not move. Shadows have neither mass nor energy and so
do not trigger formulas licensing ascriptions of momentum.

Philosophers are especially suspicious of *rotating* shadows. We
can explore why with the help of the following question: A sphere
casts a shadow (fig. 4.1). If the sphere spins, does its shadow also
spin? This riddle bears on the classic controversy about how objects change. Endurantists believe that objects persist by being
wholly located at different times. They take pride in their ability
to distinguish between a rotating homogeneous sphere and a stationary homogeneous sphere (Zimmerman 1998). Perdurantists say
that objects persist by having different temporal parts at different
times. None of these parts persists, so perdurantists have trouble
sustaining the distinction between the sphere being stationary and
it rotating.

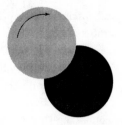

Figure 4.1 Sphere and its shadow

Most endurantists doubt that shadows endure. So *they* have trouble sustaining a distinction between the shadow being stationary and it rotating. I accept the stationary–rotation distinction for both the sphere and its shadow. A cautious perdurantist will merely insist the stationary–rotation distinction holds either for both the sphere and its shadow or for neither. He will draw attention to the shadow of the homogeneous sphere to neutralize the dialectical advantage of the endurantist.

Observability and indiscernible movement

The puzzle is not that the shadow *looks* stationary. Consider the shadow of a chipped Frisbee. When the Frisbee spins rapidly, its irregular shadow appears to become perfectly round and stationary. High-speed photography reveals that the shadow is moving and never changes its shape; at each frame, the shadow is as "chipped" as the Frisbee itself.

The real problem is that any rotation by the shadow of a sphere is *absolutely* indiscernible. Leibniz's principle of the identity of indiscernibles provides a metaphysical premise for collapsing the distinction between the shadow being stationary and it rotating. Antimetaphysical thinkers will say that the empirical equivalence makes the distinction meaningless. According to the logical positivist's criterion of significance, a statement is meaningful only if it is analytic or empirically testable. The answer "If a sphere spins, then so does its shadow" fails this test and so is condemned by the logical positivist as meaningless.

If Leibniz and the logical positivists are even-handed, they will go on to dismiss as meaningless the hypothesis "If a sphere is stationary, then so is its shadow." For how could one tell whether the stationary sphere has a stationary shadow rather than a spinning shadow?

Most people are repelled by this symmetry. They believe that the shadow of the stationary sphere is stationary. One might subtly insist that the shadow is in a neutral state—neither stationary nor spinning. Perhaps the sphere's center point achieves this neutrality by virtue of lacking proper parts. But dynamical neutrality is a strange state for a thing with parts to be in given that it is *in* space (as opposed to being an aspatial number or space itself). It is also strange that mere change (from being round to being oval) could entail a transition from the neutral state to the stationary state.

The verdict of meaninglessness has technical drawbacks. If the spin hypothesis and the stationary hypothesis are meaningless, then they should have a meaningless disjunction. But "If a sphere spins, then either its shadow spins or its shadow is stationary" is true rather than meaningless.

The truth of this statement assures us that we are not committing a category mistake when asking whether the shadow spins. Shadows move in exactly the same sense as do physical objects. A balloonist can be sure that a dark patch is moving even if he is unsure whether that patch is a black balloon or his own shadow.

G. E. Moore was puzzled by the moving pictures at the cinema. How can we see the actors move if we are only presented with a rapid succession of still pictures?

If they did move, it would be in the same sort of sense in which a shadow moves, which is very similar to that in which a wave moves: no material thing is transferred from one place to the other; but one surface after another, is lighted with a degree of illumination less than that which lights surrounding surfaces, and this happens continuously—just as in the case of a wave, a certain form of arrangement of masses of water occurs successively in many different places, & that continuously. (1962, 139)

Moore goes on to suggest that shadows (and waves) move only in the sense that "to any normal person they would look to be moving" (1962, 139). He concedes that this cannot be the only sense of "move" because we can say that Earth is moving even though in normal circumstances it does not appear to be moving (1962, 118). So Moore believes there are two senses of "move" and restricts shadows to the sense that parallels the normal observer definition of color (as in "Something is yellow if and only if it looks yellow to a healthy human being in daylight").

Moore's shadow is on Earth. If his shadow persists for one second, then it must share the motion of Earth. Since Earth's motion is objective, then Moore's shadow must also objectively move. We can generalize: all terrestrial shadows share the movement of Earth. Therefore, even shadows that do not appear to be moving in normal circumstances are moving.

Some counterexamples to Moore do not rely on common sense's traditional vulnerability to astronomy. A passenger waiting for his train to leave the station may misconstrue the motion of a neighboring train's shadow; he may think he is moving through a stationary shadow when he is really stationary and there is a shadow passing over him. We distinguish apparent motion of shadows from real movement of shadows. "The shadow moved" cannot be paraphrased as "The shadow appeared to move."

The night appears to move over us, but it is we who move into the night. The night is the shadow of Earth and thus is uniformly located on the side of Earth away from the sun. We rotate into the night. Those nearer the equator have a higher tangential velocity than those closer to the poles. For instance, when you fly north from Bogotá, Colombia, to Trondheim, Norway, twilight lengthens. This is not because the twilight zone is wider in Trondheim. Instead, those at higher latitudes have less linear speed (even though everyone on Earth has the same angular velocity). Trondheimers travel through twilight more slowly than do Bogotáns.

Shadows are in the same public space as the objects that cast them. Commensurability of direction is assumed in the historian's explanation of why clocks move clockwise: the hour hand of the first mechanical clocks mimicked the shadow of a sundial. In the northern hemisphere, where the mechanical clocks were pioneered, the shadow moves clockwise.

When we watch a lunar eclipse, we can calculate how much of the darkening is due to the movement of Earth's shadow and how much is due to the movement of the moon into that shadow. Joint effects imply commensurable causes.

Commensurability of speed is assumed in the astronomer's calculation of a solar eclipse's duration: the two variables are the diameter of the moon's shadow and its ground speed. The shadow's ground speed is affected by the curvature of Earth. Another factor is the speed of Earth and the moon. The shadow is slowed by the fact that Earth's rotation has the same angular direction as the moon's orbital motion. This effect is strongest at the midpoint of the shadow's transit where the movement of the moon's shadow and the movement of the moon are closest to being parallel.

The approach of the moon's shadow can be dramatic. A century ago, the astronomer Mabel Loomis Todd was on a hill with a view to the west. She described the moon's shadow as "a tangible darkness advancing almost like a wall, swift as imagination, silent as doom" (1900, 21).

During a solar eclipse, the ground speed of the moon's shadow near the equator is 1,730 kilometers per hour. (And that is because of a slowdown: the moon moves to the east at 3,400 kilometers per hour while Earth rotates east at 1,670 kilometers per hour. The ground speed of the shadow near the north pole is more than four times the ground speed near the equator.) A jet must travel at mach 1.5 to keep up with the shadow. Unlike a jet, the shadow does not produce a sonic boom when it breaks the sound barrier. And unlike all physical objects, shadows can accelerate beyond the speed of light (Rothman 1960).

A shadow cannot initiate movement on its own. Nor can it be directly moved. However muscular you may be, you cannot lift my shadow off the ground. To move my shadow, you must alter other things—physical objects such as my body or the lamp that illuminates me.

Aristotle and Descartes required that a mover impact the moved. Impact with a shadow is problematic. Shadows offer no resistance. The perfect ease with which shadows are penetrated makes it impossible to transfer energy to them. Shadows have no mass. The *air* inside the long shadow volume you cast at sunset weighs more than you do. (Air is surprisingly heavy.) Your shadow weighs nothing.

Those who continue to harbor conceptual reservations about the spinning shadow riddle might navigate through technical difficulties by declaring "The shadow spins" indeterminate (rather than meaningless or ambiguous). Indeterminate disjuncts can form a determinate disjunction. For instance, if you feel that the expansion of a balloon is a borderline case of movement (because its center of mass stays the same), then you cannot say the balloon is definitely moving and you cannot say that it is definitely not moving. You can say that definitely the balloon is either moving or stationary. Similarly, if you deem the round shadow to be a borderline case of rotation, then you cannot say it is definitely spinning and cannot say it is definitely not stationary. You can say it is definitely either spinning or stationary.

This hedging is incompatible with the commonsense belief that a stationary sphere definitely has a stationary shadow. Common sense privileges the rest state. We ask why a rock moved, not why it remains still. (This may be grounded on the perceptual system's parsimony in motion attribution. Given a choice, the eye prefers the interpretation involving the least movement—zero motion being ideal.)

Aristotle endorses common sense by characterizing rest as the natural state for terrestrial objects. If Aristotle were willing to extend the rest privilege to shadows, he could endorse the answer that the stationary sphere has a stationary shadow.

Aristotle's physics might not offer a complete solution. He says the natural motion of celestial objects is circular (to explain why heavenly bodies still move despite their infinite antiquity). Since the moon is a celestial object that casts a shadow, Aristotle is committed to the reverse preference for the moon's shadow (when the moon is illuminated along its axis of rotation). According to Aristotle, the moon is the only celestial body that does not emit its own light. So the lunar shadow would be the single rotating shadow in the universe.

Isaac Newton opposed Aristotle's presumption that rest is the natural state. Newton's first law promotes indifference between rest and motion: every object continues in its state of rest or of uniform motion in a straight line unless compelled to change that state by impressed forces. Perhaps Newtonians project this law onto shadows. They wince at the suggestion that the spinning shadow of a ball with a spike in it stops spinning when the spike drops off (fig. 4.2). How could sheer change of shape (to roundness) act as an instantaneous brake? Even Aristotelians have the intuition that the shadow should *gradually* slow down after the spike drops.

Spinners exploit the principle that the motion of a shadow is not affected by its contact with another shadow. Consider the separate shadows cast by a spinning gold hemisphere and a spinning oak hemisphere (fig. 4.3). The hemispheres are the same size and are revolving around a common point at equal speed. As they draw closer and make contact, their two shadows look like a single round shadow. But contact between two shadows is not enough to make them one shadow. My shadow and your shadow do not become a single shadow when we shake hands.

Spinners can also appeal to the principle that light intensity is irrelevant to motion. People readily describe the shadow of a mesh disk as spinning, for they can see the subshadows cast by the grid of wires. Under intense illumination, even the shadow of a thickly woven meshed disk can be seen as moving by virtue of the tiny specks of light peppering the shadow. As the light dims, the specks disappear

Figure 4.2 Shadow with falling spike

Figure 4.3 Spinning hemisphere shadows

because no photons are getting through. The shadow of the mesh disk becomes completely black. We are reluctant to conclude that the shadow of the disk has stopped moving, for we do not treat change of light *intensity* as relevant to shadow movement.

Do shadows even exist?

Zeno's response to the enigma of the spinning shadows would be to deny that shadows move. The most extreme premise for this extreme conclusion is eliminativism about shadows. If shadows do not exist, then there is no such thing as the movement (or rest) of shadows.

One rationale for eliminativism is ontological dependence. The dependence of shadows on the distribution of light shows that there really are no shadows. But why stop there? The distribution of light depends on electromagnetic waves that in turn depend on yet more fundamental features. Spinoza reasoned that if a substance is required to be independent of other things, there is at most one substance: Nature (or God, depending on how you look at it). If the chain of dependence is bottomless, then there are no substances. Reality is then an infinite regress of epiphenomena.

A moderate eliminativist may suggest that we only shave off the top layer of the ontological hierarchy. But shadows are not the top layer. Consider the para-wave that passes through the shadows of toppling dominoes. The para-wave moves along the row of shadows, but each shadow only moves its own length. Para-waves cannot be waves because waves must carry energy. Para-waves depend on a nonmaterial "medium" (in this case, shadows) that in turn depend on material things.

The shadow of a fence cast on a billowing sheet creates an illusion of a para-wave. There are genuine waves in the sheet. The movement of the sheet makes a wavy end slice of the shadow volume. But the shadow is not billowing; it is stationary and also has no para-waves traveling through it.

Shadows can host other "disturbances":

> A disturbance is definable as an object or entity found in some other object—not in the sense in which a letter may be found in an envelope, or a biscuit in a tin, but in the sense in which a knot may be in a rope, a wrinkle in a carpet, a hole in a perennial border, or a bulge in a cylinder. One way of telling whether an object X is "in" an object Y in the sense peculiar to disturbances is to enquire whether X can migrate through Y. (Karmo 1977, 147)

For instance, the bulge in the shadow of a freshly fed snake can move south even if the shadow is stationary. Big bulges can host little bulges, and little bulges can host littler bulges. Therefore, the chain of dependency can lengthen without limit.

Principled eliminativists would like to halt the purge at some level of reduction that respects common sense or science. They wish to spare whatever the legitimate authorities presuppose in their explanations. But this conservatism reintroduces shadows. The role of shadows in physics has been documented panoramically by Roberto Casati (2003) and in telling close-ups by historians of astronomy.

The most powerful reason for believing there are shadows is that they are in plain sight in daily life. A second important reason is that shadows guide object perception. We make out objects by seeing their attached shadows and their cast shadows. We work inward toward being from the margins of nonbeing. This hide-and-seek metaphysics evolved from an arms race of camouflage. For the hunted, to be is to appear not to be.

Psychologists who reveal the role of cast shadows in perception pre-suppose commonsense realism about shadows. Almost all their work prior to 1990 focuses on static shadows. (I am excepting the sequence of articles on rotating *silhouettes* inaugurated by Wallach and O'Connell's [1953] "The kinetic depth effect" described in chapter 1.)

In the 1990s, interest in moving shadows became more systematic. Psychologists have long studied the clues that help us turn the flat retinal image into a three-dimensional representation. They were given a running start from the theory of perspective. Shadows form one class of clues. The size and shape of an object's shadow pro-vide computationally cheap information about their casters. Thanks to advances in computer graphics, Daniel Kersten (1997) and his colleagues could test the relative strength of another clue: shadow movement. Kersten suspected that shadow size and shadow shape would prevail over shadow movement because more complicated calculations are needed to exploit movement. But shadow movement trumped the other clues.

Disappearing shadows Shadows disappear when they move too fast to be seen. But faint shadows can disappear when they move too little. This first came to my attention while marveling at how thoroughly my lawn had been cleared of leaves. To my amazement, a leaf seemed to materialize on the bare grass and then disappear. It was actually the shadow of a leaf in a tree. The shadow was too faint to see when stationary but became visible when a breeze moved the leaf. Although the leaf shadow did this repeatedly, I was unable to break the camouflage of the shadow.

Since motion is relative, you can make a stationary shadow vis-ible by moving the surface it is cast upon. Cast a shadow with a dim light source on a matte surface that is just dark enough to make the shadow invisible. When you move the surface, the stationary shadow "reappears."

Are shadows momentary? Punctualists about shadows con-cede that shadows exist—but only for an instant. They say that there is only an illusion of shadow movement akin to that caused by the frames of a movie. Punctualism can be motivated by the shadow's lack of immanent causality: each stage of the shadow depends on a light source and the object blocking the light. No stage of a shadow causes the next stage. Therefore, shadows cannot persist.

Punctualists would still face a tough question from the spinning sphere (Casati and Varzi 1994, 121): what is the difference between a series of shadows whose members are all in the same orientation and a series whose members occupy slightly different orientations? There is a difference between a sequence of photographs of a stationary sphere and a sequence of photographs of a spinning sphere. The photographs of the spinning sphere show the sphere at different orientations—even if all the photographs look identical. These photographs also record the shadows of that sphere. Why prefer the hypothesis that the photographs of the spinning sphere are photographs of shadows in a uniform orientation as opposed to diverse orientations?

The orientation riddle is the more general enigma. The riddle about spinning shadows is just a special case. Mirror reversal can also change orientation indiscernibly. When asked why the mirror only reverses DIED in OTTO DIED, we answer that the mirror does reverse OTTO. The symmetry of OTTO just makes its reversal indiscernible. Should we adopt the same stance when symmetrical shadow casters are put through a mirror reversal process? This riddle sidesteps the issue of whether the shadow persists.

The most obvious cost of punctualism is translational motion. In addition to denying that shadows rotate, the punctualist denies that shadows move from place to place. Indeed, the punctualist denies that shadows grow or change shape. The punctualist must even deny that shadows *sustain* their shapes or locations over time.

Punctualism implies that all shadows are invisible. Anything that lasts less than a trillionth of a second does not last long enough to be seen. A punctualist might reply that shadows contribute to what is seen in the way that the frame of a movie contributes to the perception of the movie.

Even if this cinematographic analogy were psychophysically viable, we would be seeing *effects* of shadows rather than shadows. The shadows themselves would be invisible.

The invisibility follows independently if the punctualist embraces a causal definition of parthood (Slote 1979). My right foot supports my body. Its contribution to the organization of my body makes it part of my body. My shadow does not support anything and so is not part of my body. Are there parts of my shadow that contribute to my shadow's organization? The shadow of my right foot does not support the shadow of my right leg. The subshadows are causally independent of each other. So an application of the causal definition of parts implies that shadows have no parts. All shadows would be simples, and simples are too small to see.

Volumes and the at-at theory of motion

Other theorists grant that shadows persist over time but deny them motion. Volume theorists say shadows are volumes of unilluminated space. Volumes of space persist even though one stage of the volume does not cause the next. Volumes have sizes and shapes. However, volumes of space cannot change shape or position. So the volume theorist denies that shadows can change shape or move. The volumist's static conception of shadows is reminiscent of Egyptian murals except it does allow shadows to be three dimensional.

A slightly more liberal theorist will concede that shadows change position but deny that this constitutes movement. This seems contradictory to we believers in the at-at theory of motion. We say motion is nothing more than change of position. Philosophers almost universally accept the at-at theory. It is simple and solves Zeno's arrow paradox (Russell 1937, 350). However, there are distinguished dissidents who think there is more to motion than change of position. Michael Tooley (1988, 244) imagines a world in which things occupy different places at random. The successive positions of one of these herky-jerky objects happen to form a smooth path. Tooley suggests that the object is not really moving because the earlier positions of the object are not causally relevant to its later positions. This requirement would forbid any shadow from moving even though it is compatible with the shadow occupying different positions.

Allowing for change of shape

The seeds of philosophical interest in moving shadows were sown by David Lewis and Stephanie Lewis (1970) in their dialogue "Holes." Bargle ambushes the materialist Argle with an unexpected counter-example: because there are holes and a hole is where there is no matter, there are immaterial things. Argle first tries to deny the existence of holes by paraphrasing talk of holes in terms of shapes. When Argle becomes persuaded that this reduction of holes to shapes cannot succeed, he changes his mind and affirms the existence of holes. Argle preserves his materialist scruples by identifying holes with hole linings. Since hole linings (e.g., a toilet roller) can spin, Argle boldly asserts some holes spin.

Given that shadows are holes in the light, the materialist Argle would identify each shadow with its shadow lining (the light immediately surrounding the unilluminated volume). So the issue of whether the round shadow spins turns on the question of whether its shadow lining spins.

The Lewises' dialogue inspired Roberto Casati and Achille Varzi to write a whole book on holes. They offer an immaterialist analysis of how shadows move. Casati and Varzi say holes are *constituted* by space just as Michelangelo's Statue of David is constituted by matter (marble in particular). Casati and Varzi regard shadows as holes in the light. Holes "are not abstractions but individuals, although they are not made of anything but space. They are not parts of the material object they are hosted in . . . ; rather, they are immaterial bodies, located at the surfaces of their hosts" (1994, 6). Holes can change location. A bubble rising through water is a hole that is constituted by successive regions of space. "Space is, in a sense, the matter of holes—or, if you prefer, space is to holes what matter is to material objects" (1994, 32). Since the hole is immaterial, it takes on the shape of its host. They compare the hole to the wine in a spinning goblet. The goblet spins but the wine stays still.

Actually, the motion of the glass is impressed upon the wine, so some of the wine will rotate. But that is only because the wine has mass. Casati and Varzi's point is that the goblet's cavity is immaterial and so cannot acquire motion from contact with the goblet.

Casati and Varzi still require an unstated premise that rest is the universal default state of shadows. If some shadows are already in motion, then their lack of mass would just make shadows all the harder to stop.

What happens if a circular hole in a rotating sphere is made elliptical? Casati and Varzi (1994, 123) deny that the hole suddenly starts to move. Instead, the hole just gently changes its shape. Thus, Casati and Varzi's theory of holes implies that all of the apparent rotation of shadows is actually deformation.

Partial rotation   Erdinç Sayan (1996, 87) criticizes Casati and Varzi for exaggerating the extent of deformation. He doubts that "gentle change of shape" can account for translational motion.

Sayan agrees with Casati and Varzi that a circular shadow cannot rotate and that any spinning shadow with a circular core cannot rotate as a whole. But Sayan thinks that an elliptical shadow can partially rotate. Specifically, he thinks the circular core of the elliptical shadow is stationary and the rest rotates. Sayan believes that space is the *medium* of a hole. Holes are a species of waves. Shadows, as holes in the light, move through space by the successive darkening of space.

The inspiration for Sayan's analysis is Peter Forrest's (1984) Achilles weed. This fictitious plant grows ten centimeters per hour but a tortoise eats one side of it at the same rate. None of the parts of the weed moves. Yet the weed winds up in a different location.

Forrest presents Achilles weed as a counterexample to the at-at theory of motion. He thinks the weed does not really move even though it is at one place at one time and at another place at another time.

Sayan thinks that the Achilles weed *does* move. He values Achilles weed as a model for the motion of holes, waves, and shadows. For the sake of clarity, Sayan cultivates a tidier descendent of Achilles weed: Achilles turf is a doormat-shaped patch of lawn grass that is composed of grass blades (fig. 4.4). The weed grows in an easterly direction by continual growth of new blades and is pruned at the westerly end by a tortoise. The tortoise moves by changing the location of its parts. Achilles turf moves in the way that waves move; successive blades are activated and deactivated as parts of the turf. In the case of holes, points of space play the role of the blades of grass. Shadows can be understood as holes in the light. As a region of space loses its illumination, the shadow grows.

Sayan grants shadows translational motion. But he denies that round shadows can rotate. For such motion does not exhibit the succession of activation and deactivation essential to waves.

Sayan's theory is geometrical, focusing on the intrinsic features of dark patches. Here he is backed by a mathematical tradition inaugurated by Jean Victor Poncelet (Gray 1993). Poncelet was left for dead during Napoleon's retreat from Moscow. After being taken prisoner by the Russians, he kept up his spirits by developing a branch of geometry in which the key features of a figure are those that it shares with its shadows. These are the projective properties of an object—the sort artists exploit when they depict a three-dimensional object on a two-dimensional surface. Another French mathematician,

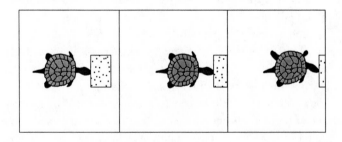

Figure 4.4 Achilles turf

Louis Poinsot, developed a simple geometrical description of how a solid body rotates. This projective geometry was extended by August Ferdinand Mobius. His barycentric calculus focuses on the object's geometrical center of gravity (which is calculated by assuming that the object has a uniform distribution of density).

Like Casati and Varzi, Sayan provides no role for the object that blocks the light. Yet movements of shadows do seem to track movements of the light blocker. Consider the shadow of a slowly spinning chipped Frisbee (fig. 4.5). Its moving shadow can be imitated by rotating a chip-shaped beam of light along the circumference of the shadow of a stationary unchipped Frisbee. The stationary shadow is being altered to look as if it is spinning.

Sayan must dismiss this description as naive. For him, there is nothing more to the shadow than the dark patch. He infers that questions about its movements never crucially depend on the means by which the dark patch is produced.

Although Sayan forbids total rotation, he permits partial rotation and distinguishes that from change of shape. He takes deformation to entail change of shape or size. Therefore, the movement of a rigid shadow from one location to another qualifies as translational motion, not as deformation. Consider a one-inch movement of my twelve-inch ruler's shadow across my desktop. Sayan says the light devoured the southernmost inch while the northern end grew an inch. The remaining eleven inches did not move. To move as whole, there must be a change in the geometrical center of gravity of each part. So Sayan thinks that the ruler's shadow only partially moves.

I agree that the ruler's shadow would move in this grudging way if it were cast by an Achilles ruler. But the shadow of my ordinary

Figure 4.5 Chipped Frisbee shadow

ruler moves all twelve inches of its shadow parts when it moves an inch. Each part of the shadow is a follower of some part of the ruler. Consequently, Achilles movement of shadows is as rare as Achilles objects. Yet Sayan's theory implies that all shadow movement is Achilles movement.

Sayan is driven to this narrow model of movement by his resolution to individuate all parts of a shadow internally (in terms of the shadow's intrinsic properties). This approach inadvertently makes contact a sufficient condition for the unification of two shadows. So on Sayan's theory, when the moving shadow of a bird grazes the shadow of a mountain, the result is a single, huge moving shadow.

We are happy to individuate parts of physical objects by other objects. The parts of a human hand individuate the parts of my glove. The hooks of a hookworm are understood relationally as devices to grasp the intestines of its host. We follow the same extrinsic policy of part individuation for shadows.

The essential connection between a shadow and its blocker is obscured by our tendency to focus on the cast shadow (the part of the three-dimensional shadow that is intercepted by a surface). This leads us to interpret shadow movement as an example of action at a distance. As dusty air reveals, the cast shadow is just an edge of a three-dimensional shadow that adheres to its blocker. The blocker is in contact with the shadow body, so movements of the shadow body naturally echo movements of the blocker. Since the speed of light is finite, the distant portions of some large shadows (e.g., the 150-million-kilometer shadow of Comet Hale-Bopp) significantly lag behind their blockers. For terrestrial purposes, however, the fidelity is virtually perfect.

To recapitulate, we need to go outside the dark patch to individuate the parts of a shadow. We need to introduce the parts of the blocker. For shadows are derivative (like echoes and reflections). There can be no shadows without blockers. The geometrical approach to the shadow ignores its causal structure and therefore obscures its anatomy—and thereby, misconstrues its behavior.

Full rotation Psychologists confirm our felt difficulty in calculating rotation (Parsons 1995). Historians of science chronicle how rotation has bedeviled theories of motion since Aristotle. This makes it tempting to infer that *rotation* is essential to the problem of indiscernible shadow movement.

Fortunately, translational motion is enough to frame the issue. Think of the shadow of a conveyor belt. When the belt is turned on, does the shadow start moving? If there are no chinks between the segments of the belt, the belt's shadow will look undisturbed. If you suspect that there is some illicit rotation in the conveyor belt, consider an unconventional conveyor belt that works by having segments grow at the left end and then disintegrate at the right end.

The shadow of the conveyor belt is moving because parts of the blocker are moving. Once we individuate shadow parts by blocker parts, we are poised to accept spinning shadows. The shadow cast by a spinning disk is made up of shadow parts that follow their casting parts. This is more salient if the disk is a round jigsaw puzzle. The shadow has as many parts as there are jigsaw pieces. When the disk is stationary, so is the shadow. Now spin the disk. The shadow looks stationary. Yet the shadow must spin because the shadows of the jigsaw pieces move.

One advantage of this solution is that it coordinates movements. Some of the desired matching is between the shadow and the blocker. Recall the ball that has a spike protruding from it. Let the spike rotate away from the light source (fig. 4.6). The spike's shadow shrinks and disappears from the left side of the ball. The shadow of the spike soon reappears on the right side of the ball. The desire to coordinate shadows and blockers nurtures the inference that the shadow of the spiked ball shares the motion of the spiked ball.

Of course, if we rely solely on the intrinsic properties of the shadow, then we cannot exclude the possibility that the round part

Figure 4.6 Shadow of rotating spike

of the shadow is stationary and a spike-shaped shadow element grows and disappears, only to reappear on the opposite side of the circle.

But why confine our attention to the shadow? The prisoners in Plato's allegory of the cave are chained so that they can only view shadows cast on the wall. We are free to examine the objects that cast the shadows. Like other animals, we attend to shadows chiefly because they provide clues to the objects that cast them.

Rules that coordinate the movements of shadows with their blockers would be more informative than rules that treated shadows autonomously. Thus, a purely geometrical approach to individuating shadow movements would be less likely to develop than a causal approach that coordinated shadows with their blockers.

Our appetite for coordination extends to matching between shadows. We are keen to keep double shadows moving together. Illuminating a wobbling cone from its apex yields a round shadow with no discernible movement. Adding a second light source to illuminate the profile of the wobbling cone produces a swinging triangular shadow. We resist the conclusion that only one of the shadows is moving. Our reluctance intensifies when we maneuver the second light source so that the two shadows overlap. It is arbitrary to describe one half of the fused shadow as moving while the other is stationary.

What goes for double shadows extends to the whole scene. We want the shadows to move in a way that makes overall sense. This is especially true when the shadows exhibit biological motion (Johansson 1973).

Scrolling Coordination between the movement of blockers and their shadows is compromised by the fact that shadows have fewer parts than their blockers. Only a minority of an object's parts blocks the light. Consider the shadow cast by Saturn's ring. Does its shadow rotate?

No. Instead, bands of shadows migrate across Saturn until they are destroyed (by virtue of that ring segment no longer blocking light). Shadow bands emerging along Saturn's daybreak replace the shadows that meet their end at Saturn's nightfall. Let us call this analogue of rotation "scrolling." As in rotation, scrolling permits an object without translational motion to have all of its parts simultaneously move. This permission is not a requirement. Just as a rotating object can simultaneously move translationally, a scrolling object can simultaneously undergo translational movement.

A cylinder can simultaneously cast a scrolling shadow and a rotating shadow (fig. 4.7). The round shadow rotates while the rectangular shadow scrolls. All the parts of the rectangular shadow uniformly move toward their destruction but are steadily being replaced at the opposite end by new shadow parts.

A landing surface is not needed for a shadow. Earth's shadow extends into empty space. Aristotle realized that a lunar eclipse is the moon's interception of this shadow. He also realized that Earth's shadow is the night. Aristotle did not realize that the night scrolls on the surface of the moon.

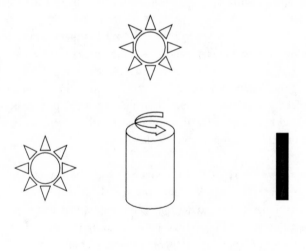

Figure 4.7 Spinning cylinder

When sunlight strikes Uranus at its southern axis of rotation, the Uranian night rotates. Uranus is the only planet that spins like a barrel. All the other planets spin upright like tops. (Astronomers suspect Uranus was knocked on its side.) If Earth rotated perfectly upright, then its shadow would perfectly scroll. The shadow of each portion of Earth would be destroyed before coming around again. However, Earth is tilted 23.5 degrees. This complicates the motion of our night. Happily geographers have terminology that can guide my description of how Earth's night moves. A *Marsden square* is a 10-degree longitude/latitude square. These are subdivisions of the grid you see on a globe. There are 936 Marsden squares. Each has its own number on a Marsden square chart. The top row of squares (ringing the north pole) number from 901 to 936. Since Earth is slightly tilted, the shadows of these uppermost squares rotate (casting a shadow throughout the rotation of Earth), but the shadows of most squares scroll (casting a shadow for only part of the rotation of Earth).

The Hawaiian-Emperor volcanic chain illustrates how a physical object can scroll. The islands composing the chain develop as the Pacific plate moves north over a fixed hotspot (see fig. 4.8). The hotspot creates a submarine volcano. Pillow lava from the volcano creates an island. The volcano becomes dormant after it rides past the hotspot. Its island begins to erode away into the Pacific Ocean. Meanwhile, the hotspot begins to form a new island.

The movement of light sources   Can the shadow of a stationary object rotate? We are slow to ask this question because human beings operate under the default assumption that objects are being illuminated from above by a single light source. (This is a special case of Bergstrom's [1994] principle that the number of light sources be minimized.) We also tend to simplify the lighting by treating the light source as a point. Finally, we operate under a default assumption that the local environment is stationary. Consequently, our first instinct is to trace any movement of a shadow to movement of its blocker.

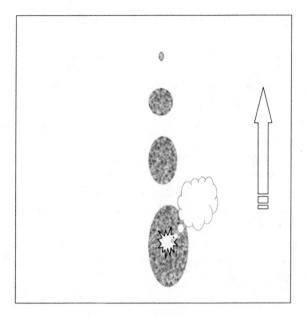

Figure 4.8 Scrolling island chain

When a light source moves to the side of a disk, the shadow changes from round to oval. Since we also operate under the default assumption that objects stay the same shape, the conflict between our default assumptions stimulates the thought that the light source is moving.

If the disk is also spinning, then the change of shadow shape illustrates how an *oval* shadow can indiscernibly rotate. The change to side lighting merely reapportions how much shadow corresponds to which parts of the disk. If the light source circles the disk, the oval shadow will indiscernibly rotate. This shows how a shadow can rotate even though neither the blocker nor the light source is rotating.

About 70% of those attending my lectures deny that the round shadow spins. My explanation is that people combine a default assumption that things are stationary with an intrinsic approach to shadows. Since the only relevant datum is the dark patch as it presently appears, there is nothing to override the stationary default assumption.

An implication for the Yale shadow puzzle

As one grants more movement to shadows, the range of viable theories shrinks, for movement becomes an extra differentiator of shadows. Recall the Yale shadow puzzle (Todes and Daniels, 1975), depicted with disks in figure 4.9. Is the shadow cast by High or Low? Since one object is enough to block the light, either object can be removed without affecting the appearance of the cast shadow. Some respond to the overdetermination by asserting that the shadow is cast by the mereological fusion of High and Low. Our meditations on spinning shadows suggest an objection. What if High and Low are disks spinning in opposite directions? In which direction does the shadow spin?

The objection cannot be avoided by restricting rotation. Let East be a high disk traveling east and West be a low sphere traveling west.

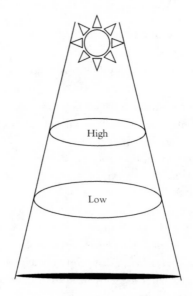

Figure 4.9 Yale puzzle

What happens when East meets West? Is the shadow below them moving east or west? Translational motion is enough to raise the objection to the fusion view.

According to the blocking theory, a shadow is an absence of light caused by blockage (as opposed to absorption, filtering, diffraction, etc.). Only High blocks the light. Low is causally idle. Therefore, the shadow belongs to High. The shadow's movement must be computed from how High blocks light.

The blocking theory suggests an intermediate case that serves as a precedent for accepting indiscernible movements of shadows. First, let the spinning sphere be perfectly black. It will look stationary but is spinning. Now consider the silhouette of the spinning sphere (which can be viewed by looking from the opposite side, into the light). The silhouette also looks stationary. But there is still no reason to conclude it is not spinning. The silhouette is the layer of the sphere that blocks the light. Unlike the shadow of the sphere, the silhouette is part of the sphere itself. You can touch it. To change the silhouette, you have to change the object—and the silhouette will carry along that mark, unlike a shadow. Just as the front surface of a black sphere is visible because of the light it fails to reflect, the silhouette is visible by virtue of the light it blocks. The silhouette has mass. Consequently, a force can be impressed upon it. This layer spins in the same way that the reflective surface of an object spins.

The shadow's boundary does not include the silhouette. Since none of the parts of the sphere is part of the shadow, parts of the sphere are not so intimately related to the shadow as to the silhouette. But there is a causal connection. Parts of the caster have parts of the shadows as effects. This encourages the inference that the shadow inherits the motion of its caster.

Superposition of shadows

John Locke said that two things of the same kind cannot be in the same place at the same time. Gottfried Leibniz replies that this is a reasonable assumption; but experience itself shows that we are not bound to it when it comes to distinguishing things. For instance, we find that two shadows or two rays of light interpenetrate, and we could devise an imaginary world where bodies did the same. Yet we can still distinguish one ray from the other just by the direction of their paths, even when they intersect. (1765/1981, bk. 2, chap. 27, 1)

Contemporary physicists would say that waves are counterexamples to Locke's principle. When an east-moving wave with a one-meter trough meets a west-moving wave with a one-meter trough, then they briefly coincide with a trough of two meters (see fig. 4.10).

After the constructive interference, the two waves then resume their one-meter depths. The two waves just pass through each other.

When waves have opposite phases, they appear to disappear on contact. But this "destructive" interference destroys only the outward effect, not the waves. The waves continue to exist through the dead spot and reemerge unscathed (as depicted in fig. 4.11). Thus, black patches that are due to the destructive interference of light waves are not absences of light. They are pseudoshadows.

Acceptance of shadow movement vindicates Leibniz's contention that shadows interpenetrate and that their paths can distinguish them. Consider two flashlights each with half of a coin taped to the bottom of its lens. Each flashlight casts a shadow of its coin half. The starting position of the flashlights is straight up. Then they pivot toward each other, making their shadows intersect (see fig. 4.12).

At the intersection, one shadow part is moving to the right while the other shadow part is moving to the left. In other words, the intersection contains two distinct shadow parts, not a single shadow part shared by two shadows. If there were a single shared part, it could not

Figure 4.10 Constructive interference

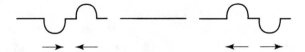

Figure 4.11 Destructive interference

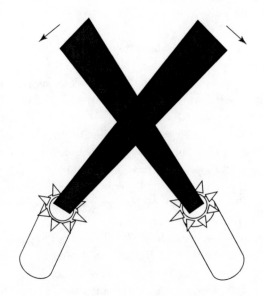

Figure 4.12 Intersecting shadows

be moving both right and left. It would be arbitrary to say it moves in one direction rather than the other. And if it is moving neither to the right nor to the left, then what about the shadow parts that lie beyond the intersection? They have a direction of movement, but the movement cannot be traced through the immobile intersection. These interruptions are avoided by allowing shadows to pass through each other.

Our tendency to accept interpenetration of shadows but not the interpenetration of objects may explain the "motion-bounce" illusion. When two dots silently cross in an X pattern, we see them as moving through each other. But if there is a collision noise at the intersection, we see the dots as bouncing off each other. My conjecture is that the noise prompts a module of the visual system to interpret the dots as objects rather than shadows.

Moon shadows

The interpenetration of shadows solves a riddle about moon shadows. A moon shadow (as opposed to the moon's shadow) is a shadow whose light source is the moon. Moon shadows are seen at night. The night is the shadow of Earth. A shadow is an absence of light. So how can there be shadows at night?

The Russian Space Regatta Consortium has already lofted reflectors into orbit to test the feasibility of illuminating cities at night. These create light spots many times brighter than moonlight. These reflectors will pierce "holes" in the night just like spotlights. Alarmed astronomers have allied with environmentalists to preserve the night. (Ecologists preserve what is not as well as what is.)

Moonlight is less destructive. The moon is not bright enough to make a hole in the shadow. Instead, the moonlight co-exists with Earth's shadow as natural light pollution. When you block the moonlight, you clean up the mess. This human-shaped fragment of the shadow of Earth was there before you arrived on the scene. You just clarified it by making it darker and providing a reason to single it out from the larger shadow that contains it as a part.

In short, there are two shadows, one contained in the other. Your moon shadow exists by virtue of you blocking the moonlight. The night exists by virtue of Earth blocking the sunlight. Earth has not been completely successful because the sun manages to ricochet some of its light on to the far side of Earth, thanks the moon's reflective capacity. But the amount of light is small enough to make it comparable to other shadows. When you cast a shadow in the afternoon, the sun manages to ricochet light into your shadow from walls and other reflective surfaces.

Our blindness to the polarization of light may impede our acceptance of interpenetrating shadows. Although light from the sun is not polarized, reflected light is. Since the polarization increases with the angle of incidence and varies with the nature of the reflecting surface, there is enough information to separate overlapping shadows from multiple light sources. The technique has been demonstrated for machine vision (Lin et al. 2006) and is probably exploited by animals that can see the polarity of light.

A total coincidence

Once we resign ourselves to superposition, we can arrange a case in which two shadows totally coincide with each other. Tape a round penny to the *center* of each of two flashlights as in figure 4.13. Aim them directly at each other. Their shadows overlap perfectly. There are two shadows, not one shared shadow. Rotate the flashlights in opposite directions. Now there are two spinning shadows in exactly the same place at the same time.

A complete theory of motion

G. E. Moore (1939) proved the existence of material things by presenting his hands as specimens. Beneath Moore's hands were shadows. They are specimens of absences.

Although Moore did not propound the shadow proof of absences, he is committed to accepting it. The preface to his proof of the external world contains an analysis of external things. After images are

Figure 4.13 Total coincidence of shadows

presented in space but cannot be met in space. Shadows can be met in space. Moore (1939, 275) denies that shadows are material things.

Physics, especially a physics that takes vacuums seriously, should cover every thing that moves, not just the movement of material things. I have focused on the movement of shadows because shadows are accessible and easy to manipulate. A complete theory of motion, however, must extend to knots and bulges and reach every nook and cranny.

5

Berkeley's Shadow

George Berkeley should fear his shadow, for it is a counterexample to the central thesis of his *New Theory of Vision* (1709/1901): sight derives its spatiality from touch.

Berkeley's untouchable shadow has a size and shape and location. Since his *left* profile differs from his *right* profile, his shadow also has an orientation. This complete array of spatial properties is not appropriated by fiat. The precision of Berkeley's shadow is earned by natural properties, specifically, by the juxtaposition of the sun, local surfaces, and the body of George Berkeley, Bishop of Cloyne.

Berkeley cannot say that his shadow possesses spatial properties solely in virtue of its *resemblance* to his body. Berkeley's mirror image, his illusory twin, more strongly resembles him than does his shadow. That is why Berkeley grooms himself by looking at the mirror instead of the ground. Berkeley's shadow resembles his body only with respect to the very spatial properties that an analogy is obliged to prove rather than presuppose.

Berkeley on the primacy of touch

Out of fear of taking on too many enemies at once, George Berkeley's first book, *New Theory of Vision*, is written from a perspective that does not challenge materialism. Indeed, Berkeley gives primacy to touch—the sense that seems so redolent of materialism. In Plato's war of the giants and the gods, the gods, in their idealism, associate reality with incorporeal ideas, while the giants, in their materialism, believe only in what they can touch, dragging

> everything down to earth out of heaven and the unseen, literally
> grasping rocks and trees in their hands; for they lay hold upon every
> stock and stone and strenuously affirm that real existence belongs
> only to that which can be handled and offers resistance to the touch.
> (*Sophist* 246 a b)

Primal needs are satisfied solely by what is tangible. ("Eating is touch carried to the bitter end" [Butler 1917, 230].) The practical man therefore sides with the giants.

Berkeley expresses solidarity with the practical man (his fellow Irish, "the vulgar," etc.). Touch is the master sense. Sight, hearing, and smell provide only indirect access to the spatial properties of objects. These more speculative senses are wholly dependent on correlations with the stable realm of tangible ideas. Thanks to the direct contact required by touch, tactile features are steadfast, invariant, and nearly foolproof. In contrast, the phenomenology of the far-ranging senses is variable, perspectival, and illusion prone. As you walk to a tower in the distance, "the appearance alters, and from being obscure, small, and faint, grows clear, large, and vigorous" (1901, 148). When you finally lay your hands on the tower, it feels the same way it always feels. From a distance, your eyes may have indicated that the tower is rounded and smooth, but now your hands reveal the tower to have sharp edges and a rough texture.

The other senses provide shortcuts to spatial judgments. The eye may eventually dominate the hand. But this is only because of what the hand has taught the eye. When experimental subjects handle a square while viewing it through a lens that makes it look rectangular, the square feels rectangular (Rock and Victor 1964). Vision "captures" touch. Irvin Rock (1966, 18n5) says this domination refutes Berkeley by showing that visual space prevails in conflicts with tactile space. But Berkeley denies that there is any independent visual space that could come into conflict with tactile space.

> What we have in Rock's experiment, according to Berkeley, is a conflict
> between two kinds of tactile information: the one coming directly from
> the hands, and the other coming from memory images aroused by infor-
> mation from the retinal image. The retinal image is one that has always
> been associated in the past with tactile rectangles. The fact that the subject
> perceives a rectangle and not a square thus indicates that previous experi-
> ence dominates over current impressions. (Morgan 1977, 177)

Visual space and auditory space are two forms of shorthand for tactile space. They are meaningful only to the extent that they can be trans-lated into pokes and pats, pinches and probes.

Phenomenologically, *feeling* the roundness of a ball is radically unlike *seeing* the roundness. Berkeley's explanation of the difference is that one is direct and the other is indirect. A number of contemporary phi-losophers embrace this asymmetry. According to Brian O'Shaughnessy, "There is in touch no analogue of the visual field of visual sensations . . . in touch a body investigates bodies as one body amongst others" (1989, 38). Michael Martin thinks that there is tactile sensory field but that it plays a different role from the visual field:

> [Sight] is experience of objects external to one as arranged in physical
> space. [Touch] is experience of objects as they come into contact with
> one's body; one is aware of one's body and its limits and so aware of
> objects coming into contact with one's body as they discernibly affect
> those limits. Normal visual experience is essentially experience of
> objects as they fall within the visual field; tactual experience is essen-
> tially experience of objects as they press from the outside onto the
> limits of a felt sensory field. (1992, 210)

This structural difference explains why sense datum theory is more attractive when we concentrate on *visual* experience. Hallucination motivates the postulation of sense data for vision but not for touch. Or so says Martin.

As an opponent of innate knowledge, Berkeley thinks babies begin with an uninformative color mosaic. From *learned* correlations between tactile sensations and visual sensations, the baby builds a stock of visual cues to distance, shape, and size. For instance, the child learns that proximity correlates with the sharpness and size of the retinal image.

Here is my exegetical thesis: Berkeley's tenets concerning the primacy of touch imply that intangible things cannot have spatial properties. Berkeley can count shading as a visible sign of contour, size, and distance. But he cannot count the shading as itself spatial. Berkeley must regard the belief in his shadow as a reification of the way in which he is illuminated.

Berkeley must deny that his shadow exists even though it scores well by the criteria he later endorses, as an idealist, to distinguish illusion from reality. In *The Principles of Human Knowledge* (1710), Berkeley audaciously agrees with John Locke that real things are coherent, lively, and independent of the will (unlike dreams, hallucinations, and imaginings). The coherence of shadows is evident from their amenability to geometrical analysis. There are tight (and useful) connections between the metrical properties of shadows and of their casters. In addition to meticulously meeting their mathematical obligations, shadows go beyond the call of duty with surprising gifts, such as Girard Desargues's (1591–1661) theorem: extending the sides of a triangle and the sides of its shadows yields intersecting points that form a straight line (Casati 2003, 185–87).

Shadows satisfy the criterion of liveliness by mimicking the lively movements of their casters. The involuntariness criterion is satisfied by our reactions to surprising shadows. We are startled by shadows that suddenly loom. Real shadows contrast with dreamt shadows, hallucinated shadows, and imaginary shadows just as real stones contrast with dreamt stones, hallucinated stones, and imaginary stones.

My critical thesis targets eliminativism about shadows: refusal to ascribe spatial properties to shadows exposes Berkeley to two objections, one at the level of appearance, the other at the level of reality.

The very fact that Berkeley's shadow *appears* to have a shape and size and location is an anomaly. Berkeley explains the spatial phenomenology of vision as an effect of conditioning. Even if the appearance of size and location is an illusion, how is it generated? Since there can be no correlations between sightings and touchings of shadows, there should not even be an appearance of size, shape, location, or orientation. In Berkeley's phraseology, shadows should seem as though they are "in the eye" instead of being "without the mind"; shadows should not have "outness." An observer in the remarkably long and straight Pontcysyllte Aqueduct sees the banks converge to the vanishing point. He treats this convergence as an artifact of his *representation* of the banks, not an external aspect of the banks themselves.

Whimsical observers *can* treat the convergence externally—as if they could travel to the vanishing point and take a close look at it. From the belfry of a church, Berkeley can see the people below as being small as dolls. For comical effect, Berkeley can see distant birds as tiny, intrinsically blurry, dots. The visual humor lies in an analogue of the use-mention ambiguity: properties of the visual field are being treated as properties of what they represent.

But the "outness" of shadows is no joke. We have trouble conceiving shadows internally on a par with fuzziness. We compulsively see shadows as being out in the landscape. Shadows are open to public inspection. The appearance–reality distinction for physical objects translates fluently into the domain of shadows. Mountaineers, mindful of the foreshortening illusion, distinguish between the triangular appearance of their mountain's shadow (as viewed from the summit) and the shadow's real shape. Spear fishermen, mindful of refraction, distinguish between the virtual location of the fish's shadow and the shadow's actual location.

The student of shadows is also surprised by their fidelity. When the sun is behind you, a cloud appears to cast a shadow that is smaller than itself. The distortion seems to fall in line with your experience of distorted shadows created by campfires and lamps. When an extended light source is near the object casting the shadow, the light rays are not parallel. Given this affine projection, it is difficult to make an envelope cast a rectangular shadow. *Sunlight* eases the task; the sun is so far away that its rays are nearly parallel. Once we appreciate why the shadow so faithfully mirrors the size and shape of the envelope in sunlight, we rethink our inference that the cloud and its shadow are not congruent. We realize that the "distortion" must be an illusion of a perspective (like the illusion of railroad tracks converging into the distance). The shadow of the cloud is the same size and shape as the cloud.

If shadows were merely appearances, then there should not be a difference between where a shadow is and where it appears to be. Nor should there be a difference between the shadow appearing to have a length and it really having a different length. Yet psychologists do think the horizontal–vertical illusion applies to ⊥-shaped shadows. Although the horizontal line of the ⊥ equals the vertical line, the vertical line looks longer.

The simplest explanation of the appearance–reality distinction for shadows is that there really are shadows out there. Astronomy encourages this realism. Galileo could not scale the lunar mountains. But he could measure their shadows with a telescope and infer the height of the mountains. If lunar shadows do not have shapes and sizes, Galileo would have been reasoning from false premises.

My interest in these anomalies is not restricted to Berkeley. Although few believed Berkeley's idealism, nearly everyone believed his perceptual thesis that distance is not immediately seen. John Stuart Mill writes,

> The doctrine concerning the original and derivative functions of the sense of sight, which . . . is known as Berkeley's Theory of Vision, has remained, . . . one of the least disputed doctrines in the most disputed and most disputable of all sciences, the Science of Man . . . the warfare which has since distracted the worlds of metaphysics, has swept past this insulated position without disturbing it; and while so many of the other conclusions of the analytic school of mental philosophy . . . have been repudiated with violence by the antagonist school, that of Common Sense or innate principles, this one doctrine has been recognized and upheld by leading thinkers of both schools alike. (1973, 84)

Phenomenalists, representative realists, and direct realists such as Thomas Reid were in near universal agreement with Berkeley. There was near unanimity that we visually represent distance in the indirect way we visually represent anger in a facial expression.

In the twentieth century, prominent dissent with Berkeley emerged. Is this recognition that Berkeley has been empirically refuted (as Bertrand Russell alleged) by *inventions* such as Charles Wheatestone's stereoscope? Or by *experiments* such as Gibson and Walk's (1960) visual cliff? Has Berkeley been conceptually undermined through refinements of *theory* such as the direct realism of late-twentieth-century philosophy and psychology (Gibson 1976, 1979)? Or is the apparent disagreement with Berkeley a volcano of verbal disputes occasioned by subterranean changes in the meaning of key terms? For instance, Robert Schwartz (1994) argues that eighteenth-century distinctions just do not mesh with twentieth-century distinctions, so the issue is a verbal deadlock. Schwartz's line of defense risks making Berkeley irrelevant to contemporary psychology and philosophy. Barriers to genuine disagreement are also barriers to genuine agreement.

There is genuine agreement with Berkeley, especially as we go along with the charitable tendency to dilute Berkeley's theses (as an antidote to minor inaccuracies). Berkeley continues to exert a diffuse but significant influence over psychologists and philosophers. He is invoked in discussions of the surprising ways touch guides vision. Echoes of Berkeley's *New Theory of Vision* can be heard in behaviorist theories of perception (Taylor 1962), inference models of perception, contemporary discussions of Molyneux's problem, the development of spatial perception, perceptional adaptation to abnormal conditions, sensory substitution, the role of action in perception (Noe 2004), and the study of touch. Shadows provide evidence against contemporary descendents of Berkeley's *A New Theory of Vision*. For the modernizations were not made with an appreciation of how shadows blindside Berkeley's original thesis.

Berkeley overlooked the significance of shadows just as pre-seventeenth-century astronomers overlooked the significance of the night sky being dark (Harrison 1987). Only in the seventeenth century did astronomers notice how anomalous the dark night is given that there is a star shining in any direction one points. Only a narrow class of theories can accommodate this observation. The banality of the fact that the sky is dark at night masks its status as a powerful clue to the structure of the universe.

Shadows provide a simple argument for the negation of Berkeley's thesis that all spatial things are tangible:

Intangibility Premise: All shadows are intangible.

Spatial Premise: All shadows have spatial properties (indeed the complete array).

Existence Premise: There are shadows.

Anti-Berkeleian conclusion: Some intangible things have spatial properties.

There are other candidate counterexamples: fog, rainbows, the sky, heavenly bodies, microscopic entities, and holes. Berkeley can handle some of these as his theory stands. For instance, Berkeley can say fog and rainbows are bodies of water droplets—which feel wet. Mars can be touched—at least hypothetically by a giant hand. I shall show how the remaining anomalies can be handled by patient application of Berkeley's theory or by fruitful (and therefore not ad hoc) adjustments to that theory. Shadows are the exception. Berkeley is forced to stonewall against the existence of shadows. This rigid hostility to shadows is ironic given Berkeley's later revelation that he is an immaterialist. More substantively, Berkeley's shadow eliminativism fails to "save the appearances" entrenched in both common sense and science (including vision science).

To get a better grasp of the challenge posed by shadows, I first review the highlights of Berkeley's theory of vision. There is controversy about the exact nature of Berkeley's theory. Does Berkeley think our spatial vocabulary is *ambiguous* across the sense modalities? What is the difference between direct and indirect perception? Does Berkeley think our visual perception is two dimensional? Shadows pose riddles regardless of how these exegetical questions are answered. And answers to these expected questions may depend on the constraints imposed by shadows. The challenge posed by shadows is as bluntly interesting as the challenge posed by the darkness of the night sky.

Berkeley's critique of the geometrical theory of vision

In the *Optics*, Euclid answered "What do people see?" by drawing straight lines from the eye to the surface of the nearest object. These rays collectively constitute the visual field. In the *Caloptics*, Euclid show how this field is supplemented with mirrors and other media that bend visual rays. An observer's ability to glean the dimensions and configuration of objects is explained by his ability to apply geometry. This mathematical approach to vision was rejuvenated by the development of spectacles, telescopes, and microscopes. Geometrical calculation led to improved lenses and elegant explanations of surprising optical effects. Berkeley took René Descartes and Nicolas Malebranche to be the most prominent philosophical advocates of the geometrical theory of vision.

The geometrical approach did not resolve all of its anomalies. Some of the recalcitrant issues were old. Aristotle had noted that the moon looks bigger when situated along the horizon. The image made on the retina does not change size, so why does the moon seem bigger?

Other anomalies date from 1602. Johannes Kepler had surmised, from the hypothesis that the eye incorporates a lens, that the retinal image is inverted. When René Descartes checked the conjecture by looking through the eyeball of an ox, he saw that the image was indeed upside down and left–right reversed. Descartes' subsequent brain dissections did not yield any mechanism that reinverts the image.

Geometrical explanations of distance perception were also compromised by the fact that each seen point in the environment corresponds to a single point at the retina. A ray of light is like a rod. You get no information about its length from being poked by it. That is why we are vague about the sizes of clouds; the cloud might be small and nearby or large and far away.

Some theorists had suggested that we disambiguate by comparing the image presented by the left eye with the image presented by the right eye. Berkeley doubted that anyone other than a geometer could exploit this binocular disparity. In any case, those born with only one functioning eye, such as the logician Augustus De Morgan, report having depth vision. Animals with wide-set eyes behave as if they have depth vision. Whales cannot be exploiting binocular disparity even if they are proficient at geometry.

Consequently, there was general agreement, prior to Berkeley, that we must *infer* distance. Berkeley's contribution was to streamline this psychological thesis. He restricts to touch *all* direct perception of distance, size, shape, and orientation. *All* visual judgments of spatial properties are inferences from patches of color and light. These patches do not correspond one to one with features of the environment. Contrary to the geometers, the eye's project is not to map a mental picture on to the external environment. There are no natural visual units that can be mapped on to tangible things. Color patches are like spoken sounds. The sounds do not gain their meaning from a resemblance or isomorphism with the objects they represent. Connections between visual ideas and tactile ideas are as arbitrary as the connections between names and their bearers.

Berkeley elaborates the analogy between visual ideas and words. The signs we use for objects must be learned. They are arbitrary. But once we have learned to connect a visual idea with a tangible object, the association is so strong that we instantly read through the sign to the object. The transition is so effortless that we are prone to confuse the sign with what it signifies. We seem to see the heat of a red iron when we actually see only a pattern of light. Berkeley thinks a similar confusion arises for distance cues. We are so fluent in translating cues for distance that we take ourselves to be directly seeing distance, shape, and magnitude. Thus, in ordinary language, we are said to both see and feel the roundness of a ball.

Berkeley believes that this error is exposed by William Molyneux's thought experiment featuring a blind man who suddenly has his sight restored. Can the newly sighted man distinguish a ball from a cube without touching it? No, answers Berkeley. The blind man must *learn* to see roundness by correlating what he sees with felt roundness. Prior to acquiring the spatial cues, Molyneux's man will see everything as being "in the eye" rather than as being out in the environment. Berkeley thinks this is actually a more philosophically accurate way of seeing than normal vision; Molyneux's man does not mistakenly think that he is directly seeing distances, sizes, and shapes.

Berkeley also illustrates his thesis by imagining an unembodied spirit who can see but cannot touch. This spirit brings to mind Dante in the second canto of Purgatorio (II, 74–77). The poet tries to embrace an affectionate shadow but his arms fail to clasp anything:

> *O shadows vain!*
> *Except in outward semblance: thrice my hands*
> *I clasped behind it, they as oft returned*
> *Empty into my breast again.* (Dante 1321/1957)

But Berkeley's unembodied spirit has no arms to grasp and no memory of any tactile contact. Since geometry is the study of *tangible* distance, this benighted soul "could have no idea of a solid or quantity of three dimensions, which follows from its not having any idea of distance" (1901, 154, 203). The unembodied spirit would be a complete ignoramus with respect to geometry: "He cannot even have an idea of plain figures any more than he can of solids; since some idea of distance is necessary to form the idea of a geometrical plane, as will appear to whoever shall reflect on it" (1901, 204).

Berkeley's gloom about the unembodied spirit and Molyneux's man should envelop the prisoners in Plato's allegory of the cave. Plato's immobilized prisoners would not be able to attribute spatial properties to the shadows. They would be like the unembodied spirit who sees only colors. Berkeley would disagree with Plato's view that the prisoners become experts on the shadows. On Berkeley's view, the prisoners could not see the distance between shadows or recognize their shapes or see some shadows as bigger than others. There is little more to a shadow than its spatial properties. So Berkeley should doubt that the prisoners could even see shadows. At best, the prisoners see merely effects of shadows just as we see merely effects of shadows behind pebbled glass (which is designed to disorganize the information carried by light).

Once Berkeley establishes that the spatiality of our visual ideas is completely derivative, he can dissolve the problem of the inverted retina. Since there are no direct visual ideas of up and down, there was never any conflict to begin with. The eye has no innate spatial ideas that might come into conflict with empirically learned connections.

Berkeley handles the moon illusion with an appeal to nongeometrical cues such as faintness. When the moon is viewed along the horizon, there is more atmosphere between the viewer and the moon. Particles in the atmosphere scatter light rays, making the moon blurrier. Blurriness is a sign of distance. Because the image size is constant, we adjust and infer that the moon is large. When the moon is high in the sky, there is less atmosphere, so we see the moon more sharply and therefore do not attribute as much distance.

Incidentally, astronauts on the atmosphereless moon refuted Berkeley by witnessing Earth perform a "moon illusion" along the lunar horizon. (The illusion is inadvertently documented by the photographs of Earth at different positions in the lunar sky.) There is no shame in being refuted by an observation that requires such a remote vantage point. But some embarrassment is in order for overlooking the significance of observations that no sighted man can avoid making. Berkeley's writings contain not a single literal remark about shadows.

On Berkeley's theory, an extended thing might be silent or odorless or tasteless or invisible. But it cannot be intangible. Only tangible things can be perceived as having spatial properties. So if I am conceiving an extended thing, I am imagining a thing that could, in principle, be touched.

For Berkeley, the proper objects of touch are the physical objects themselves. When a hand touches a dog, it touches the dog itself, even if the hand is that of a cadaver. Given that you are a healthy human being, your hand's contact with the dog causes tactile sensations. You touch perceptually, not just physically.

The immediacy of touch insures its intrinsic spatiality. When you touch a dog, you do not merely touch a sign of the dog; you touch the dog itself. In contrast, when you smell a wet dog, you only have contact with his odor. As the odor intensifies, you may infer that you are approaching the malodorous canine. But odor intensity does not intrinsically represent increasing proximity. Similarly, when you hear a dog, you are really hearing the sounds produced by the dog. You can infer that the dog is leaving by the decreasing intensity of its barks. But the sounds are not intrinsically spatial. When you see the dog recede into the distance, you attend to visual cues. The dog occupies a progressively higher position in the visual field. He becomes more faintly perceived with distance. There are more interpositions by other objects. Your eyes converge less tightly. Whereas you directly see color, you do not directly see the distance between you and the dog.

Or so I say Berkeley says in his *New Theory of Vision*. I next consider how Berkeley might meet the challenge posed by shadows.

Thermal sensing of shadows? Given that there are no tactile sensations of shadows, there is no hope of verifying that a shadow is round by feeling it. Size and distance judgments would also be unverifiable by virtue of their tactual unverifiability. Since shadows are *necessarily* intangible, such attributions would be worse than unknowable or false. Given Berkeley's *New Theory of Vision*, they should count as meaningless.

Do we thermally sense shadows? Hot travelers feel the cool shade of a tree. In principle, a blind man could learn the dimensions of a shadow by stepping in and out of the shadow, sampling its coolness.

The blind man could also get a clue about the boundaries of shadow by feeling the dampness of the ground on which the shadow is cast. Blocking the light retards evaporation and promotes condensation.

However, only things composed of particles can hold water. The *ground* is damp, not the shadow cast on the ground.

Asking "What is the temperature of a shadow?" is like asking "What is the temperature of a vacuum?" Temperature is defined as the average kinetic energy of molecules. Things that lack positive constituents lack temperatures. An object in a vacuum can have temperature but not the vacuum itself. Since electromagnetic radiation can travel through empty space, objects in space cool down as they radiate their energy. The "coldness of outer space" alludes to this effect.

The space suits of astronauts need to tolerate temperature drops of 240 degrees centigrade as the astronaut moves into the shadow of a space vehicle. But this is a change in the temperature of the space suit, not the shadow. Strictly speaking, heat is not radiated through a vacuum. Instead, the heat of the sun is transformed into radiant energy, and the radiant energy travels through space until it strikes an object. It is then retransformed into thermal energy, which can be felt as heat.

When I hold my hand in the sunshine, radiant energy from the sun is transformed into thermal energy, so I can feel my hand heating up. When a ruler casts a shadow over my palm, I could (at least in principle) feel the temperature difference. The issue is whether this would constitute feeling a shadow.

I could feel *that* there was a shadow. That is, I could infer a shadow on the basis of what I feel. This is the epistemic sense of perception (Dretske 1969, 88). I am interested in nonepistemic feeling of shadows.

I cannot feel radiation and so cannot feel absences of radiation. I can feel the effects of radiation. I am feeling a band of coldness because there are cold receptors in my hand. There are also heat receptors, so I can feel an absence of heat. But I have not got any radiation receptors in my skin.

Some animals have photosensitive skin patches and so can sense radiation. But this counts as seeing rather than feeling. If the human pineal gland is photosensitive (as speculated by those who characterize it as a vestigial eye), then we might have more shadow perception than previously considered. But this would not be a counterexample to the *intangibility* of shadows.

If shadows had temperatures, then shadows could be warmed. A leaf on a frozen pond melts down (and eventually tunnels through surface) because it absorbs heat from the sun. The ice in the shadow beneath the leaf is warmed by the leaf. But the leaf does not warm the shadow.

Thermal *detection* of a shadow would not suffice for thermal *sensing* of a shadow. A golfer, wary of lightning strikes, detects an electrical charge by feeling his hair stand on end. But he is only feeling an effect of the electric field, not the electric field itself.

It is also doubtful that Berkeley should attribute any intrinsic spatiality to thermal ideas. The contact rationale of spatiality through direct perception does not work because we often sense temperature at a distance. The prudent feel the coldness of dry ice by holding a hand *above* it. Touching dry ice produces a sensation of burning heat rather than cold. We correlate the intensity of heat to proximity to the stove. Once the association is learned, we may read through thermal sensation to get an idea of proximity to the source. But the idea of proximity is not immediately available from the idea of heat intensity.

Kinesthetic sensing of shadows?   In addition to your outward-directed sense of touch, you can also feel your own muscles, tendons, and joint orientations. Your "muscle sense," kinesthesia, tells you how your limbs are oriented. Although little aware of any kinesthetic sensations, you can tell how far apart your fingers are without looking. If your kinesthetic sense is impaired, you must look at your fingers to tell whether they are splayed.

Berkeley shows awareness of kinesthesia when he emphasizes the importance of movement through an environment. In World War II, German soldiers overlooked the informativeness of kinesthesia when they permitted blind French men to stroll along the Normandy coast. Some of the blind men paced out the distances between trench lines (and relayed their findings to the French Resistance, which in turn passed the information to the planners of the Allied invasion of Normandy).

Berkeley presupposes that kinesthesia is used in conjunction with other senses. It is doubtful that Berkeley thinks the inner sense of kinesthesia can function *on its own* to measure external things. Kinesthesia cannot autonomously supply boundaries. Consequently, a man relying solely on kinesthesia to measure something does not know when to stop pacing or stretching.

The tactile sense can delimit an object. Sight can as well. However, given that the sight of a shadow has no intrinsic spatiality, vision helps only if correlations with touch have been previously established. In the case of shadows, these correlations cannot be established by the tactile sense because shadows have no tactile properties. So, on Berkeley's account, kinesthesia could not deliver the dimensions of a shadow.

More fundamentally, measurement by kinesthesia *presupposes* that the agent knows that shadows are out in the environment rather than "in the eye."

Kinesthesia *supplements* our understanding of the immensity of large objects. It is less informative for very small things such as a sand grain. You are too big to maneuver around it and too big to feel its weight.

A four-year-old can be persuaded that a grain of sand weighs something by pouring many grains into his hands. The heft of the collective is attributed partly to each grain. If we assume that this whole to part reasoning is cogent, then the sense of touch can get a foothold on intangibly small things that can form tangibly large collections.

But most microscopic entities cannot be understood on this model. They are completely unprecedented to the naked eye. With drastic reduction of scale, we lose all other aspects of touch. For this reason, Berkeley believes that what we see with a microscope is completely unrelated to what we see in everyday life:

> A microscope brings us, as it were, into a new world: it presents us with a new scene of visible objects quite different from what we behold with the naked eye. But herein consists the most remarkable difference, to wit, that whereas the objects perceived by the eye alone have a certain connexion with tangible objects, whereby we are taught to foresee what will ensue upon the approach or application of distant

objects to the parts of our own body, which much conduceth to its preservation, there is not the like connexion between things tangible and those visible objects that are perceived by help of a fine microscope. (1901, 204)

Thus Berkeley denies that our eyes would be improved by turning them into microscopes. We would have lost the connection to the tangible realm and would be left with "only the empty amusement of seeing" (1901, 170).

Amateurs who peered through the microscopes of Berkeley's era saw little more than a confusing swirl of colored lights. Even the experts experienced severe difficulties. In the preface of *Micrographia* (1665/1894), Robert Hooke admits,

> It is exceedingly difficult in some objects to distinguish between a *prominency* and a *depression*, between a *shadow* and a *black stain*, or a *reflection* and whiteness *in a color*. Besides, the transparency of most Objects renders them yet much more difficult than if they were *opacous*. (23)

Notice that Hooke's concession presupposes that the microscopist is still seeing black stains and shadows even when he cannot tell which is which. If these microscopic things were inhabitants of a separate world, Berkeley would have trouble explaining how we could perceive them as being spatially related to each other. The microscopist could not have meaningful worries about whether his lenses exaggerate the relative size of the specimen, whether left and right have been reversed, and whether the specimen is concave rather than convex, for the microscopist cannot correlate what he sees with what he feels.

Microscopes improved during Berkeley's lifetime. Hooke's realism about what the microscopist sees becomes more compelling when one considers the equipment of modern microscopy. Ian Hacking (1983, 202–5) points out that microscopists buy lettered grids that have been shrunk through photochemical processes. The difference between the original grid and its microscopic copies is just a matter of size.

A buoyant Berkeleian could characterize the grid as an opportunity. The grid helps microscopists maneuver and poke cells. Ian Hacking (1983) counts these interventions as sight–touch relations. Why not liberalize Berkeley in this direction? True, Berkeley writes as if touch requires direct contact. This would exclude specimen staining, knob turning, and microscopic pushing, pulling, and puncturing. But Berkeley could adopt a more expansive conception of touch.

Advances in nanotechnology could make this expansion even more compelling. With big tools, we can make smaller tools. A servomechanism can enable a big tool to control the movements of a small tool. Smaller "slave" tools set up another round of miniaturization. Given enough rounds, the big "master" pliers in the microscopist's hands can control the tiny "slave" pliers under his microscope. Ditto for tiny screwdrivers, tiny hammers, and tiny saws. If Berkeley witnessed such a workshop, he would be tempted to count this as touching microscopic entities.

The metaphysician sends the bill. Touch loses its privileged status as the only sense that directly links the observer to physical objects. Like the other senses, touch would involve a distinction between the proximate cause of a perception and what is perceived. We could speak of a tactile sensory field comparable to the visual field.

Whatever the price, this wide conception of touch is correct. For instance, a blind man feels the curb with his cane. He is focused on the curb and ignores how the handle of the cane feels in his palm. His hand is like the retina.

"Distal" touch can occur *within* the body. Consider a woman who awakes because her arm has fallen asleep. To get some feeling back into her numb limb, she drags her arm up across the sheets. At shoulder level, she feels the sheets through her unfeeling arm.

Coverings tend to "deafen" touch. However, a student can feel a book through a padded envelope. A guard can feel a gun concealed beneath a coat by frisking a suspect. A physician can feel the enlarged liver of an alcoholic by palpating his abdomen.

More surprisingly, interposing a medium can *enhance* touch. Some people read Braille better with gloves or through an intermediate cloth. Automobile body inspectors examine the finish on surfaces by wiping it with a rag. In laboratory conditions, subjects are more discerning of the orientations of a surface undulation when they run a thin paper across the surface rather than their bare fingers (Gordon and Cooper 1975). Some possible explanations of the improvement are negative. Maybe the paper turns off the light-pressure system that masks deeper receptors. Or the paper might eliminate distracting temperature sensations. Other explanations are positive. Maybe the paper works like an amplifier; rough paper is more likely to snag on surface irregularities than bare skin (Lederman 1982).

Our buoyant Berkeleian could argue that microscopes amplify *both* touch and sight. The novice learns to see through a microscope by coordinating what he feels with what he sees. His laboratory experiences are as much tactile and kinesthetic as they are visual.

When the microscopist punctures a cell with a microneedle, his tactile attention is at the sharp point. He touches the cell with this instrument. But it is genuine touching despite the indirection.

The buoyant Berkeleian embraces Grover Maxwell's (1962) continuum of vision: "looking through a window pane, looking through glasses, looking through binoculars, looking through a lower power microscope, looking through a high power microscope, etc." The price is that the Berkeleian loses this sharp contrast between the directness of touch and the indirectness of vision and hearing. (In *The Principles of Human Knowledge*, Berkeley discreetly pays the price because idealism discounts pedigrees.) The more indirect the relationship, the more room there is for mistakes and illusions.

But this only increases the *amount* of illusion we can attribute to touch. There are many illusions involving direct touch. Aristotle notes that a stick held between crossed fingers feels like two sticks. In the first half of the twentieth century, it was established that there are systematic, tactile counterparts of visual illusions. Homer Bean (1938) showed that 28 blind subjects experienced the following illusions: the Mueller-Lyer illusion, the vertical–horizontal illusion, plus the Poggendorff, Ponzo, and the Zollner illusions. A subject who lets his hand ride on a surface rotating around him feels like *he* is rotating

(Shone 1984, 250–51). In the size–weight illusion, a big container feels lighter than a small container of equal weight (because lifting the big container is easier than expected).

Opponents of representative realism tend to overestimate the epistemic benefits of direct perception. Direct perception of an x that is F does not suffice for knowledge that x is F. The perceiver still needs to know he is directly perceiving x and that its appearance of being F is veridical.

Hypothetical touching   In his defense "Theory of Vision Vindicated and Explained," Berkeley emphasizes that one need not actually touch an object to see it as having spatial properties:

> And here it may not be amiss to observe that figures and motions which cannot be actually felt by us, but only imagined, may nevertheless be esteemed tangible ideas, forasmuch as they are of the same kind with the objects of touch, and as the imagination drew them from that sense. (1901, 402)

If the shadow of Berkeley were the same type of thing as a man, then the spatial properties of Berkeley would warrant attributing spatial properties to his shadow.

But the shadow of a man's body is a radically different sort of thing than his body. I came across an unexpected illustration of this metaphysical contrast amongst the reminiscences of the World War II pilot C. E. "Bud" Anderson. A Messerschmitt was pursuing him; desperate to escape, Bud flies straight up. He hopes that the Messerschmitt will stall first. The Messerschmitt shudders. The pilot breaks off the pursuit. Roles now reverse: Bud's Mustang can now dive and fire upon the Messerschmitt from behind. So the Messerschmitt is forced to fly straight up. The Messerschmitt is hit. He rolls and then dives too steeply for Bud to safely follow:

> Straight down he plunges, from as high as 35,000 feet, through this beautiful, crystal clear May morning toward the green-on-green

checkerboard fields, leaving a wake of black smoke. From four miles straight up I watch as the Messerschmitt and the shadow it makes on the ground rush toward one another . . . and then, finally, silently, merge. (Anderson and Hamelin 1990, 9)

An oil drop can merge with an oil puddle. But the Messerschmitt pilot cannot literally merge with his shadow. It is worse than trying to mix oil with water. This explains part of the absurdity of pictures that depict shadows commingled with objects (fig. 5.1).

When people are asked how a shadow resembles the man who casts it, they allude to similarity in motion, shape, size, and location. But these are the very similarities Berkeley needs to explain. Berkeley would be reasoning in a circle if he claimed his shadow has spatial properties because the shadow resembles his body with respect to its spatial properties. Since Berkeley cannot cite spatial attributes as the points of resemblance, too little remains for an analogy between his body and its shadow.

Feeling absences by feeling presences   Many philosophers have affirmed the principle that only material things can be touched: Armstrong (1962, 26–27), O'Shaughnessy (1989, 38), Schwayder (1961, 307), Strawson (1959, 107–8), Warnock (1953/1983, 50–52). Samuel Johnson was assuming this principle when he kicked a stone with the intention of refuting Berkeley. But we do *speak* of feeling holes and cracks. If these locutions can be vindicated, shadows might be shown to be tangible after all.

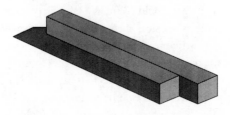

Figure 5.1   Shadow commingled with object

Psychologists compare how big a hole feels to how big it looks (Antis and Loizos 1967). The smaller the hole, the more its size is overestimated by the finger and especially the tongue. Dental patients who lose a filling often notice that the cavity seems absurdly large when probed by tongue. A surprising amount of psychology presupposes that holes can be touched. So science offers a helping hand to Berkeley.

But Berkeley may be forced to decline the assistance. Berkeley denies that vacuums are visible, and in later work he seems to deny that they are even conceivable. After dismissing the geometer's abstract triangles, Berkeley rejects the suggestion that "pure space, vacuum, or trine dimension to be equally the object of sight and touch" (1901, 189). In *The Principles of Human Knowledge*, Berkeley explains

> that it is not in my power to frame an idea of a body extended and
> moving, but I must withal give it some colour or other sensible quality,
> which is acknowledged to exist only in the mind. In short, extension,
> figure, and motion, abstracted from all other qualities, are inconceivable.
> (1901, 263)

In other words, no object can possess only primary qualities. There must be some secondary qualities. (The thesis was later embraced by David Hume, further refined by David Armstrong [1961, chap. 12], only to be later repudiated by Armstrong [1968a, 282].)

Frank Jackson (1977, 131) thinks Berkeley's secondary quality requirement precludes holes. Holes have spatial properties but nothing else. People can only sense what is, not what is not. So they cannot even imagine what would count as a secondary quality of a hole.

If black counts as a color, then shadows (just barely) satisfy the requirement that each thing must have secondary qualities. However, Berkeley says the proper object of vision is light (1901, 191). (Berkeley is seconded, in detail, by Bede Rundle [1972, chap. 8].) Since blackness is the appropriate visual response to an absence of light, this definition implies that black objects are not directly visible; when I see a black patch, I infer the black patch only from my failure to see. The absence of a secondary quality is not a secondary quality. The *conjunction* of Berkeley's account of the proper objects of vision and his requirement that each thing have some secondary quality implies that shadows cannot be directly perceived (and may even be inconceivable).

Roberto Casati and Achille Varzi (1994, chap. 11) contend that holes can be *indirectly* perceived by perceiving their linings and sometimes by perceiving their fillers (as when we see a pink oil bubble in transparent water). Perhaps Casati and Varzi would agree that we can also perceive absences by scattered presences. If you move your hand gently over the bristles of a stiff brush,

> you will feel a discontinuous space filled with points, a tactual figure. The points give the impression of a great numerosity, whose estimation might seem a completely hopeless task. Between the points, there is not "nothing" in a tactual sense, but rather empty tactual space that is not covered by matter. The tactual space is covered discontinuously with the tactual matter of the brush points; the space between forms the *tactual ground*. Unlike the case in vision, the tactual figure and ground are not reversible in this or other cases of a similar nature. (Katz 1989, 61)

Just as the perception of a lining guides the perception of the hole, the perception of scattered bristles guides the perception of the empty spaces areas between the bristles.

Casati and Varzi take as their precedent the perception of abstract things; we see the north pole by seeing a patch of ice at 90 degrees North latitude. They make the case for

> the perception of abstractions only in order to show that it could be of help in the development of a theory of the perception of holes. Consider now the hypothesis that holes are not abstractions, but are similar to abstractions at least insofar as they are not material. To perceive an immaterial entity would be to perceive it *mediately*, through perception of some material entity on which it depends (e.g., the host) or to which it is spatially linked in some relevant way (e.g., the filler). (1994, 157)

Berkeley would reject the assimilation of the perception of holes to the perception of abstractions. Berkeley is a nominalist: since abstract things are inconceivable, nothing counts as perceiving an abstract thing.

Casati and Varzi believe that the causal theory of perception precludes any direct perception of holes. However, once we accept that absences can be causes (Lewis 2004), we can make the case for direct perception of holes. Consider the hole in my pocket. This absence causes my finger to drop through the lining. The slipping sensation and penetration to my bare thigh constitutes the feeling of a hole in my pocket. I can ascertain the diameter of the hole by inserting more fingers into the hole. My fingers are active hole fillers. I am not feeling the hole by feeling my fingers. I am feeling the hole.

Skin is sensitive to a surprisingly wide variety of effects that can be produced by holes: vibrations, weight, pressure, wetness, plus changes in temperature.

In addition to the effects of a single hole (e.g., the low heft of a hollow walnut), there are joint effects of collections of holes. Cheese is thumped to get a feel for its overall volume of holes: "In a first-class cheese the holes must be of the right size and number, and this can be determined by the percussion method" (Katz 1989, 86).

We also feel holes through intermediate objects. A dentist feels cavities with a probe. Drivers feel a pothole through a jolt passed through the car.

The perception of a hole need not be through an inference. The computer paper illusion shows that one can feel a hole without feeling that there is a hole (Wolfe 1979). Old-fashioned computer paper had a column of holes that mesh with the sprockets of the printer. When you run your finger over the holes, the holes feel like bumps. The illusion of feeling concavities as convexities could fool a blindfolded individual.

We are apt to infer that a hole cannot be felt if we assume that the primary mode of touch is stationary. A hand suspended in the empty space of a hole does not feel the hole. Feeling holes requires a holistic experience that encompasses transitions between the hole and its host. Motion has the same primacy for vision. The eyes piece together the scene through saccades; the visual system is relentlessly comparative. An immobile eye is blind.

When a batter waits for a pitch, he keeps the bat in motion. The feedback helps him control the swing. Similarly, when a potter waits for a bowl to form, he continually shapes the inner cavity as the wet clay spins on the wheel. The feedback helps him control the hole.

Feeling nothing differs from an absence of feeling. The leper with numbed fingers cannot feel the buttons or buttonholes of his shirt. His failure to feel the buttonholes is a failure to feel absences.

Casati and Varzi concentrate on conditions that lead speakers to *report* that they perceive a hole. However, we need to distinguish between perceptual reports that embody an inference, reports of effects, and reports of perceiving the thing itself. After I pump a bicycle tire, I feel *that* there is a hole by squeezing the tire. When I feel a tiny jet of air, I feel *an effect* of the hole. And when I rub my forefinger over the puncture, I feel the hole *itself.*

The sky   The tangibility of holes suggests a (highly hypothetical) way in which the sky can be touched. The sky is like a hole except its volume is dictated by the face of a planet (or other large heavenly body) rather than a lining. The sky projects indefinitely up from the planet, and is bounded by the horizon. The sky inherits the egocentricity of the horizon; when I travel, the sky shifts with shifts in the horizon.

Satellites orbit above the atmosphere but not above the sky. There is as much atmosphere (indirectly) below us as above us. But the sky is only above us.

The *atmosphere* is tangible. Wind can be felt. But the atmosphere is not the same as the sky because a planet does not lose its sky when it loses its atmosphere. The sky contains air in the way the hole of a ring contains air. If the ring is put in a vacuum chamber, then the hole remains after the air is pumped out. The sky cannot be material because it would survive the disappearance of any of the material things found in the sky.

The only material thing on which the sky depends is the face of the planet from which it projects. We can imagine a giant hand caressing the face of Earth much as a blind man explores the face of his wife. A blind person can understand the sky by this sort of analogy.

The motivation for coining the word "sky" is visual, but nothing in the definition guarantees that the sky holds anything of visual interest. Astronomers think earthlings are lucky to be able to see anything of note in the daytime sky (Lynch and Livingston 2001, 21). If the amount of air were doubled, the sky would be opaque from perpetual overcast. If the amount of air were halved, no water would be carried aloft and the sky would be clear but featureless. If Earth were a few percent closer to the sun, the surface water would evaporate entirely. If Earth were a few percent farther from the sun, the water would freeze out as ice.

The sky cannot be touched by reaching up. True, the daytime sky appears dome shaped, and the ceilings of domes can be touched. But the sky dome is an illusion. The clouds directly above are nearer than the ones toward the horizon. Because clarity is a sign of proximity, the dome appears to have a flattened top (Humphrey 1964, 453). But there is no real dome up there.

At night, the sky is black and dotted with stars. Because they move in unison, the Greeks postulated a rigid sphere that moved around Earth. Many of their astronomers believed that the stars are just holes in the celestial sphere through which we see light from a celestial fire. Where contemporary astronomers see a scattering of matter in a field of emptiness, these ancient astronomers "saw" a scattering of immaterial entities in a substantial sphere. Even if there were such a sphere, the sky would extend beyond it.

The sky lacks any surface that can be touched. The blue color of the daytime sky is produced in the same way as the blue light from a colored light bulb. The atmosphere transmits light only with a limited range of wavelengths.

Because there is neither a dome nor a sphere nor any other surface, the sky cannot be touched in the way that first comes to mind (reaching up). And because we are very small compared to the surface of Earth, we cannot normally feel the sky by feeling the face of Earth. But we can imagine a giant feeling the face of Earth, and that satisfies Berkeley's tangibility requirement.

As a historical footnote, Berkeley should have been primed to the relevance of giants. In 1752, he lived a month with the Irish giant Cornelius Magrath—whose skeleton is on display in the museum of Trinity College (Luce 1949, 187).

The recalcitrance of shadows

Tangible holes (and cracks) owe their tangibility to the tangibility of their linings. As the lining becomes less tangible, so does the hole. Shadows are holes in the light and so cannot derive tangibility from their intangible host.

A shadow can be cast on a surface that feels rough. But that experience does not count as feeling the roughness of the shadow. Contrast this with feeling the roughness or jaggedness of a hole.

Contact with the casting surface qualifies as touching the shadow physically (in the way a flag touches the ground) but never perceptually. Contact with the lining of the hole often counts as feeling the hole.

The dimensions of a cast shadow depend on several factors: the dimensions of the caster, the relative position of the light source, and the orientation of the casting surface. If the surface cuts the three-dimensional shadow at oblique angle, the shadow will have a different shape and size. Some shadows are projected into empty space and so lack a casting surface.

Shadows must have casters. But feeling the caster does not count as feeling its shadow. One reason may be that the dimensions of the shadow also depend crucially on the relative position of the light source. An object can cast shadows that differ widely in size and shape. Figure 5.2 depicts a wedge that casts a round shadow from the top, a square shadow from the side, and a triangular shadow from another side. One genre of shadow art consists of a jumble of wire that casts coherent shadows (in the shapes chairs, words, or other familiar forms).

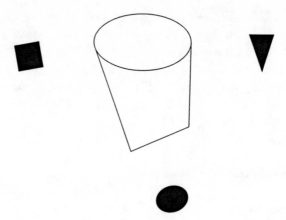

Figure 5.2 Triple shadow

Geometers ask the general question: what is the relationship between the different projections (shadows) set in a three-dimensional
space? Kenneth Falconer used fractal geometry to answer: none
whatsoever! Falconer (1990, 88–90) illustrated his answer by imagining a digital sundial crafted from iterated Venetian blinds (Stewart
1991). This static suspension of tiny shapes casts a shadow that accurately displays the time in *digital* form. For instance, at 4:52, there is a
shadow in the shape of 4:52.

Summary

My core objection to Berkeley's theory of vision runs as follows:
No shadows are tangible yet all shadows have size, shape, location,
and orientation. Therefore, shadows are robust examples of intan-
gibles that have spatial properties. I concentrate on the most conservative reply to this argument: rejecting the intangibility premise.
As Berkeley himself anticipated, many apparent counterexamples to
"All that is spatial is tangible" can be handled by reading "tangible" as
"can be touched in principle."

Although Berkeley did not apply this strategy to explain how we see microscopic things, he could have. Given later revelations about his idealism and given later advances in microscopy and the scientific understanding of distal touch, Berkeley should have made compromises to accommodate microscopic entities.

No hypothetical improvements in our perceptual situation bring us closer to touching of shadows. But "touch" covers many submodalities: pressure sense, kinesthetic sense, hot, cold, and, perhaps, a vibratory submodality. The thermal and kinesthetic submodalities held some promise as avenues toward touching shadows. Neither idea panned out. The thermal suggestion failed because shadows lack particles. The kinesthetic suggestion failed because the kinesthetic sense relies on the tactile sense or vision to delimit the object. Since shadows are not accessible to the tactile sense, and Berkeley denies that they have purely visual spatial properties, he has no way to guide the kinesthetic sense.

I also considered the tactic of first arguing that some holes can be felt and then using this as a precedent for concluding that shadows can be felt as well. Although a surprisingly good case can be made that some holes can be felt, the extension to shadows founders on the fact that shadows lack tangible linings. We cannot say that shadows are instead felt by feeling their casters because the spatial dimensions of the caster are just one variable in a three variable *calculation* of shadow dimensions. Consequently, the dimensions of a shadow can vary widely from the dimensions of shadow. There just is not enough information.

Touching something differs from reckoning its existence by touch. A blind physicist can infer the existence of a shadow by feeling a lamp a cube and a tabletop. But his tactile explorations do not constitute feeling a shadow. He detects the shadow in the same way he detects hydrogen leaking out of a balloon by feeling its loss of buoyancy over time.

Berkeley's second possible reply is to deny that shadows really have spatial properties. Pains, sounds, and afterimages appear to have spatial properties. But many philosophers characterize these appearances as illusion.

This line of reasoning is unpromising because scientists frequently argue from spatial properties of shadows to spatial properties of their casters. Some of these arguments are within vision science itself. For instance, in 1853, H. Mueller used shadows within the eye to prove that the light-sensitive stratum of the retina is the layer of rods and cones (Le Grand 1967, 150). (Mueller moved a light source across blood vessels and by parallax measured the distance between the vessels and the rod-cone layer.)

Vision scientists also cite shadows as spatial cues. Shadows help us discern whether an object is concave or convex, attached to the ground or above it, moving horizontally or floating. These are just the sort of visual cues Berkeley encouraged us to catalog.

Berkeley anticipates adverbial analyses of sensing in his discussion of abstract ideas. But shadows cannot be paraphrased away in this or any other fashion (for much the same reason holes cannot paraphrased away [Lewis and Lewis 1970]).

Shadows cannot be reduced to the perception of lightness and darkness because the postulation of shadows influences brightness (the apparent amount of light). Adding a shadow to an object makes the object appear *darker* (Beck 1971). Considerations of contrast give the opposite prediction: because the shadow is darker than the object, the object ought to seem lighter when compared to the dark shadow. Instead, the visual system infers from the shadow that the object is being spotlighted. It therefore *lowers* its estimate of the object's intrinsic brightness. Shadows are among the founding characters that the visual system uses to build up its representations of the shape, size, distance, and brightness. Shadows play an early role in the visual process.

The history of the eye gives us reason to conjecture that shadows are deeply entrenched in our conceptual scheme. The eye developed 530 million years ago (possibly triggering the Cambrian explosion of life forms). It developed from a skin patch that became photosensitive. An early function of this patch was shadow detection. Possibly, our concept of a physical object is an enrichment of the concept of the shadow. In any case, shadow detection helps an organism to discern shape, orientation, and water depth. The primitive eye delivers spatial information because it is just a modest extension of touch. There is strong pressure for the eye to keep this spatial fluency throughout its evolutionary history.

A similar story can be told for hearing. Touch has no monopoly on spatiality because sight and hearing evolved from touch. Touch does have primacy with respect to origin. But this historical primacy undermines perceptual primacy. We see spatial properties just as directly as we feel them. Evolutionary history explains why we see distance, feel distance, and hear distance, all in the same sense of "distance." The evolution of eyes is just the evolution of spatial vision (Land and Nilsson 2002, 5). It is not as if sight begins as a toy that is later adapted to a practical function (in the way radio men threw Slinkys over branches to create aerials during the Vietnam War).

Berkeley wrote his *New Theory of Vision* well before Charles Darwin's revolution. From the perspective of divine design biology, there is no reason for the senses to be homogeneous with respect to spatial concepts. The theobiologist then has a problem of coordinating the spatial concepts of the separate sense modalities. Shadows become an anomaly for Berkeley because his explanation makes touch the master modality for spatial concepts. But from the evolutionary perspective, there is no problem to begin with. All the modalities will be commensurable. And shadows will be as fully spatial as material objects.

6

Para-reflections

Picture a white beach ball and a black beach ball afloat on a smooth lake (fig. 6.1). The sun is shining from behind you and to your left. The white ball has a reflection because light is bouncing off the ball and onto the flat water. What about the black ball? If no light is bouncing off the black ball, then textbook definitions of "reflection" imply that it lacks a reflection. But most onlookers (unguarded physicists included) would say that the black oval adjacent to the black ball is its reflection.

The invisible red herring

Actually, a little light is reflected off the black ball. The blackness of a black surface is compatible with it reflecting light. Ancient Egyptians made mirrors from polished black granite.

Even a surface with a matte finish will reflect some light. The blackness of the object is only a relative indicator of how much light it reflects. A patch that looks black against one background will look gray against a darker background and even white against a much darker background (Land 1977, 109–16). Our visual systems are sensitive to the ratio of light

Figure 6.1 A reflection and a para-reflection

differences between parts of a surface. The absolute amount of light is of minor significance. That is why we continue to see colors fairly uniformly indoors and outdoors. When I go outside, the amount of light increases tremendously but the ratios stay about the same. Objects will look black when they contribute *relatively* little light.

This emphasis on contrast *supports* rather than undermines my thesis that we see a "para-reflection" of the black beach ball rather than its reflection. The absolute amount of light reflected by the black ball is visually insignificant. If one were to subtract photons from that region, people would still see an elliptical black patch. Indeed, the subtraction of photons would *increase* the sharpness of the image.

I want to stress my concession that the black ball has a perfectly standard reflection. Physicists impose no minimum light requirement for reflection. In addition to reflecting the balls, the lake has reflections of the stars even though their light is swamped by sunlight. Nor is there any restriction to the visible portion of the electromagnetic spectrum. The black ball has a rich array of reflections: ultraviolet, infrared, radio, and so on.

But none of these invisible reflections is singled out when we point at the black patch adjacent to the ball. We are referring to a privational phenomenon.

The faint reflection of the black beach ball is an irrelevant distraction. We should not let its existence mask the existence of the black ball's para-reflection. The black ball's reflection and para-reflection exist in the same place at the same time. The reflection does not *camouflage* the para-reflection. We see only the para-reflection, not the reflection. The culprit is our pre-Newtonian visual system. The visual system does not treat darkness as a privation of light. This tendency to treat darkness as if it were substantial (or at least as substantial as light) is recapitulated in the history of optics, as I describe below.

Para-reflections are mind independent

Privations such as vacuums, holes, and silence are not subjective phenomena. The para-reflection of the black ball is not like an afterimage. The para-reflection can be photographed. If there had never been any observers, there would still have been para-reflections. They are as independent of minds as reflections.

Not all para-reflections look like reflections. Consider a fluorescent button attached to a black velvet curtain. When viewed in a mirror without any further light source, many people regard only the glowing button as reflected, not the curtain. Para-reflections look most like reflections when they take center stage in a figure–ground relation. When para-reflections form a homogeneous black backdrop, many people assume there is nothing there. The assumption is overridden if viewers start to picture the blackness as a tablecloth or an oil slick. Happily there is no need to linger over these peculiarities of gestalt organization. Para-reflections do not depend on the quirks of human perceptual psychology. They are objective.

The black ball's para-reflection works by contrast rather than by the electromagnetic energy emitted by the ball. Most of the black ball's environment is being reflected in the positive way described by physics textbooks. But the area adjacent to the black ball is dark because of a combination of what the black ball's environment does (reflect visible light) and what the black ball fails to do (have a visually significant reflection).

Some privational phenomena, such as vacuums, behave according to distinctive principles. Others mimic their positive counterparts. Cold regions conform to the low-level generalizations that govern hot regions. Ernst Mach regarded heat and cold as equally real. According to Mach (1886/1986), cold is the absence of heat and heat is the absence of cold. He dismissed debate about which is fundamental as a verbal dispute. Only with subsequent realism about atoms did physicists (led by Ludwig Boltzmann) come to a consensus that the debate does not involve notational variants. In the hot and cold debate, hot wins. Cold is the absence of heat but not vice versa.

The first part of the law of reflection states that the angle at which a ray strikes a surface equals the angle at which that ray is reflected. (The second part of the law specifies that the incident ray, the perpendicular to the surface, and the reflected ray all lie in a plane.) The ancient Greeks inferred the law of reflection with the help of mirrors. Euclid's *Optics* and *Caloptics* show that the Greeks had a basic grasp of geometrical optics. However, their beliefs about light differed from ours. Anaximenes and Aristotle explained colors as modifications of light and dark. If these pioneers had been asked about para-reflections, they would have extended the law of reflection to them. Just as black balls and white balls are equally balls, the Greeks would have insisted that black reflections and white reflections are equally reflections. Johann Wolfgang von Goethe (1840) and other continental rivals of Newton would have applied the law of reflection with Greek impartiality, for Goethe agreed with the Greeks that darkness is no less fundamental than light.

Goethe and the Greeks could have used the optics diagrams of some contemporary physics textbooks. For these contemporary physicists often illustrate the law of reflection with black figures. Rays are drawn from these dark objects to the reflecting surface in strict accordance with geometrical optics.

And this works surprisingly well. Para-reflections behave just as this unblinking application of the law of reflection predicts. Major corollaries of the law of reflection go through.

For instance, a single para-reflection changes a right-handed system into a left-handed system. If you hold a right-handed black glove to a mirror, the image will be of a left-handed black glove.

The nature of the reflection varies with the surface. An irregular surface creates a diffuse reflection, so, for example, if the lake becomes choppy, the para-reflection becomes more diffuse.

The sharpness of the dark image is also affected by one's point of view. The amount of light reflected from a surface increases with the angle of incidence. When you look at a puddle from straight above, it looks murky. When viewed from a distance, it is quite reflective. The artist John Ruskin spoke up for the puddle:

> It is not the brown, muddy, dull thing we suppose it to be; it has a heart like ourselves, and in the bottom of that there are the boughs of the tall trees and the blades of the shaking grass, and all manner of hues of variable pleasant light out of the sky. (1906, 347)

From a distance, you can observe an eclipse reflected by the puddle. Increasing the angle of incidence strengthens the para-reflection because the extra reflected light strengthens the contrast.

Modern mirrors are highly regular and so provide sharp para-reflections. A dark mirror image is the same perpendicular distance behind the mirror as the object is in front of it. Thus, the smallest plane mirror that can reflect your entire blackened body is half your height (with its upper edge lowered by half the distance between your eye and top of your head). Convex mirrors slenderize your para-reflection. Concave mirrors widen your para-reflection. Such conformity to optical principles tempts us to classify para-reflections as reflections.

The fidelity of para-reflections to standard optical principles is dramatized by images that are mixtures of normal reflections and para-reflections. Consider the mirror image of a black and white checkerboard. The black squares seem to behave with the same optical propriety as the whites squares. Indeed, we regard the reflection of the checkerboard as a unitary phenomenon. But only half of the checkerboard's squares have genuine reflections.

Physics and its parasites

Isaac Newton demonstrated that darkness is the absence of light and not vice versa. Since there are no rays of darkness, the law of reflection does not directly apply to para-reflections. Para-reflections only obey the law of reflection parasitically. In this respect, they resemble holes (Casati and Varzi, 1994). Much of the environment is reflecting light in accordance with the law of reflection. Because the environment's pattern of reflection is molded by this law, the contrast image inherits most of its optical properties. But it is the host that is governed by the law of reflection, not the parasite.

The mere fact that para-reflections owe their existence to reflections does not make them reflections. Consider Newton's rings. If you place a spherical glass surface on a flat glass surface, the multiple reflections will create circular interference patterns. The dark rings are not reflections even though they are products of reflections. When you make a soap bubble, a black spot appears just before the bubble bursts. This is also due to destructive interference between light coming from two surfaces of the bubble. When the wall of the bubble thins, light reflected at the air-to-soap surface of the soap bubble undergoes a phase reversal. Light reflecting from the soap-to-air surface has the same phase as the incident light. The two reflections come back with opposite phase and so cancel out.

There are some geometrical differences between para-reflections and reflections. Reflections require surfaces. Since light cannot bounce off of a hole, no hole has a reflection. But holes can have para-reflections. Hold a sealed Styrofoam cup in front of a mirror. The entire front surface is reflected. Now punch a hole in the middle of this white cup. You will see the hole para-reflected in the mirror. But you cannot see a reflection of the hole.

Now fill in the hole's para-reflection with a black marker. This act destroys the para-reflection. The defaced mirror has a black dot but no longer has an image of the hole. If you fill in the para-reflection carefully, the result may be an overall image of the cup that is indistinguishable from the original. However, even a perfect resemblance to an image of a scene is not sufficient for being an image of that the scene. An artist could paint the whole mirror so that scene involving the cup is qualitatively identical to that originally produced by the unpainted mirror. The painted mirror is no longer reflects the scene because the mirror no longer causally sensitive to the scene. Para-reflections inherit the causal requirements of reflection. Although a para-reflection may originate from a nonsurface, it must land on a surface.

Para-reflections disappear when isolated. If the environment of a para-reflection is draped in black velvet (which reflects only a negligible amount of light), then the para-reflection goes out of existence. There is only darkness. No host, no parasite.

Reflections are autonomous. If the area around the white ball is darkened, the white ball still has a reflection.

The black beach ball's para-reflection can also be destroyed by focusing more light on just the black ball. This will increase the amount of light reflected by the black ball and thereby decrease the contrast with the environment that constitutes a para-reflection. When the amount of light reflected by the black ball equals the amount of light being reflected by the ball's environment, the para-reflection ceases. The black ball will itself look grayer. If enough extra light is focused just on the black ball, it will look as white as the white beach ball. And the black ball will have a white reflection.

Silhouettes have the same relational nature as para-reflections. A ship forms a silhouette as it sails in front of the setting sun. But once the sun goes down, the silhouette of the ship disappears. If a curtain with a single puncture is placed in front of a single light source, then we see the silhouette of the curtain. If the hole is mended, then the scene is completely dark. The silhouette has gone out of existence.

The relational aspect of silhouettes and para-reflections does not render them subjective. An object's weight depends on the body to which it is gravitationally attracted. But weight is still an objective property because the relatum is not a perceiver. An object's para-reflections are similarly independent of observers.

Since many reflections are invisible, many para-reflections are also invisible. Only high-speed photography can capture the para-reflection of a black bullet being shot past a mirror. Since the speed of some reflections exceeds the speed limits of photochemistry, there are para-reflections that cannot be seen with any recording device.

A comparison with shadows

A para-reflection forms on the side of the object nearest the light source. The shadow of the object forms on the side opposite the light source. The difference between shadows and para-reflections is dramatized by objects that simultaneously cast shadows and para-reflections (fig. 6.2). The black ball has a para-reflection on the side near the sun and a shadow on its far side. Since there is light striking the illuminated side of the object (it merely is not being reflected), the para-reflection is two dimensional. In contrast, the shadow is three-dimensional, for the back side of the object is not receiving light. A hot duck who wants to be sheltered from the sun will paddle to the shady backside of the ball, not toward the ball's para-reflection.

The difference in dimensionality between shadows and para-reflections can be underscored by having our two beach balls drift onto a dirty oil slick. The dirty oil forms a dull black plane. Neither ball casts a visible shadow on the blackened water. However, there is some dust in the air, so each ball has a shadow that is visible above the water. As architects stress, shadows are three-dimensional volumes. People focus

Figure 6.2 Simultaneous reflection and para-reflection

on the surface of the shadow that makes contact with objects. This misleads them into thinking that shadows are two dimensional. They are tempted to conclude that neither ball on the oil slick has a shadow.

Para-reflections also differ visually from shadows. I can see a black crow by seeing it para-reflected in a mirror. But I cannot see the crow by seeing its shadow. I can visually detect the presence of the crow by seeing its shadow. But I do not see the crow itself.

How science has coped with privations

Scientists, like philosophers, are uncomfortable with privations. This discomfort issues from a deep conviction that reality is *positive* (Gale 1976). It is difficult to square this view with truths about absences such as shadows and para-refractions. Thus, scientists and philosophers have a tendency to substitute positive entities for these nonentities.

Physicists have overcome this prejudice in the past. In 1672 Otto von Guericke undermined the long-held notion that nature abhors a vacuum with the help of his new air pump. After evacuating the air from attached two copper hemispheres, he had two teams of eight horses try to pull the hemispheres apart. After the horses failed, Guericke let air into the hemispheres by opening a stopcock. The hemispheres then separated easily. This showed that the hemispheres stayed together because of a failure to counter the pressure of the atmosphere. Similarly, beginning physics students learn that there is no need to postulate a positive force of suction. When students suck beverages through a straw, they are not pulling the liquid up. They are merely letting the atmosphere push the liquid up the straw.

But this style of negative thinking does not come naturally to us. We tend to revert to positive species of causation.

What goes for hydraulics goes for optics. Our preference for positive thinking leads us to mischaracterize phenomena that we encounter daily. Whenever we look into the mirror, we see a para-reflection. Our pupils are holes in our eyeballs that trap light. As a consequence, our pupils are very black. Indeed, they approximate blackbodies. Since the pupil fails to reflect light while the iris does reflect light, the mirror para-reflects the pupil.

The pupil itself conducts para-reflections as well as reflections into the eye. Whenever a dark thing is seen, the retina must contain the corresponding image as a para-reflection. No dark object could be seen without a para-reflection of it. Para-reflections are literally inside our heads because our eyeballs are inside our heads.

A good theory of optics should not talk around such pervasive phenomena. To describe para-reflections accurately, we need to take privations seriously. We must resist the temptation to reconstrue privational phenomena as positive phenomena.

In commerce, we are warned of those who say they will give us something but wind up giving us nothing. In optics, we should be wary of those who say they will give us nothing but wind up giving us something.

7

Para-refractions

Shadowgrams and the Black Drop

Can a flame cast a shadow? When placed on a white background in bright sunshine, the shadow of a candle appears to include the shadow of its flame (fig. 7.1). It dances with the flame. The "shadow" disappears when you blow the flame out.

Yet the flame is not an opaque object. The flame is a bright source of light, not a blocker of light. Thanks to the flame, there is more light in the scene, not less. Is this a counterexample to the blocking theory of shadows?

Para-refractions contrasted with shadows

No, the flame is not casting a shadow. Fire heats a pocket of air, and that pocket operates as a weak lens. Undulating waves extend beyond the flame's "shadow" because the air continues to be heated invisibly above the flame.

This chapter is devoted to dark effects of refraction. We often overlook these effects because they are often mixed with genuine shadows.

Figure 7.1 Shadowgram of candle flame

For instance, when smoke came out of my neighbor's chimney on cold winter afternoons, it cast a shadow on the snow. When he installed an efficient furnace, there was no more smoke to be seen. But it looked like the shadow persisted. A plume of hot air still created lens effects on his roof and on the ground.

Since shadows are absences of light, they cannot be refracted. However, shadows can be para-refracted. If you are viewing a black fish in clear water, there is a virtual image that makes the fish appear higher in the water than it really is. The exact discrepancy is predicted by the law of refraction (Snell's law). However, the law cannot directly explain the success of the prediction. The law only applies to the black fish's environment.

If the water is clear, you may see the shadow of the black fish. The image of the shadow cannot be refracted, but it can be para-refracted.

Shadowgrams

Physicists do not discuss para-refractions as such. They do discuss particular species of para-refractions. F. J. Weinberg (1963) coined the term "shadowgram" to cover "shadows" created by the bending of light rays through anomalies in transparent media. Instead of blocking the light, the shadowgrammer refracts light rays.

Robert Hooke (1894/1665, 217–19) discovered shadowgrams when he studied a candle burning in the sunlight (as in fig. 7.1). He realized that the plume of hot air has a different density, so the heat of the candle was refracting light rays.

The steam immediately emerging from a kettle is invisible because it takes the form of individual water molecules. Light is scattered by the molecules in different phases that cancel each other out. Once the steam cools enough for the molecules to form droplets, the light they scatter has approximately the same phase. This reinforcement makes a visible cloud. If you look at the shadow cast by this cloud, there is no gap separating the shadow of the kettle and the shadow of the cloud. A shadowgram bridges the gap.

Shadowgrams are of practical interest to aquatic predators that hunt transparent prey. Instead of looking for the prey directly, the predators study shadowgrams on the sea floor.

The scientific utility of shadowgrams was first appreciated by those studying fire. The notorious French revolutionary Jean-Paul Marat made substantial contributions by studying shadowgrams.

Ernst Mach combined shadowgrams with high-speed photography to study shock waves. This led to the development of Schlieren photography, which helps engineers photograph the flow of air around objects (Settles 2001).

Shadow bands

The most common refraction phenomenon for the night sky is the twinkling of stars. This "stellar scintillation" is caused by the lenslike behavior of air currents. The stars wink in and out and appear to move a bit. Stars near the horizon twinkle more because there is more atmosphere to randomly refract the light. The effect is usually too small to make the planets twinkle. Planets are bigger than a point source of light.

The sun may also twinkle—from the vantage point of other planets outside the solar system. The only time it twinkles from Earth's vantage point is during solar eclipses. When only a sliver of light remains, the scintillations form shadow bands. The bands move across the ground at jogging speed. The contrast is low. This makes them hard to photograph. The eye works better than the camera for this kind of phenomenon. Mabel Loomis Todd (1900, 28) published a famous drawing of shadow bands on an Italian house (see fig. 7.2). Shadow bands resemble the "shadows" in ripple tanks. Picture the crests and troughs as a sequence of positive and negative lenses. Each positive lens focuses light onto the bottom. Each negative lens refracts light out of the beam. These additions and subtractions of light create a network of light and dark. Because the waves propagate smoothly along the length of the tank, so does the network. If the medium is turbulent, like the waves in a swimming pool, then the network will be less orderly. Shadow bands remind us that we are at the bottom of an ocean of air.

The English astronomer George B. Airy recalled seeing his first shadow bands in 1843: "As totality approached, a strange fluctuation of light was seen . . . upon the walls and ground, so striking that in some places children ran after it and tried to catch it with their hands" (Airy 1970, 4).

Figure 7.2 Drawing of shadow bands

The black drop

In 1716, Edmund Halley published a scheme for calculating the Astronomical Unit (the average distance between Earth and the sun; all the planetary orbits were to be measured in terms of this unit). To obtain the unit, observers from all over Earth needed to precisely observe the transit times of Venus (scheduled for 1639, 1761, 1789, 1874, and 1882). Each observer was to record exactly when Venus made first contact (the first moment Venus is partially silhouetted), second contact (the first moment Venus is completely silhouetted), third contact (the last moment Venus is completely silhouetted), and fourth contact (the last moment of partial silhouetting). The duration of the transit was defined as the time between the second and third contacts. Ideally, this could be done with an accuracy of one second (thereby yielding an Astronomical Unit to the accuracy of 0.17%).

Halley's program was the first example of "big science"; a huge international effort was made to dispatch expeditions all across the globe, often at government expense. The project was undermined by a phenomenon called the "black drop." A representative description:

> The planet seemed quite entered upon the disk, her upper limb being tangential to that of the sun; but instead of a thread of light, which he expected immediately to appear between them, he perceived Venus to be still conjoined to the sun's limb a slender kind of tail, nothing so black as her disk, and shaped like the neck of a Florence flask. (Bevis 1769, 190)

You can see this "bridge" or "ligament" by holding your thumb and forefinger lightly together against the bright sky. A "black drop" appears between your fingers.

The black drop exposed unanticipated indeterminacy in the observational meaning of "contact." Does "second contact" mean the first moment when light goes all around Venus? Or does it select the first moment when the best-fit circle of Venus is tangent to the best-fit curve of the sun? There was as much as a 52-second difference between the rival definitions.

The black drop can be photographed. It is also observed for transits of Mercury, so it cannot be due to refraction from the atmosphere of Venus (Mercury has no atmosphere). The black drop effect is too big to be explained as diffraction of the sun's light around Venus.

The correct explanation of the effect is the smearing of the image (Schaefer 2001). This loss of resolution is chiefly due to atmospheric refraction. Diffraction within telescopes can also contribute to the fuzziness. The smearing can be simulated. A dark circle silhouetted against a bright circle will develop a black drop as the resolution declines (fig. 7.3). Since I am near-sighted, I can simulate the black drop effect just by removing my glasses.

The main cause of the smearing is the scattering of light by temperature variations in Earth's atmosphere. Black drops are the

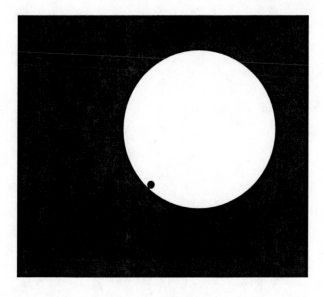

Figure 7.3 Black drop

dark side of twinkles. We tend to focus on light when we consider the stellar scintillation, but the smattering of darkness is also part of phenomenon—as underscored by shadow bands.

The diffraction of telescope apertures is a second cause. Older telescopes had additional smearing because of chromatic aberration and other optical imperfections. Telescopes have improved so much that most observers of the 2004 transit of Venus did not witness the black drop. The absent absence of light was the subject of an article in *Sky and Telescope* (Shiga 2004).

8

Goethe's Colored Shadows

For in and out, above, about, below
'Tis nothing but a Magic Shadow-show
Played in a Box whose candle is the Sun
Round which we Phantom Figures come and go.

—The Rubaiyat of Omar Khayyam

The cinema is often compared to Plato's cave. But G. E. Moore denied he was seeing shadows:

What name is there for the ? thrown upon the screen in a cinema?

They are not shadows, because they are not produced by the introduction of an opaque object between the source of light & the screen, but by the introduction of transparent (= translucent) objects between the 2—translucent in different degrees....

Nor is it natural to call them "patches of light". When an electric torch is turned towards the wall in a dark room, a patch of light appears on the wall & may move. And if the glass is blue or a piece of transparent blue paper is pasted over it, a blue patch of light is thrown on the wall; and in a *colour* film many of the blue patches that appear on the screen seem to be blue patches of light in just this sense. But I think this is not so: I think to say there is a patch of light on a surface implies that the surrounding part of the surface is dark, & this is not in general the case with ? in a film. Perhaps this is why you can't have

a *black* patch of light; whereas you can have a black ? on the screen.
(1962, 142)

Moore is correct to insist that a shadow can only be cast by an object that blocks the light. But the black patches satisfy this condition; they are shadows caused by opaque patches on the film. Only the colored patches warrant a question mark; they behave like shadows but are positive entities rather than absences.

Do color scientists think the colored patches are shadows? When they discuss prisms, their attention goes back to Isaac Newton, and they agree he showed that shadows are absences of light. When they discuss color mixing, their attention goes back Edwin Land's research culminating in the Polaroid camera—and they take the existence of colored shadows to have been experimentally established. Yet the scientists also assume that *absences* of light cannot have a hue.

Scientists would be less inconsistent if their historical attention were more uniform. Colored shadows predate Edwin Land's (1959, 1977) spectacular strengthenings of colored shadow effects. Wolfgang Goethe used colored shadows in a controversial challenge to Newton. The Newtonians prevailed. As the victors, they purged Goethe from the annals of color science.

Incomplete retrospective adjustments generate inconsistencies. Consider the retouched photographs of Joseph Stalin's enemies in David King's album of absences, *The Commissar Vanishes*. Unpersons were expurgated from official photographs to avoid embarrassing the regime. If the excised person is deleted without deleting his shadow, the photograph becomes optically incoherent.

Goethe has been excised from color science, but his colored shadows remain. Newtonians must purge Goethe's colored shadows—or at least demote them as colored "shadows." Once the Newtonians review the history of colored shadows, they will be more likely to view "colored shadow" as a misnomer like "peanut." (Peanuts are not nuts; they are legumes related to peas—a kind of dried fruit related to peas, beans, and alfalfa.)

Botanists who do not wish to appear pedantic shy away from correcting common (mis)usage. Color scientists who come to believe that colored shadows are not shadows may share this reticence. However, "colored shadow" is not nearly as entrenched, and so there is an opportunity to remove the misnomer (or to at least dilute its currency). To that end, I offer a competitive term, "filtow." I hope "filtow" will displace "colored shadow" just as color scientists hope "color deficient" will displace the misnomer "color blind." Scientists couple linguistic recommendations with substantive remarks about the phenomenon they wish redescribed. I follow their example in chapter 9. But first I need to set the stage by reviewing the history of "colored shadows."

The modification theory of color

The filtow theaters of ancient Java (around 1000 A.D.) used translucent colored figures cut out of leather. Possibly, G. E. Moore's mysterious ? dates back to antiquity.

The earliest scholarly reference I have found to colored shadows is an observation by Otto von Guericke of Magdeburg, inventor of the vacuum pump, in 1672: "This is how it happens, that in the early morning twilight a clear blue shadow can be produced upon a white piece of paper [by holding] a finger or other object . . . between a lighted candle and the paper beneath" (quoted in Land 1977, 126). When outdoors, this blue tint is most salient with shadows cast on to snow; the shadowed area receives no direct sunlight but is illuminated by light from the blue sky. (Perhaps blue gets its association with coolness from this phenomenon.) Subsequent commentators note the phenomenon as a curiosity.

This modification theory of color goes back to Anaximenes but was best known through Aristotle's analysis of rainbows. Under this view, darkness is not the mere absence of light. Light and dark are persisting entities in their own right like salt and pepper. When directly mixed, light and dark yield gray. But when mixed through media, they produce colors. For instance, when light is darkened by smoke, it looks blue. When light is darkened by a less turbid medium, it looks yellow. Light and dark retain their integrity as ingredients of color. Depending on the proportions, light and dark yield "shadows" that vary from deep purple to light yellow.

This approach should appeal to reductionists. The strategy is to explain chromatic phenomena in terms of achromatic phenomena and ordinary media. Black and white are simple and primitive. The hues are complex. Thus the modification theory aims to explain the complex in terms of the simple.

Aristotle regards perception as the detection of forms in particular objects. When you see Spartan black gruel, your eye is becomes acquainted with the form of darkness as it inheres in the gruel. This model of perception would lead us to infer that Aristotle believes that we can see the darkness of an unlit cave. However, with questionable consistency, Aristotle insists that we need light to see. He voices the requirement in his discussion of extromission theories of vision. According to Empedocles, Plato, and Euclid, we see by virtue of light being emitted from the eye. This visual fire reaches out to objects. This explains the structure of our field of vision. Draw straight lines from an open eye to the nearest object. The eye sees whatever the rays touch. Nothing more. In chapter 3 of *On the Senses*, Aristotle states the basic objection to extromission theories:

> If the eye was made of fire as Empedocles says, and as it is suggested in *Timaeus*, if vision were produced by means of a fire emitted by the eye, like the light emitted by a lantern, why then are we not able to see in the dark?

All extromission theorists were aware of this anomaly. The most popular solution (adopted in Plato's *Timaeus*) was to postulate a second ray that emanated from objects. We see when these two types of light unite.

Aristotle rejects this marriage. What could such a union be like? The union is also unparsimonious. If there is a light ray extending from the object to the eye, the eye-to-object ray is redundant.

In his preface to Euclid's work, Theon of Alexandria replies that the eye-to-object ray is needed to explain why we sometimes fail to see objects even though we are looking right at them. A reader may fail to notice a gnat resting on a page and so be startled when the refreshed gnat flies away. Theon is right about our occasional failures to see what we are looking at. But this insight is of no help to Euclid, for it conflicts with Euclid's postulate that we see whatever is in our line of sight. It is doubtful that the extromission theorists ever provided a good explanation of the datum Aristotle found so damning: we need light to see anything.

But I doubt that Aristotle could *consistently* make this influential objection. He is committed to their being a visual form for darkness; he should maintain that we see shadows without light and that we see darkness in a lightless cave. Aristotle should be the greatest friend of blackness.

The objection would issue far more fittingly from the lips of Augustine. He emphasizes that darkness is the absence of light. Augustine associates darkness with deficiency and imperfection. Evil itself is just a privation in being. In a sense, evil does not exist. (That is one of his solutions to the problem of evil.) Darkness is not there to be seen.

Isaac Newton conferred scientific credentials on the Augustinian view that darkness is just the absence of light. With a prism, he divided "white light" into colored lights. With a second prism, he recombined colored lights into white light. Darkness was not necessary to explain the hues, so Newton rejected the modification theory of colors.

Goethe's revival of the modification theory

Goethe (1840, pt. I, sec. 6) is the first to regard colored shadows as revealing the fundamental nature of color. Goethe revived the modification theory that colors are mixtures of light and darkness.

Goethe's initial interest in color was ignited by art and natural beauty. This aesthetic call of the wild echoes through passages of his *Theory of Colors* (1840).

Goethe relished science. His work in biology was praised by Charles Darwin as "path breaking." Goethe's characteristic method was Platonic: analyze complex things in terms of ground phenomena. These basic archetypes recur and evolve through nature like variations on a musical theme. In botany, Goethe claimed that the leaf was the basic organ from which all other parts develop. He intimates that a primal plant may still grow in some remote corner of Earth. As far as geology and mineralogy are concerned, the ground phenomenon is granite (which Goethe takes to be at the base of Earth's crust). Goethe regarded the antipathy between light and dark (and their visual correlates of white and black) as the ur-phenomenon for optics. Color arises when media such as prisms and lenses elicit cooperation from the polar opposites of light and dark.

Colors are differential darkenings. We most readily apply "shadow" to darkenings that match the contour of an object. But this representative aspect is not essential. Nor does Goethe require the object to block the light. Goethe is result oriented. What is essential to shadowhood is the reduction of light, not the manner in which the light is reduced.

Whereas Newton takes the primary bearer of light to be the light that strikes the retina (and so thinks objects are only derivatively colored by virtue of how they alter light), Goethe thinks *objects* are the primary bearers of color by virtue of the fact that their surfaces are light darkeners. All colors are shadows because all colors result from light being stopped by objects. For instance, grass is green because it darkens most light except green. Although grass reflects some red light, this relative deficiency of red light is what counts. Black is the maximal darkener. White is the minimal darkener.

"Nothing can be both green and red" is true because green cancels out other colors. Green is defined in terms of what it is not. Goethe conceives of colors holistically, as tied to a color scale like numbers are tied to the number line. When we think of the number seven, we must consider the entire number line. Seven could not become the successor of five by the disappearance of six; numbers come as package, situated essentially at their respective positions. Just as numbers cannot move along the number line or exit from it, colors cannot migrate through or out of color space. Each color gains its identity in this contrastive, competitive way, marking out territory in color space by what it excludes. Jonathan Westphal (1991, 105) suggests that Georg Hegel has in mind this definition by rivals when Hegel writes in the *Science of Logic*:

> Thus something *through its own nature* relates itself to the other, because otherness is posited in it as its own moment; its being-within-self includes the negation within it, by means of which alone it now has its affirmative determinate being....The negation of its other is now the quality of the something, for it is as this sublating of its other that it is something. (1812/1989, 125)

Colors interlock in a motionless struggle of opposites. Red cannot prevail over green as Rome vanquished Carthage. Nor can the balance of power be altered by the introduction of a novel color. Anything other than stalemate is inconceivable.

Goethe's critique of Newton

As an intellectually serious person, Goethe naturally turned to Isaac Newton's celebrated analysis of light. In the eyes of many, Newton's *Optics* was his premier achievement.

Goethe was profoundly disappointed. The experimental procedures did not work when he tried them. Newton's successful predictions concerned a narrow band of phenomena—essentially those in a room with a pinhole opening for the light. Goethe was repulsed by the artificiality of the observations, arranged as though a straitjacketed observer is viewing a specimen impaled on a pin.

Goethe regarded the fruits of such confinement as meager. Newton could not consistently count the number of spectral colors. (For religious reasons, Newton wanted the number of colors to come out to *seven*; that is why he distinguishes indigo from violet in the ROYGBIV sequence: red, orange, yellow, green, blue, indigo, violet.) Newton could not account for the dark rings that form on thin films. Newton could not explain why the sky is blue.

Goethe felt *he* could explain color as it occurs in the great outdoors. For instance, Goethe's explanation of the blueness of sky starts with the observation that the white of the sunlight borders the black of outer space. Blue arises along the border of light and dark.

Goethe complained that the Newtonians ignored evidence. Phenomena such as afterimages and contrast phenomena suggest that the eye and mind contribute to color. But Newton set a precedent by bracketing subjective phenomena:

> I speak here of colours so far as they arise from light. For they appear sometimes by other causes, as when by the power of phantasy we see colours in a dream, or a madman sees things before him which are not there; or when we see fire by striking the eye, or see colours like the eye of a peacock's feather by pressing our eyes in either corner whilst we look the other way. Where these and such like causes interpose not, the colour always answer to the sort or sorts of the rays whereof the light consists. . . . (1704/1952, 160–61)

In Goethe's era, the Newtonians treated the eye as an imperfect spectroscope rather than as an instrument for vision.

Lastly, the Newtonians conspired to suppress rival views. Instead of promoting a fair, open-minded inquiry into the phenomena, Newton and his lackeys resorted to the arts of politics to promote their viewpoint above all others. Historians of physics will confirm that this was not entirely paranoia on the part of Goethe.

Goethe thought that he was one of the few thinkers who had the intellectual stature to challenge the Newtonian conspiracy. At times Goethe's challenge takes the form of counterpropaganda. But Goethe's more systematic reaction to Newton's program of intellectual repression was a special emphasis on the Baconian virtues that Newtonians publicly endorsed. Goethe's own scientific work on colors was intended to be purely observational.

Interpretation of the phenomena is left for the metaphysicians

This division of labor pleased Goethe's compatriots Hegel and Arthur Schopenhauer. Each extolled Goethe as a model of scientific restraint (Lauxtermann 1990). Each agreed that Goethe had established the centrality of colored shadows in a correct theory of light.

Ludwig Wittgenstein (1951/1977) interprets Goethe as half-consciously engaged in a *phenomenological investigation* of color. Indeed, Goethe often seems to being trying to limn out the deep structure of color *appearances*. His experiments seem more like illustrations rather than tests of hypotheses. Despite Goethe's genuflection to Francis Bacon, Wittgenstein thinks Goethe is forging a template for color experience. Goethe regards colored shadows as revealing the deep nature of all color. All colors *are* shadows.

The official death of phenomenology within optics

Newton explained color appearances in terms of an underlying model of light particles. He presupposes Robert Boyle's distinction between primary and secondary properties. Colors are joint effects of the perceiver's psychology and the primary properties of mass, shape, and velocity.

Goethe thought colors are more real than the entities theoreticians use to model them. This phenomenological tradition is not entirely dead within German philosophy (witness the continued influence of Edmund Husserl's phenomenology), but it did die within German optics. As a good German, Hermann von Helmholtz praises Goethe's literary appreciation of color. Nevertheless, he defends the distinction between primary and secondary properties that underlies Newton's approach:

> For the investigation of physical phenomena he [Goethe] demands such an arrangement of observed facts, that the one always explains

the other, so that one comes to an insight about the overall connections without leaving the realm of sense-experience. This demand
may appear insidious but it is basically false. Because a phenomenon
of nature is physically explained only when it has been brought back
upon those forces of nature that constitute its ultimate basis. Since we
can never observe these forces in themselves we must, at every explanation of natural phenomena, leave the realm of the senses and proceed
to those non-sensuous things that are determined only by concepts.
(quoted in Sällström 1979, 480)

Helmholtz's emphasis on the primacy of unobservables does not
entail allegiance to Newton's particle theory. Helmholtz believed
that Newton's particle theory of light had been refuted by Christian
Huygens's theory that light consists of waves. The wave theory was
in turn displaced by a partial revival of the particle theory. Light is
thought to behave like a wave under some circumstances and like
a particle under others. Since no familiar object behaves this way,
William Bragg lamented, "God runs electromagnetics by wave theory on Monday, Wednesday, and Friday, and the Devil runs them by
quantum theory on Tuesday, Thursday, and Saturday." An anony-
mous wit added, "And on Sunday we pray for enlightenment."

None of this resuscitated Goethe. His *Theory of Colors* is read only
in an antiquarian spirit by scientists who study light. They (and I)
accept Newton's view that shadows are absences of light just as cold
is the absence of heat and silence is the absence of sound.

Unnatural support for colored shadows

Goethe disparaged *artificial* observations. Natural colored shadows are
weak effects, noticed only by careful observers. But artificial observations ultimately provided the most striking support for the proposition that shadows can be colored.

Let me first mention a modest effect induced by the rapid movement of dark lines. It is based on the phenomenon of "subjective

color," which is generally credited to G. T. Fechner (1838). Subjective colors arise when an achromatic stimulus that triggers colored images. The best-known specimen is C. E. Benham's rotating disk, first used in 1894. When the black-and-white disk is rotated at between five and ten revolutions per second, you see colored rings. The eye has three types of cones. Each is sensitive to white light. The subject sees white light when all three types of cones respond equally. But one type of cone is most sensitive to red light, one to green light, and one to blue light. The cones also differ in latency time (the time needed to respond to light stimulus) and persistence time (how long they keep responding after the light stimulus has been removed). When a subject gazes at the spinning disk, his cones are being stimulated by alternating white flashes. Given the variation of latency and persistence times, the cones respond unequally, and so he will see unsaturated streaks of green, red, and blue.

If an overhead transparency is made of Benham's disk and it is spun over the light of an overhead projector (turned on its side), then the *shadows* projected on the screen have the same colors as the opaque disk.

Retinal moiré patterns are "stationary" examples (fig. 8.1). Moving the eye gently down the rectangle yields a faint pastel of unsaturated yellows, greens, and reds. Your quivering eyeballs are supplying the movement. Mesh window screens and the teeth of fine combs form retinal moiré patterns when lying on a white background. If these detailed artifacts are lifted above the surface, they form retinal moiré shadows. There is little temptation to describe these as colored shadows because the color does not seem to be *in* the shadow.

Is it enough to get colored light into the shadow? A photographer's "dark room" is illuminated by a red light bulb. The shadows in the dark room contain a little light of the wavelength associated with red light (around 650 nanometers). Red light is reflected off the walls and into the shadow.

We can increase the amount of red light in the shadow by adding a second red lamp. Now we have a double shadow from the object. Each of the two shadows has twice the light as the original

Figure 8.1 Retinal moiré

shadow. But doubling the light within the shadow does not affect the appearance because we have also doubled the amount of red light in their surroundings. The visual system is sensitive to *ratios* of light. The absolute amount of light is of minor importance. If the visual system went by the absolute amount of light, objects that look one way indoors would be unrecognizable outdoors. By tracking the ratios of illumination between surfaces (and especially across borders) rather than the absolute amounts of reflected light, the visual system can uniformly represent objects in disparate light conditions. (The ratio approach is good, not perfect. The red fabric you see under the store's fluorescent bulb will look different in the daylight.)

Nevertheless, the shadows are not called colored shadows. They do not *look* red. The shadows in a red dark room still look black or gray. Can a shadow that has color in it also look colored? Yes! Substitute a white light bulb for one of the two red light bulbs (fig. 8.2). The shadow associated with the blocking of the white light source is some-what red. But there is an amazing side effect: the shadow associated with the blocking of the red light source is now *green!*

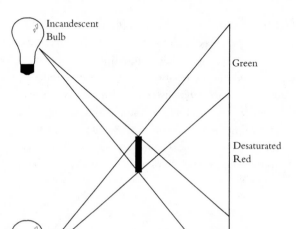

Figure 8.2 Green-colored shadow

Combining red and the yellowish white light of an incandescent bulb yields a desaturated red light. Blocking the white light stops the desaturation. Therefore, interrupting the beam of white light generates a red shadow. Interrupting the red beam results in a "shadow" of yellowish white light ensconced in a desaturated red background. A common explanation of the green appearance is that the visual system operates with the default assumption that the background is white light. Through the psychological mechanism of simultaneous contrast, we obtain a body of light that looks green (even though it has the wavelength associated with yellowish white light).

This green light appears to be a colored shadow in the phenomenal sense. We need not fret about whether it is *really* green (by virtue of its appearance) or is *really* yellow (by virtue of its wavelength). As long as the body of light is a shadow of some hue or other, it is a colored shadow.

This classic double-shadow demonstration of colored shadows is presented in most introductory textbooks to color science—a legacy of Edwin Land's spectacular demonstrations of colored shadows in his *Scientific American* presentations of his Retinex theory of vision. Although Land did not initially realize that his demonstrations were colored shadows, he did adopt the historically well-precedented position of construing the phenomenon as counterexamples to Newton's objective approach to light. Dennis Sepper (1988) accurately aligns Land with the subjective tradition inaugurated by Goethe's *Theory of Colors*.

A scientific inconsistency

Newton maintained that white light sufficed to explain color because he had shown that white light is composed of lights that look colored when separated. Goethe emphasizes that this reverses the expected order of explanation. Chromatic phenomena are being used to explain achromatic phenomena. White light, which Goethe regarded as paradigmatically simple, is being treated as a complex fusion of colored lights. Darkness is demoted to a mere privation of white light.

Newton's reversal is not quite as severe as Goethe asserts. Like many of Newton's followers, Goethe underweights Newton's remark that "indeed rays, properly expressed, are not coloured. In them there is nothing else than a certain Power or Disposition to stir up a Sensation of this or that Colour" (1704/1952, 124).

Still, according to Newton, there is no need to appeal to shadows in explaining colors. In addition to being explanatorily unnecessary, shadows are antithetical to color because shadows are absences of light. Color scientists think Newton is correct. Therefore, they ought to deny that colored shadows are shadows.

Color scientists should instead consider "colored shadow" as a misleading a term—like "color blind." Color scientists make an effort to avoid the phrase "color blindness" because it conveys the impression that no hue is seen at all (Hurvich 1981, 241–42). In fact, nearly all "color-blind" people see in color; they merely have less color sensitivity. Color scientists therefore substitute "color deficient" for "color blind." Color scientists should have parallel misgivings about "colored shadow." The phrase is misleading in two respects. First, "colored shadow" falsely suggests that all colored shadows are shadows. Second, even when a shadow is involved, "colored shadow" falsely suggests that it is the *shadow* that has the hue. In fact, the bearer of the hue is the body of light that has leaked in. Just as a dental cavity can be filled with gold without being itself gold, a shadow can be filled with blue light without being itself blue.

Shadows do not produce light (like a neon sign) or reflect light (like an apple) or refract light (like colored glass) or diffract light (like a pigeon's feather). Shadows are privations and so can only be colored in the parasitic way a void can be colored.

Spectacular scientific demonstrations often owe their persuasiveness to a spurious connection with an intrinsically interesting effect. When students learn that solid objects are mostly composed of empty space, they wonder why they do not sink through the floor. Their science teachers explain by placing a disk over a layer of marbles in a cylindrical beaker. When the beaker is put on a shaking machine, the disk is held aloft by the many collisions with little marbles. Thus, students are invited to infer that the floor supports their feet by virtue of collisions with the constituents of the floor. But actually the students are kept aloft by electrical repulsion. Similarly, the standard demonstrations of colored shadows actually exhibit different phenomena.

9

Filtows

Roberto Casati (2003, 170) propounds a slippery slope argument for colored shadows: Blocking a light source with a blackened glass disk produces a black shadow. Follow this disk–shadow pair with a progression of dark gray to light gray filters hanging from a mobile (fig. 9.1). Below the first dark gray disk is a patch virtually as dark as that of the black disk's shadow. The extra light is insignificant. Therefore, the gray disk casts a shadow. The next dark patch is only insignificantly lighter than its predecessor, so both are shadows. By continuing the smooth sequence of comparisons, we conclude that even a light gray glass disk casts a shadow.

Next substitute a dark *blue* disk for the dark gray disk. Since the patches below them are equally dark, both cast shadows. The same goes for blue disks that are progressively lighter. Therefore, there are blue shadows. Similar slippery slope arguments show that there are shadows of every hue.

My reply to Casati's slippery slope argument focuses on his second step: I deny that Casati's dark gray filter casts a shadow. The process is wrong and the product is wrong. Shadows require a *blocking* procedure. Filtering is the wrong process. The filter also produces the wrong product. Casati's dark gray filter only produces a "filtow":

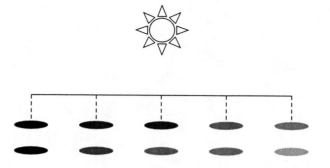

Figure 9.1 Slippery slope of filters

a body of filtered light. No body of light is a shadow; therefore, no filtow is a shadow.

Plugs and filters

As filters let less and less through, they approach being plugs. But a filter must let something through (a sink strainer is a filter but a sink stopper is not). All shadow casters are plugs. None are mere filters.

As G. E. Moore noted about the mysterious ? (see chapter 8), the film used to project light patches on a cinema screen is not opaque— it filters light. An opaque object can behave as a filter when there is more than one light source. Consider a fusion of red, blue, and green lights as in figure 9.2. Mixing red, blue, and green lights yields white light. The interposed object is commonly said to produce multiple colored shadows. But the only genuine shadow is the one that results from blocking all the light sources—the black shadow. The bodies of light that form from incomplete blockage are filtows.

Being nearly opaque is not sufficient for being a plug. You cannot see through a thin sheet of gold leaf. But the gold leaf lets green light pass through. Hence, the gold leaf gives the (incorrect) impression that it is casting a green shadow.

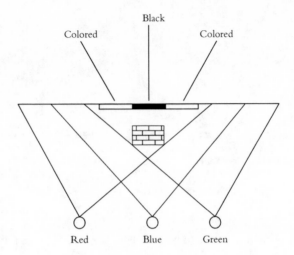

Figure 9.2 Filtow–shadow comparison

Filtows are weaker than shadows. A shadow can penetrate a filtow but cannot penetrate another shadow. When I walk under my patio umbrella, my shadow can still be seen. When I walk under the shadow cast by my overhanging roof, my shadow disappears.

Invisible shadows and the domain of discourse

A polarized lens filters out half of the light (fig. 9.3). Is the "darkened" region a shadow? It does not look much darker than the gray patch created by ordinary glass (at least to the unaided eye). Adding a second lens of the same polarity only slightly darkens the patch. But when the second lens is twisted so that its polarity is opposite that of the first lens, a dark shadow forms. The two lenses collectively constitute a plug. Since it is now clear that all the light is blocked, the darkened region is clearly a shadow.

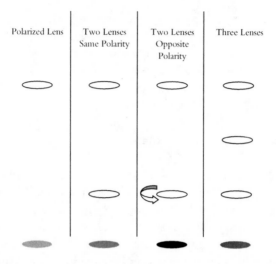

Figure 9.3 Polarized lenses

There is a further surprise when a third polarized lens is sandwiched between the earlier two. When this middle lens is at an angle of forty five degrees different from the axis of the first lens, light passes through the bottom lens! The middle lens is twisting the light that survives the first lens. Some of that twisted light can pass through the third lens. The middle lens reintroduces our ambivalence about whether there is a shadow.

The right answer to the question of whether there is a shadow is "It depends on the domain of discourse." A shadow must plug all the light. But what are we counting as the "light"? If we are counting light of only one polarity, then a shadow is formed. If we are counting both polarities, then the lens is only acting as a filter, not a plug.

William Herschel used the term "invisible light" when describing how directing infrared light on a thermometer expands the mercury. Blocking the infrared light creates an invisible shadow. Panes of glass are opaque to most infrared lights and must cast infrared shadows. The phrase "infrared shadow" helpfully signals that the speaker is limiting the domain of discourse to infrared light.

Biologists have discovered many organisms that are sensitive to forms of light to which we are not. Bees are sensitive to ultraviolet light. Suppose a bee is in a room illuminated with a hydroponic gardener's single "black light." Only the bee can see the shadows formed by interruptions of the ultraviolet light.

Privational character of shadows

The plug/filter distinction is sensitive to context. Many sink stoppers actually let a little water leak down the drain. But because the amount is too small to heed, we still count the stopper as a plug. Of course, there is often unclarity as to how small is small enough to be ignored. But cases that are borderline between "plug" and "filter" are not counterexamples to the thesis that the plug/filter distinction sorts cases into substantive categories. We want to avoid the twilight fallacy of inferring that there is no difference between day and night because there are cases that are borderline between day and night.

If some shadows were filtered light, then they could be projected from flashlights. A beam of colored light cannot be a shadow because the beam itself creates shadows when pointed at other objects. Shadows cannot beget shadows. Shadows cannot power photoelectric cells. Shadows are absences rather than positive entities. Shadows cannot do anything on their own. Nor can they be projected or directly acted upon. When I cast a shadow, I interact only with the light.

Nevertheless, shadows inherit the subtleties of light. In his book *Opticks*, Newton wrote, "Light is never known to follow crooked Passages nor to bend into the Shadow" (1704/1952, 363). If light were a wave, it would bend around corners like water waves. We would be able to see around corners just as we can hear around corners.

What Newton did not realize was that the wavelengths of light are very short. For instance, the wavelength for green light is only 1/50,000th of an inch. The predictions derived from the particle theory of light were fairly accurate for medium-size objects.

Nevertheless, Newton might be faulted for overlooking the evidence. Newton had been attracted to optics by Francesco Grimaldi's treatise *Physico-mathesis de lumine* (Cajori 1898, 88). Grimaldi mentions that on a very small scale, light can bend around the shadow caster. If light is shown through a small hole, light bends a tiny bit behind an obstacle just as water waves bend slightly around a jetty.

According to Ernst Mach, Grimaldi was right for wrong reason. What Grimaldi actually observed was an illusion. In figure 9.4, there appear to be thin dark and light borders separating the blocks. This is an illusion induced by the contrast between the blocks. A light meter reveals only a stepwise decrease in luminescence. Mach bands can be "observed" along the edges of almost any shadow cast in sunlight on a uniform surface.

Dark Mach bands alternate with bright Mach bands. This is all that Grimaldi was "seeing" when he inferred that the bright bands were due to constructive interference and dark bands were due to destructive interference. So Mach denies that Grimaldi discovered the wave nature of light: "Grimaldi makes a remark which would appear to indicate that the superposition of rays of light can also produce darkness. . . . Had not this conclusion been based on an illusion, it would have formed an important anticipation of later knowledge" (1926/1953, 134). In the terminology of post-1964 epistemologists, Grimaldi was "gettiered." Grimaldi had justified true belief without knowledge. A correct theory of shadows depends on a correct theory of light.

Plugging light is a necessary but not sufficient condition for casting a shadow. A shadow forms only when that plug darkens a region.

Figure 9.4 Mach bands

If too much light leaks in from other sources, then the plug does not create a shadow. For instance, photographers stop shadows from forming behind their subjects by adding back illumination.

Some light leakage into a shadow is acceptable because the plug needs only to darken the region, not make it lightless. The region is darkened if it is made darker than its environment. The environment is not always identical to the shadow's *immediate* surroundings. A shadow can be completely surrounded by another shadow. My wedding ring casts a circular shadow. By positioning a penny above the ring, I replace the circle of light with the shadow of the penny. There are now two shadows even though the outer shadow snugly surrounds the inner shadow.

Seeing inside shadows

When I sit on my patio in the shade of my house, I have enough light to read. Light is being scattered into the house's shadow by dust and water particles and is being reflected in by surrounding buildings and trees.

Since the moon lacks an atmosphere, astronauts confront harsh light that produces nearly pure black shadows. The first practical comments men made on the moon concerned the extraordinary darkness of the shadows; bolts that fell into the shadows were very hard to find. When Neil Armstrong entered a shadow, he could initially see nothing but darkness. The first man on the moon had to spend precious time adjusting to the dark—and then would be dazzled when he left the shadow.

If Mars becomes colonized, the settlers will need shelter from the intense radiation of the sun. They are likely to take refuge in the shadows of mountains.

Fortunately, the biggest mountain in the solar system, the volcano Olympus Mons, is on Mars. It soars 29 kilometers above it base, triple the height of Mount Everest. Olympus Mons is about 600 kilometers across, making it the size of Missouri. Olympus Mons is so big that no observer on Mars will able to see its overall shape. If the observer tries to back off to see Olympus Mons from a distance, it will disappear over the horizon.

In addition to providing the widest zone of protection, the shadow of Olympus Mons might make a streak of stars visible during the day. Thanks to the foreshortening effect, the streak would look neatly triangular to an observer on Olympus Mons.

The idea of a search beam shadow goes back to Anaxagoras. He used it to explain the appearance of the Milky Way: when the sun passes underneath Earth, the light from the Milky Way is no longer swamped by sunlight.

Anaxagoras overestimated the selectivity of Earth's shadow (the moon does not get dark when the Milky Way lies in its background). But there is merit in his general idea. The shadow casts by a boat makes fish more visible on the shady side. Why can't a shadow cast into space have the same effect? A shadow could sweep across a region allowing stars to be seen (stars that we are otherwise prevented from viewing because their light is swamped by a stronger source of illumination—the sun). Olympus Mons's height, relative to the thin Martian atmosphere, makes it a promising candidate.

Unfortunately, Mars is a dusty planet. When there is heavy dust in the atmosphere (as is commonly and may be invariably the case), the colonists would only see a giant dark streak in the sky. This dusty shadow of Olympus Mons would be impressive but would not be a search beam shadow because stars could not be seen with it.

An observatory on the mountain itself would be above much of the dust. If there is a search-beam shadow, the telescope should be dedicated to Anaxagoras. When a meteorite landed on Earth in 467 B.C., Anaxagoras concluded that the heavenly bodies were not divine beings. He reasoned that they are like things on Earth. Anaxagoras was imprisoned by Athenians for his impiety, narrowly escaping the fate of his pupil Socrates.

Filtows that coincide with shadows

I am not prejudiced against colored light. Recall that I conceded that a photographer developing pictures in a dark room does cast a polluted shadow even though a single red light bulb illuminates his room.

I am not prejudiced in favor of black and gray. A pane of glass does not cast a shadow (with respect to visible light) even though it appears to have a gray shadow. I say that the imperfectly transparent pane operates as a filter and so does not cast a shadow. I concede that the darkened three-dimensional volume created by the pane looks like a shadow and acts much like a shadow. But this filtow is a body of light rather than a shadow. In addition to having a different genesis, filtows stand in a different relation to the photons it contains. The photons in a shadow are contaminants. They are not part of the shadow. They are like the bits of matter that pollute a vacuum. The photons in a filtow are constituents. They compose the filtow in the way water molecules compose a cloud. If all the photons are subtracted from a shadow, then the shadow remains. If all the photons are subtracted from the filtow, the filtow ceases to exist.

Filtows can also coincide with shadowgrams and other privational look-alikes of shadows. My eyeglasses both refract light and filter light and so create both a shadowgram and a filtow in the same place.

Because a filtow is a positive entity, it can directly interact with other objects. For instance, a beam of colored light can penetrate a pane of glass. A shadow cannot penetrate anything. True, a shadow will form on both sides of the pane of glass. But only light penetrates the glass. The shadow is just where the light has failed to penetrate.

No filtow is a shadow. But some filtows exactly coincide with shadows. Figure 9.5 depicts a projector that can emit feeble light. The light would be too weak to destroy the shadow that would form if the strong lamp were turned on. The lamp and projector are connected to the same switch. So a shadow and filtow both form when the switch is turned on and are extinguished when the switch is turned off a minute later. An impatient experimentalist then destroys all the apparatus responsible for both the filtow and the shadow. Thus, the shadow and the filtow also coincide in their life spans.

This example is patterned after Allan Gibbard's (1975) tale of Lumpl and Goliath and challenges the conclusion Gibbard was trying to draw. In the original example, Goliath is a statue and Lumpl is a piece of clay that constitutes Goliath. The sculptor first fashions the top half of Goliath,

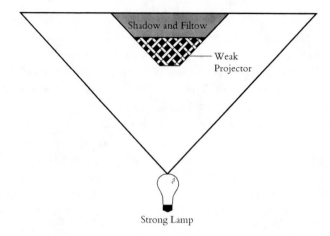

Figure 9.5 Coinciding filtow and shadow

and then the bottom half. When he joins them, Goliath comes into existence and Lumpl comes into existence. After the clay dries, the sculptor becomes dissatisfied and smashes the sculpture—thereby simultaneously destroying Lumpl and Goliath. This appears to be a counterexample to the principle that two distinct things must differ temporally or spatially. One might defend the principle by insisting that Lumpl and Goliath are identical. However, they have different modal properties. Goliath could survive the loss of a finger and Lumpl could survive flattening. Thus, by the principle that identical things have identical properties, Goliath and Lumpl are distinct. Gibbard replies that Lumpl and Goliath are *contingently* identical. They are the same thing that can be, as it were, viewed from different possible worlds. According to Gibbard, water and H_2O are the same in the actual world but are distinct in other possible worlds. Lumpl and Goliath stand to each other as water and H_2O.

My objection to Gibbard does not turn on the ingenious details of his revival of the doctrine of contingent identity. Just note that a shadow is *necessarily* distinct from the body of light that may occupy it. Metaphysically, an absence of light could not have been a body of light. Absences are essentially absences.

A similar point holds for ordinary holes and their fillers. Suppose I have two halves of a ball. Each half is filled with clay. Bringing two halves together simultaneously creates a cavity and a cavity filler of clay. Cavities are essentially distinct from their fillers (distinct in every possible world). Therefore, Gibbard's contingent identity solution to the problem of Lumpl and Goliath fails to be a complete solution. There is no point in reviving the doctrine of contingent identity if another solution to puzzle must be adopted anyway.

The metaphysical peculiarities of shadows cause noteworthy collateral damage. All accounts of the nature of the art object assume that the object is a material object, an abstract object, or a mental entity. But the shadows displayed by puppeteers do not fit in any of these three categories.

Nor can artifacts be defined as material things. Consider the shadow clock cast on the floor of the Manchester-Boston airport. The clock is a shadow, not the shadow of a clock. (Pedestrians walk through the clock; they do not tell time by looking at the contraption in the ceiling that casts the shadow.) The "multiple-realizability" of clocks extends beyond material things.

Overextensions of "shadow"

Filtows are confused with shadows because we tend to focus on the products of light darkenings rather than the process. Filtows behave like shadows. So do shadowgrams and shadow bands and para-reflections and pockets of destructive interference between light waves. A second cause for confusion is that filtows often coincide with genuine shadows and with privational phenomena, such as shadowgrams, that are often themselves mistaken as shadows.

The best way to distinguish shadows from other phenomena is to attend to the process rather than product. But there are differences at the product level. Sometimes the difference is obvious enough to make it clear that "shadow" is being applied only metaphorically, as when a man's freshly sprouted beard is described as a "five o'clock shadow."

Roberto Casati (2003, 15) extends "shadow" to dark marks on surfaces. For instance, a permanent "shadow" was left by Japanese man who happened to be sitting on some steps when the Hiroshima bomb exploded. Early research in photography was encouraged by phenomena such as the outlines old furniture leaves on walls. Sunshine bleaches the room except where the light is blocked by furniture. The "shadows" left on the wall are enduring images. Early chemists experimented with optically sensitive surfaces in the hope that they could "catch shadows."

These images on surfaces are not shadows because they are physical marks. Each stage of the mark causally sustains the next. In contrast, each stage of a shadow is sustained by objects blocking light sources. In Wesley Salmon's (1984, 144) terminology, shadows are pseudoprocesses. Although each stage of a shadow provides a basis for predicting the next stage, none of the stages is causally relevant to each other (recall fig. 1.10). If a passing car deforms my shadow, the deformation does not cause the next stage of the shadow to be deformed. The car cannot permanently mark my shadow. But if the image of the Japanese sitter is scratched, then that leaves a lasting mark on the image. In contrast, shadows cannot be defaced.

Shadows typically have a penumbra because the light source is not a single point of light. When only some of the points of light are blocked, the light is being filtered rather than blocked. Light is needed for a penumbra. If we could somehow subtract all the photons from a penumbra, it would cease to be a penumbra. Thus, the penumbra of a shadow is not itself a shadow—it is a filtow. Filtows normally surround shadows. Only the umbra of a shadow is a shadow.

If filtows were shadows, there would be implausibly many shadows. Cathedrals would be illuminated by shadows. Shadows could be divided into spectra with prisms. Our eyes have a slightly yellow pigment, so all that we see would be shadows.

One may fear that my attempt to stop the flood of shadows is still too anthropocentric: "A plug with respect to light need not be a plug with respect to cosmic rays. A door plugs the light but does not plug the sound. A red filter is just a plug with respect to all wavelengths of light except red light. Thus, the filter/plug distinction fails to stop the flood of shadows." There is no denying that plugging is relative to the stuff plugged.

Light is the *visible* portion of the electromagnetic spectrum. But visible to whom? Although we normally relativize "visible" to human beings, biologists frequently relativize it to different species. Given that we are relativizing "visible" to bees, we should agree that there are shadows in the ultraviolet range. This relative conception of "light" does not require that shadows always be visible. The shadow might be too quick to be seen even for a bee. The relativization of "light" only fixes the relevant interval of the electromagnetic spectrum.

Applications to the classic demonstration of colored shadows

The distinction between shadows and filtows also applies to the classic demonstrations of colored shadows. In colored shadow demonstrations, the opaque object acts as a gatekeeper, blocking one source of light but not others. A gatekeeper is a filter. Therefore, the green shadow in the classic demonstration is actually a body of filtered light.

The cause of the *greenness* of the filtow in figure 8.1 is controversial. I do not need to enter this controversy. After all, I reject shadows of any hue. My goal is to apply the shadow/filtow distinction against the demonstration of there being a colored *shadow.*

Those who do not bother to distinguish shadows from filtows are reminiscent of those who slough over the distinction between reflection and refraction. The distinction between reflection and refraction attracts little interest from laymen. Yet it is important for theoretical purposes and for practical purposes such as the construction of telescopes and cameras. Reflection and refraction involve distinct laws of nature. Where there is one phenomenon there is usually the other. But this co-occurrence is no excuse for regarding them as the same phenomenon. Aristotle uses the Greek words for reflection and refraction in his analysis of the rainbow. However, he never disentangles refraction from reflection (Boyer 1959, 54). This sloppiness handicaps Aristotle's otherwise agile account of a complicated natural phenomenon.

A parallel case can be made for observing the distinction between filtows and shadows. Since filtows are bodies of light while shadows are absences of light, they are essentially different kinds of phenomena. Their resemblance is largely due to the fact that shadows abide by the laws of physics of parasitically—by virtue of the obedience of their casters and surroundings.

I do not deny that there are colored shadows in the sense that there are shadows that are *associated* with certain colors. The number seven on my house is black. Ask any child on my block! Pythagoras thought numbers were unchanging. If I paint the number green next year, will I have refuted Pythagoras?

Numerals can change color. The numbers themselves are colorless. The distinction between numbers and numerals is necessary for understanding mathematical propositions. There are only finitely many numeral tokens but infinitely many numbers. Distinct numeral tokens can represent the same number. Numeral tokens can be destroyed. Numbers are indestructible.

Just as distinctions are needed for number theory, distinctions are needed for shadow theory. Just as various abstract beliefs about numbers survive sundry empirical challenges, some abstract beliefs about shadows survive the empirical demonstrations of color scientists.

Shadows that create light?

By the principles of color addition, beams of blue, red, and green light sum to white light. Consider a standard array of three white incandescent light bulbs whose light converges on the same spot of

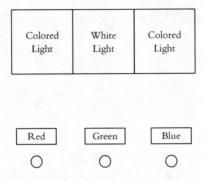

Figure 9.6 "White shadow" scenario

a screen. If filters produce shadows, then a blue shadow is formed by interposing a blue block of glass in front of one lit bulb. Turn that bulb off and place an identically shaped green block of glass in front of the second bulb. Turning that bulb on produces a green shadow. Now turn the second bulb off and go through the same procedure for a blue block of glass. Finally, turn all the bulbs on as depicted in figure 9.6. The fusion of red, green, and blue light forms white light. The center region on the screen is white surrounded by colored lights. Casati's slippery slope argument for colored shadows stops just short of affirming the existence of white shadows.

The white shadow would lack a boundary with its environment. This is not a problem with the scenario depicted by figure 9.5. The white patch is well defined against a dark background. The difficulty is that a shadow cannot be brighter than its environment.

Have blue, red, and green *shadows* combined to create light? No, there is white light, but no shadow is composed of white light. Everybody, especially Goethe, would agree that shadows cannot create light.

10

Holes in the Light

Sunshine fills a wigwam from an opening at the top (fig. 10.1). When you lift a lid from the ground, it forms a shadow. As you raise the lid, the shadow gets bigger. When the lid seals the opening, is the whole wigwam engulfed in the shadow?

Shadowhood and figurehood

From within the wigwam, there is only darkness. Shadows are hard to recognize when they lack a visible boundary with lighter areas.

The visual system is even fussy about how this boundary with light is demarcated. Ewald Hering illustrates:

> If I suspend a bit of paper from a thread before a lamp in such a way that a faint shadow is cast upon my writing pad, I see the shadow then as a casual dark spot lying on the white of the paper. If however, I now draw a broad black line about the shadow, so as to cover the penumbra completely, what I see within the black line is a grey spot, which looks exactly as if the white paper had been coloured with grey paint or a grey paper with a black border had been pasted on the white. (1874/1964, 8)

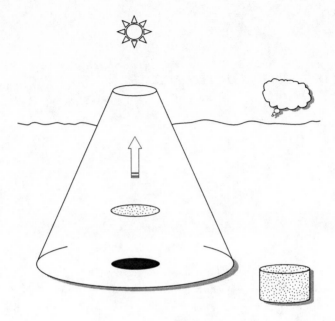

Figure 10.1 Wigwam shadow

When Hering erases the black line, he does not bring a new shadow into existence. He merely removes the disguise of the old shadow. If Hering peels away the wigwam (but leave the lid suspended), an *old* shadow is revealed.

Shadows with invisible boundaries can serve as the ground to another figure. Shafts of light in a dark room resemble shadows (fig. 10.2). This appearance exactly reverses the correct interpretation of the scene.

A shadow can also appear to reverse roles with a caster (fig. 10.3). The visual system assumes light is coming from above, so in the absence of other clues, the shadow is regarded as the object. Because we attend primarily to objects and only secondarily to shadows, we overlook the greater detail present in the figure below the shadow. So the object passes as a shadow and its shadow as an object.

Figure 10.2 Shafts of light

Figure 10.3 Upside-down bicycle shadow

The figure–ground relation marks our preoccupation with objects. Instead of attending to the scene impartially, as a mosaic of color patches, we organize the visual field to promote our practical ends. Those goals are served by what we can predict and control. *Objects* stand out as opportunities for knowledge and power. This is why figurehood correlates well with objecthood. Election to figurehood is influenced by the extent to which the candidate is surrounded, smaller, convex, and symmetrical, plus the extent to which the candidate contrasts with most of the scene and has a gravitationally stable orientation.

The shape of an object is highly instructive—much more instructive than its color. We remember the shape of an object but not the shape of spaces between objects. The spaces between objects are accidents of juxtaposition.

So why do we see *holes* as having shapes? Why do ordinary observers recognize holes, classify holes, and remember holes? Why bother? If *objects* are the beacons attracting the figure–ground relation, we should remember the shape of the lining of the hole (the inner contour of the host object) but not of the hole itself. The hole is just part of the background. Why remember the shape of the scenery viewed *through* an object but not the shape of the scenery viewed *around* the object? Why the greater interest in internal object complements than external object complements?

Psychologists have considered the possibility that this enigma rests on an overestimate of our knowledge of holes. Maybe we do not know as much about holes as we think we do! However, these circumspect psychologists have gone on to empirically verify that the shapes of holes can be recognized and classified about as accurately the shapes of material things (Rolf and Palmer 2001). People remember the shape of holes about as well as they remember the shape of an object.

Attention to holes is innate. Psychologists have verified the common impression that people, from the time they are infants, can track holes with the same ease as material objects (Giralt and Bloom 2000).

Knowledge through illusion?

People have far more perceptual knowledge of holes than is predicted by object-oriented perceptual psychology. Have observers been tricked into collecting this information? Perhaps holes fool the visual system into construing them as objects. Maybe holes cheat in the competition for attention.

Many of the distinguishing features of objects are shared by holes; holes achieve figurehood by being surrounded, smaller, symmetrical, contrastive, and stably oriented. This overlap in distinguishing features also explains cases in which we fail to distinguish the object or hole from its environment. Some islanders fail to realize they are on islands because they cannot see that they are surrounded by water. Canadians who lived in the Holleford meteor crater did not realize they were living in a huge hole. The rim was only disclosed in a 1955 study of 200,000 aerial photographs.

Under the illusion hypothesis, the visual system lavishes attention on holes in the same way a hedge sparrow lavishes attention on a cuckoo egg. The cuckoo egg looks like a sparrow egg. The sparrow is tricked into rearing a bird that is not its offspring.

The illusion hypothesis conflicts with the fact that holes are normally correctly perceived *as holes* rather than *as objects*. True, we are sometimes uncertain as to whether we are seeing a hole or seeing a smaller object in front of a larger object. But the visual system has criteria for distinguishing holes from objects. A figure tends to be interpreted as a hole if it has the same pattern as the background. For instance, this continuity makes the inner circle in figure 10.4 look transparent.

Holes also need to be *in* objects. They are metaphysical parasites. Therefore, the perception of a hole generally involves the perception of another *object* that serves as the host of the hole.

Holes are revealed by their fillers. Stuff flows in and out of holes. We identify some holes by spotting their guests.

The second problem with the illusion hypothesis is that holes are useful. Orifices are critical to your survival. Several diseases are just absences of these absences.

Our ordinary vocabulary for holes is rich because holes are of practical importance. They provide access, storage, and refuge. Holes shape and filter. Consequently, an engineer can explain holes by appealing to their function. Why does my washer tub have holes? To separate water from the clothes. At high speed, the tub interferes

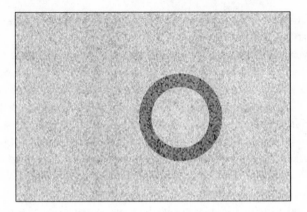

Figure 10.4 Ring with continuous background

with the trajectory of the clothes but not with the trajectory of the water. The engineer subtly continues: we picture the water as being forced from the clothes by a center fleeing "centripetal force." But actually the clothes are being forced away from the water.

The nature of holes

In 1767 Claude-Nicholas Lecat declared that shadows are holes in the light (Baxandall 1995, 156 fn. 1). This is a surprising assertion because familiar holes are in *objects*—generally solids that sustain their own shape. Liquids are poor hosts for holes because they passively assume the shape of their containers. Gases are worse. Smoke rings are paradigms of instability.

The only virtue light has is that its short wavelength limits the extent it can bend around corners. A stable pocket of darkness forms.

Light is a cryptic host. Light only contrasts with its surroundings in special cases (as when a beam forms in a dusty room). Normally, light is pervasive and so is not singled out as a host for a hole.

Yet "Shadows are holes in the light" gets the metaphysics right. Holes are concrete absences; they have positions in space and time.

Unlike a volume of space, holes can move. Holes have histories in which they undergo changes.

Holes are not abstract objects like numbers or squarehood. They are not material things. Roberto Casati and Achille Varzi (1994) characterize holes as "immaterial beings." But holes do not sit any more comfortably on the side of being than of nonbeing. They do not betoken a *special* problem for materialism. The idealist should be equally bothered by absences. In the mental realm, there are lexical gaps, objectless emotions, and lapses of consciousness. In the abstract realm, there are gaps in numeric sequences and absences of pattern. Absences affect all ontological categories. Absence is a generic metaphysical problem like the issues of existence and identity.

Typically, the linings of holes are material. And they are often filled with material things such as debris, water, or air. But holes are not themselves material; they have no mass or texture.

Holes depend on objects. The doughnut hole depends on the doughnut. Holes in the light depend on light. Without light there would be darkness, but there would be no shadows.

All languages have words for holes. English is typical in embodying a rich folk taxonomy of holes ("tunnel," "cavity," "depression," etc.). This gives topologists a running start in their precisified accounts of holes just as geometers get a running start from ordinary words for shapes.

There is often uncertainty as to whether a term denotes a hole or its filler. Is a window an opening in an external wall or is it the transparent glass that fills that hole? Can a river dry up and still exist? Or is the river the body of water contained by the riverbed? Heraclitus said that one cannot step into the same river twice. But perhaps he was confusing the river with its filler.

Shadows and their fillers

A fumarole is an ice tunnel created by a volcano's vent. The fumarole of Mt. Erebus in Antarctica extends into the air through a tower of ice. Explorers climb the tower and descend into the fumarole. The tunnel is filled with blue light. The fumarole is a hole and so lacks any intrinsic color. Analogously, the light that pollutes a shadow can be blue without the shadow being blue.

When a shadow contains a material thing (e.g., ice, glass, or light) that filler can possess properties such as a wavelength, polarity, and mass. Shadows, on the other hand, are absences that can only have properties in a negative way.

Most philosophers concede that two things can be in the same place at the same time—as long as they are different sorts of things. They distinguish Edinburgh's statue of David Hume on the Royal Mile from the bronze that constitutes it.

Michael Burke has influentially objected that things, which share all their parts, cannot differ in kind. If the statue and piece of bronze consist of the very same atoms arranged in the same way, then what "could *make* them different in sort? . . . Given the qualitative identity of these objects, what explains their alleged difference in sort?" (1992, 14). Happily, shadows and their fillers share no parts. Just as Burke allows that a statue could coincide with a region of space, he should allow that a shadow can exactly coincide with its filler.

Color scientists systematically confuse holes in the light with their guests (the light polluting the shadow). Materialists have a philosophical motive to resolve ordinary uncertainty between holes and fillers in favor of the filler interpretation.

Classical atomism models the universe as atoms moving in the void. Hence, it is only materialistic with respective to objects. Unlike plenism, classical atomism permits empty space. Physicists exploited this in their discussions of vacuums. Authors of physics textbooks stress that when you suck on a straw, you are not *pulling* the beverage up. You are merely enabling the atmosphere to *push* the liquid up into your mouth. If you were in outer space, no amount of sucking could get the beverage into your mouth.

If you have no protection in the void, this would be the least of your worries. Your blood would boil. Not because empty space is hot. Rather because empty space fails to exert the pressure needed to keep your blood from boiling. Empty space is deadly. But not because of what it does. Empty space is lethal because of what it *fails* to do.

The services rendered by empty space also take the form of omission. A thermos keeps coffee hot by means of a vacuum between the inner and outer walls of the container. Manufacturers of incandescent bulbs keep their filaments bright without burning them out by encasing the filament in a vacuum.

We have a tendency to misconstrue omission as commission and then reify an agent. We readily infer that coldness acts on us in the same way as heat. Homeowners feel the cold enter through open doors. They see it shrink columns of mercury in thermometers. They discover that the cold has burst plumbing pipes.

Ludwig Boltzmann denied that coldness has any positive properties. As an atomist, Boltzmann insisted that cold is the absence of heat. The metaphysical status of privations is problematic. Boltzmann was ambivalent about whether coldness was real. On the one hand, a complete account of heat would leave nothing for coldness to explain. So coldness seemed explanatorily superfluous. On the hand, it seems pedantically evasive to deny that Alaska is cold in the winter. But Boltzmann was adamant that coldness cannot possess properties in the direct way heat possesses properties. Coldness has properties indirectly. Moreover, he had to show that, contrary to Ernst Mach, this was not just a notational preference for describing situations in terms of heat.

Holes in the light that are not shadows

To dramatize the fallibility of memory, Bertrand Russell (1921, 159) formulated the hypothesis that the entire universe began five minutes ago complete with "fossil" records, "memories," etc. These "traces" make everything *look* like the universe has a long past. All of our beliefs about the past could be mistaken.

Russell's five-minute hypothesis was formulated to raise questions about how we know propositions about the past. But metaphysicians use it to show that some concepts have a causal requirement.

Under the five-minute hypothesis, dinosaurs did not make the footprints of ankylosaurs, and so these are not footprints. The foot-shaped cavity exists, but it is only a hole in a rock, not a fossil hole.

At the moment of creation, are there shadows or only "shadows"? These holes with no past *look* like shadows. But none of these ahistorical holes is a genuine shadow. For none of these dark regions have been darkened by anything. To cast a shadow, an object must cause the shadow to form. If nothing preceded the holes in the light, then none of the objects has darkened anything.

Very soon after the five-minute creation time, the holes in the light will become shadows because they will be sustained by objects that plug the light. Thus, some shadows can begin their existence as nonshadows. Just as an acorn can become an oak tree, a hole in the light can become a shadow.

Shadows cannot pop into existence. They must be caused by shadow casters (even though they have *originated* by a causal process other than blocking). Every shadow has a history. Consequently, shadows do not supervene on a single time slice of the world. Although shadows depend on positive reality, that positive reality is extended over time.

The causal basis of shadow attribution lies behind criticisms of shadow depictions. In episode five of the Star Wars series, *Return of the Jedi*, Luke Skywalker and Darth Vader duel with light sabers near a precipice. Just before Luke cuts off Darth's hand, you can see shadows from these beams of light. This is *conceptually* impossible. Shadows must be caused by blockage of light.

Another impossibility is embodied in a poster for episode one of Star Wars, *The Phantom Menace*. It features a good boy, Anakin Skywalker, casting an evil man's shadow. This alludes to the fact that Anakin will mature into the villain Darth Vader. Prospective shadows are impossible because things in the future cannot cause events in the past. This may be only a physical impossibility. If time travel is coherent, then your shadow could precede you.

The process is as important as the product

"Shadow" is a causal concept; a shadow is a shadow in the light created by an object that blocks the light. No blocker, no shadow.

You cannot tell whether something is a shadow by looking at it alone. You also need to consider the caster of the shadow. Lecat is being incomplete when he identifies shadows with holes in the light.

There is an absence of light inside a solid, continuously opaque object such as a snowball. But there is no shadow inside of it. When light is antecedently precluded by the nature of the substance, no shadow results. I cannot bury my shadow my shoveling snow on it. The problem is not that my shadow climbs to the surface of the snow. Instead, the snow that destroys the bottom layer of my shadow becomes a surface on which a higher portion of my shadow becomes visible.

If a very big, very cold snowball is quickly heated from the inside, then its core becomes transparent liquid while its shell remains solid opaque snow. Now there is an opportunity for light to be present— which is frustrated by the surface of the snowball. The snowball has a new shadow even though there has been no change in the distribution of light.

Shadows surrounded by shadow

Not all shadows are islands of darkness in a sea of light. There can be shadows that are completely surrounded by a contiguous shadow. Punch a hole in a card and save the chad (the little piece you punched out). Put the card on an overhead projector. You will see the shadow of the card on the projection screen. The big shadow has a little hole of light. Now neatly replace the chad. The hole of light disappears. The newly darkened region is the shadow cast by the chad.

Roberto Casati and Achille Varzi believe all holes depend solely on their hosts. Thus, they deny that a hole can be completely surrounded by a larger hole (1994, 100–102).

Casati and Varzi overlook holes that also depend on hole makers such as craters and footprints. But shadows also have blockers. The hole maker provides an extra way of individuating shadows. In the case of the chad, one hole in the light is created by the chad, and the card creates a surrounding hole.

Metaphysical baggage of shadows

Shadows entail the existence of more than a hole in the light. There must be a light source, light from this source, something capable of blocking this light, plus the space and time needed for the formation of the shadow.

In addition to the ontological demands of shadows, there are cosmological requirements. There must causation. There are no shadows in a Leibnizian world of preestablished harmony. There are no shadows in a Humean world of mere correlations.

Where there is causation, the causation must be of the right type. There are no shadows in Nicolas Malebranche's occasionalist universe in which God is the immediate cause of each effect. According to Malebranche, my body does not block light to create a shadow; God creates the dark patch. Although God causes the hole in the light, it is not a shadow of God, for God is not causing the hole by *blocking* the light.

The phenomenology of shadows

Because shadows are a species of holes, lessons about the phenomenology of holes transfer to shadows. The transfer is especially smooth to the extent that we can focus on "cast shadows" ("two-dimensional" shadows). Only three corrections are needed.

First, shadows are less visibly dependent on a host. We overlook light for the same reason we overlook air. Except for spotlights, we have a hard time making out any host for a shadow.

Second, the lack of a salient host diminishes the effectiveness of figure–ground continuity as test against objecthood. (This is the fact that makes holes look transparent.) This loss is exacerbated as the shadow gets darker. For the background covered by the shadow becomes invisible. So although shadows are translucent, this is not enough to make them look like holes. They look more like ghostly objects.

The third correction goes in the opposite direction, favorable to recognition. Shadows are more apt to have meaningful shapes than host-only holes because they mimic the shape and movements of their casters.

This mimicry revives the cuckoo bird analogy. Even if our attention to holes is not due to an illusion, shadows might distract us into attending to them. Holes in the light are not as useful as holes in objects.

Shadows are still useful for solving visual problems. Shading helps us ascertain the shape of an object and its relation to the environment. For instance, the attached shadow and the cast shadow in figure 10.5 help us interpret the object as a ball and as attached to the ground. Since shadows are parts of our normal environment, they are useful in preventing illusions. For instance, the Pulfrich phenomenon occurs while observing a pendulum with two eyes but with one eye looking through a neutral gray filter such as a sunglass lens. The pendulum has a flat trajectory but looks like it is moving through an elliptical orbit. Adding moving shadows sharply reduces the number of people who experience the illusion (Price et al. 1998).

Figure 10.5 Ball with cast shadow

This illusion hypothesis also conflicts with the fact that some of the hardware of the retina and brain is dedicated to shadows:

> Clearly, highlights and shadows are two of the most fundamental features of images. In all vertebrate visual systems studied thus far, highlights and shadows are universally represented, not only by separate sets of ganglion cells, but by separate systems of cells throughout the retina and central nervous system. (Nelson and Kolb 2004, 260)

So it is not as if all of our attention to shadows is due to a short circuit of object-oriented brain tissue. Parts of the organ are there just for the shadows. Of course, shadows are not being tracked because of their intrinsic interest. Shadows are being exploited to perceive objects. To a certain extent, we see objects by seeing their shadows (though seeing only the shadow is never good enough for seeing the object).

Possibly, all vision of objects began as an ascent from shadow seeing to object seeing. Objects may have evolved from being theoretical entities to observational entities.

II

Black and Blue

Consider an ambiguous sundial (fig. 11.1). The three o'clock position has a mark in the shape of the gnomon's shadow. So at three o'clock it is impossible to tell whether you are seeing a shadow or whether you are seeing a black mark. Do you see something *black* at three o'clock?

Most people answer yes. After all, the shadow is indistinguishable from the black mark. They acknowledge that color appearances can be misleading in poor light. The dark red frame of a stained glass window can appear to match a black patch on the glass. While in a dimly lit church, the possibility of attributing the wrong color warrants caution in attributing blackness to the frames.

We should be cautious if the specimen is adulterated. Black rhinos are really gray; they just enjoy mud bathes. A soot-covered metal ball is black but looks silvered when submerged in water. (Soot forms an uneven surface that traps a layer of air. Most of the incident light on this layer is reflected creating the misleading appearance.) And we need to think twice if hallucinating or if an illusion is afoot.

But you are a sober, normal observer in the daylight. You are just uncertain as to whether the thing you see is a black shadow or a black mark.

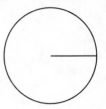

Figure 11.1 Sundial

The possibility that one is actually viewing a *shadow* does not warrant caution in the claim that one is seeing something black. For at least the shadow is black (even if the thing it darkens is not itself black). News that you are viewing a *shadow* does not overturn the judgment that you are seeing something black.

Your confidence is reinforced by the example of a shadow crossing a burnt branch in the snow. The shadow and the branch form an X pattern. The point of intersection is black even though the overshadowed portion of the branch is not absorbing any light. Since the shadow is black at the point of intersection and does not change color, the shadow is black beyond the intersection.

Many interesting facts about black objects are predicted and unified by their absorption properties—especially when combined with the insight that good absorbers of radiation are also good emitters. White mugs are better than black mugs because black mugs cool the hot beverage too fast—first by efficiently absorbing the heat, and second by efficiently passing heat to the environment.

A more exotic illustration of the connection between absorption and blackness involves asteroids. Around 1900, Ivan Yarkovsky pointed out that a rotating asteroid will be unevenly heated. Its dusk side will be hotter than its dawn side. Because the asteroid would be absorbing photons on one side while radiating energy out into space from the other, its orbit would gradually change. In principle, blackening half of an earthbound asteroid (say, with soot) could deflect it.

Color scientists are rightly impressed by the discovery that "all indiscriminate light absorbers are black." But this does not warrant their inference to the converse "all black things are indiscriminate light absorbers."

Of course, if we do infer the converse, there are strong implications for the sundial scenario: when the shadow falls on the black mark, the mark is not absorbing light. Black things need light to manifest their disposition to absorb light. Given that blackness is confined to absorbers, the shadow prevents you from seeing anything black. The shadow is not like a strip of black tape placed over the black mark. The tape is itself black, so you still see something black when it covers the black mark. Shadows do not absorb light. So they can only be dark, not black.

A grasshopper earns its green color by being a heavy absorber of all the wavelengths of light—except those associated with green. A carpenter ant earns its black color by heavily absorbing all wavelengths of light without exceptions. In this sense, black ants are more industrious (and more impartial) than green grasshoppers. Because shadows do not absorb light (or do any other work), they should not have any color (not black, not gray, and nor any chromatic color). Accordingly, color scientists are constantly disciplining attributions of achromatic colors.

Whereas the arctic explorer Robert Peary describes the sky as gray during the day and black during the night, the color scientist Irvin Rock denies that the sky is ever gray or black. He dismisses descriptions of the "black sky" as metaphorical.

The negative connotations of "black" (*black mood, black market, black heart, black magic, black Friday*) are commonly explained by the association with the dangers of the night. However, this explanation of the metaphorical usage of "black" presupposes that the night is literally black.

Whereas the philosopher Michael Tye (2002, 157) takes the visual experience we get from being in a completely dark "pitch black" room as a paradigm of blackness, the color scientist Rock insists,

A completely dark room can be considered to be a special case of a Ganzfeld, and a dark room looks dark, not black. Darkness is the experience correlated with the absence of light, but this is not true of blackness. For the colour black to be experienced, certain specific conditions of contrasting luminance must obtain. (1975, 503)

Ordinary speakers attribute blackness to many nonabsorbers: the night (which is the shadow of Earth), the pupil of an eye (which is just a hole controlled by the iris), and "reflections" of black objects. The first man in space, Yuri Gagarin, recalls: The sky was blacker than it ever appears from the Earth, with the real, slate-blackness of space" (Burgess et al. 2003, 23).

Midwinter, my boys grumble about eating breakfast before dawn. Looking out into the cold darkness, my eleven-year-old Maxwell pessimistically generalized: black is the most common color. I cheerfully sampled the kitchen to demonstrate that other colors were more common than black. Maxwell explained that he was thinking about the vastness of the universe.

Physicists relate how their predecessors were astonished by the black Fresnel ring (in which a white spot of light forms by constructive interference within a dark fringe caused by destructive interference).

The restriction of blackness to indiscriminate light absorbers is an example of overlearning a discovery. After logicians discovered the rule of double negation, grammarians, such as Robert Lowth in his 1762 guide *A Short Introduction to English Grammar*, characterized all double-negative constructions as actually meaning the opposite of what the speaker intends. Some double negatives do cancel each other. However, other negatives, such as those in "I don't want nothing," reinforce each other. They operate as two halves of an emphatic denial. Survey of how "black" is actually used by both ordinary people and scientists discloses that blackness can be produced by a variety of means: blocking light, destructive interference, and light capture.

Blue has notoriously disparate causes. Blue shirts are made with pigments that absorb everything except blue light. Blue eyes are caused by the scattering of light. Peacock feathers are blue because of interference.

Black also resembles blue in its metaphysical diversity. Earth's sky is blue because the atmosphere scatters light with wavelengths of

light associated with blue less than it scatters light of other wavelengths. But the sky is distinct from the atmosphere. Earth's sky pre-
dates its atmosphere and will postdate it. The sky is not a material
object.

Philosophers and scientists are uncomfortable with absences and
so gerrymander discussion to disenfranchise black shadows, black
space, and the black sky of the lunar day. Their discussions also have
a terrestrial bias. They neglect astronomical objects such as sunspots
and black holes. Once the generalization "All black things are indiscriminate light absorbers" is broken by astronomical examples, we
more easily acquiesce to the blackness of absences.

The scientific anomalies of black

Kurt Nassau begins *The Physics and Chemistry of Color: The Fifteen
Causes of Color* by disambiguating "color":

> The term *color* is properly used to describe at least three subtly dif-
> ferent aspects of reality. First, it describes a property of an object, as
> in "*green* grass." Second, it describes a characteristic of light rays, as
> in "grass efficiently reflects *green light* while absorbing light of other
> colors more or less completely." And third, it describes a class of sensa-
> tions, as in "the brain's interpretation of the specific manner in which
> the eye perceives light selectively reflected from grass results in the
> *perception of green*." By careful wording one can always indicate which
> of these three meanings of "color" is intended in any given usage.
>
> Sometimes the difference is critical: "Black" is used for the color of
> the surface of an object has an exact meaning, namely, zero transpar-
> ency and zero reflectivity; as the property of a light ray it has no mean-
> ing at all; in perception it can be viewed conveniently as being merely
> the total absence of sensation. (2001, 3)

Nassau underrepresents black. No surface on Earth has *zero* reflectivity. Nothing can be black in the sense of being *light* of that color. And

if black is the absence of color sensation, then there is no *color* black in the perceptual sense.

Talk of black *shadows* is further damned by the color scientists' predilection for treating illumination as something that is not seen or not ordinarily seen. Ewald Hering stresses,

> Seeing is not a matter of looking at light-waves as such but of looking at external things mediated by these waves; the eye has to instruct us, not about the intensity or quality of the light coming from external objects at any one time, but about those objects themselves. (1874/1964, 23)

Consequently, as Ernst Mach writes, "We generally perceive, not light and shadow, but objects in space. The shading of bodies is scarcely noticed" (1897, 90). Indeed, Hermann von Helmholtz intimates that we need to eliminate illumination to stabilize the appearance of objects. Despite the radical variation in lighting presented by bright sunshine, overcast sky, twilight, and candlelight, things look amazingly uniform in color. Because we are factoring out variations in illumination, shadows are not normal objects of perception. (Nevertheless, Helmholtz does say blackness results from an absence of light: "A spot in the visual field that sends no light to the eye is seen as black" [1866/1962, 131].)

If shadows are just aspects of illumination patterns, then they are not normally visible. When seen, they could only have the color that light has. But since shadows are absences of light, they can only be dim or dark. They cannot be colored in any of the senses Nassau lists.

Westphal on black

Scientifically minded philosophers inherit the scientists' troubles with black. Jonathan Westphal's general project is a Kripke-Putnam style rejoinder to Ludwig Wittgenstein's *Remarks on Color* (1951/1977). Wittgenstein denies that a contingent *theory* of color can explain the necessity of propositions such as "There cannot be a transparent

white," "There is no blackish yellow," and "There cannot be a shining brown." Wittgenstein thinks we cannot imagine what it would be
like for these propositions to be false. Consequently, he thinks *science*
cannot explain why they are true; "We not want to establish a theory
of colour (neither a physiological one nor a psychological one), but
rather a logic of colour concepts" (Wittgenstein 1951/1977, sec I, 22).

Westphal disagrees. He thinks science explains the statements on
Wittgenstein's list (or at least the true ones) by empirically revealing
the essences of colors and the relations involved in color perception
such as "opaque" and "shine." According to Westphal, "white" is a natural kind term or something close to a natural kind term.

Westphal systematically assimilates Wittgenstein's puzzle statements to Saul Kripke's *a posteriori* necessities. Ordinary speakers dub
a substance "water" and scientists later reveal the necessary properties of this natural kind. Given the empirical (yet essentialist) definitions of "white" and "transparent," Westphal can demonstrate that
transparent white is contradictory:

> So what would a transparent white surface be? It would be a surface
> which (i) transmits all the incident light—it is transparent—enabling
> us to see what lies beyond it, and (ii) scatters back almost all the inci-
> dent light—it is white—and transmits almost none. A transparent
> white object would reflect almost all the incident light and transmit
> almost none of the incident light (it is transparent). This is a straight
> double contradiction.... [I]n the proposed connection 'X is white and
> X is transparent' turns out to be an ordinary contradiction of the form
> p & ~p. So there is no peculiar logic of colour, but only logic applied
> to ordinary statements about the distinctive facts and phenomena of
> colour. (1991, 22–23)

Westphal's account of color science is influenced by Wolfgang Goethe:
color science reveals the laws that connect our perception of color
with the illumination and reflectance properties of surfaces. Westphal
emphasizes, "The basic principle is that colours are a certain sort of
shadow" (1991, 2).

Westphal defines black as the opposite of white: "Something is white if it does not significantly darken any light incident upon it, in the sense that the spectrum of the light incident upon it is the same as the spectrum of the light reflected from it, near enough" (1991, 78). Equivalently, "Something is white if it reflects a high enough proportion of the light incident upon it, regardless of the colour of this light." Whereas white things refrain from darkening or uniformly reflect, black darkens or refrains from reflecting:

> Something is black, or more strictly is black coloured, if it more or less completely darkens any light incident upon it. Or something is black if it refuses to reflect light of any colour. It robs the incident light of its entire spectrum, as opposed to preserving the entire spectrum, as white does, or selectively preserving it, as objects and materials of other colours do. (1991, 78)

Westphal's two definitions do not exactly coincide. Shadows "refuse to reflect light of any color," so they would qualify as black under the omissive definition. But shadows would not qualify as black under the *commissive* definition because it is false that a shadow "darkens any light incident upon it." A beam of light pierces a shadow without being diminished by the shadow. If the light is diffuse, it makes the shadow look grayer. Increasing the light throughout the shadow just destroys it.

Shadows reveal a conflict between Westphal's omissive and commissive definitions of blackness. The omissive definition looks more vulnerable. It is too broad. Electrons are too small to reflect light. This refusal to reflect light is not enough for them to qualify as black. Electrons are colorless.

The omissive definition cannot be rescued by restricting it to visible things. The hole in a sewing needle is small but can be seen under bright light. If the hole were invisible you would not be able to thread the needle. Yet the hole does not reflect light. This does not make the hole black. Instead, the hole is transparent.

Ludwig Wittgenstein declares that black is a surface color (1951/1977, sect. III, 70, 156). This restriction is also popular amongst psychologists. Alan Gilchrist begins his book *Seeing Black and White* by emphasizing

> this book is about the perception of surface color, which is the property of an object. It is not about the perception of light. This is implied by the word "black" in the title. Only a surface can be black; light is not black. We will be considering the perception of objective properties of the real, everyday world, not isolated patches of light in a dark laboratory. (2006, 9)

"Surface color" contrasts with "aperture colors." Aperture color is a rigorous development of what artists call "local colors" (color isolated from influences of background and lighting). To ascertain the most basic aspects of color vision, scientists have subjects view small, disembodied patches of color, which are usually seen on a black backdrop with no other objects visible. To further neutralize extraneous factors, observers are dark adapted. The study of aperture color isolates the effects of wavelength on color vision, the effects of light on cones in the retina, and explains aspects of color matching and discrimination. The price of these analytical advantages is diminished guidance as to how things look outside the laboratory. The isolated viewing conditions confer an ethereal appearance to aperture colors; they appear to lack a definite location in space. Some colors cannot be seen at all in this artificially noncomparative setting. For instance, the aperture color of a chocolate bar is a dark yellow. Brown requires simultaneous contrast and so can only be seen as a surface color.

Like Gilchrist, I am only interested in surface colors. Shadows have surfaces. After all, they occupy volumes of public space. The surface begins where this volume ends.

When the shadow is produced by a point source of light, there is no penumbra and the surface of the shadow can be precisely measured. When the shadow has a blurry penumbra, the boundaries can be as vague of those of a column of smoke or an oil smudge. But even diffuse shadows have locations in the natural environment and can be surveyed by objective means such as light meters.

The blackness of shadows can be documented with photographs—though their blackness is manipulable:

> The blackness of shadows can be controlled to some extent by your exposure. An average exposure reading recommended by the camera meter for a sunlit part of a scene usually accommodates some visible shadow detail. Underexposing the scene by about one stop to enrich the color of the sunlit parts will render the shadow mostly black; underexposures of two or three stops will create totally opaque shadow images. Generally, the blacker the shadow, the more it contrasts with the sunlit parts of the image, and thus gains in compositional strength. (Braasch 1990, 100)

If I accurately photograph a shadow that is free of significant light pollution, then the photograph will be black where the shadow is represented. The shadow is accurately photographed only if the color matches. Therefore, the color of the shadow is black.

In an accurate photograph, the color matches are due to an appropriate causal connection with the scene. The color of the shadow must cause the same color in the photograph. Faithful color photography does not need to replicate the same kind of mechanism. Photographic processes exploit metamerism; two things can look the same color even though light coming from them have distinct spectral contents. Sodium yellow (589 nm) light from a street light is monochromatic but can be matched with a mixture of red light and green light. The blue of a peacock's feather is due to iridescence. The blue of a color photograph of the feather is due to an entirely different mechanism. Likewise, the blackness of the shadow can be due to a different mechanism than the blackness of the photograph. Mach bands complicate this color matching argument. For an accurate photograph will pass along the dark illusion.

Mach bands can be "observed" along the edges of almost any shadow cast in sunlight on a uniform surface. They make shadows seem slightly larger than they are. The discrepancy is significant for astronomical purposes when the size of an object is inferred from the size of its shadows. For instance, the diameter of Earth will be overestimated if astronomers went by the apparent size of its shadow. During a lunar eclipse, Earth's shadow looks about 1/55th bigger than what the geometry of the situation predicts (Ratliff 1965, 214–17). Observers mistakenly assimilate the dark band to the shadow of Earth. They have a clue that something is amiss because there is also a light Mach band just inside the shadow.

In addition to exaggerating the extent of blackness, Mach bands exaggerate its intensity. Experimenters measure the apparent darkness of Mach bands by having subjects compare the bands to other dark stimuli. But Mach bands can be darker than the dark:

> When they are very dark, these bands cannot be matched by a simple comparison stimulus of any intensity because they are darker than the darkness produced by total absence of light in the comparison field. To extend the range of the comparison stimulus downward to match this unusual darkness, it is necessary to subject the comparison stimulus itself to contrast influences by the surrounding visual field. (Ratliff 1965, 52)

These darker than dark Mach bands are the privational counterparts of hyperstimuli. They elicit an even stronger blackness response than situations for which the blackness response was designed.

Big eggs are hyperstimuli for gulls because they prefer to sit on these artificial eggs rather than they own. The artificial stimulus is more powerful than the natural stimuli for which the response was designed. Candy is a hyperstimulus for human beings. We are designed to choose riper fruit by means our desire for sweeter alternatives. Candy is sweeter than any fruit.

One objection to the behaviorist's stimulus–response psychology is that creatures react to the absence of stimuli. In Harry Harlow's maternal deprivation experiments, monkeys respond to an absence of a mother. Deer respond to a sudden silence. Children are frightened by the dark.

Blackness is the appropriate visual response to an absence of light. Dark Mach bands are absences of absences of light. The "darker than dark" Mach bands are the privational counterpart of hyperstimuli.

Blackness without darkness?

Perhaps Westphal could shrug off the apparent counterexamples by simply abandoning his omissive definition of "black." After all, he also offered a commissive definition. All the man needs is *one* good definition. Westphal would be free to retain the omissive definition by demoting it to a heuristic adjunct. He does not employ his omissive definition to explain anything.

Victor Hugo's dying words were reported as "I see the black light!" Westphal employs his commissive definition to explain why "black light" is an oxymoron:

> A black light would be darker than what lies around it—this follows from the proposition that it is black—and brighter than what lies around it—it is a light. If something is brighter than what lies around it, it is not darker than what lies around it. So a black light would be both darker than what lies around it and not darker than what lies around it. This is a contradiction. (1991, 79)

Westphal also shows the impossibility of black light by considering how it would affect other colors. Vermillion light darkens blue, cyan, and green patches, turning them black. It lightens yellow and red patches; they retain their color pretty much as they would if white light were cast upon them: "A white light lights up samples of all colours. A black light, however, would darken a sample of any colour. So it would not light up anything coloured. Accordingly it would not be a light" (1991, 79).

Are sunspots black lights? On the one hand, sunspots are so dark as to be easily confused with the silhouette of Mercury (when Mercury makes a transit across the Sun). Sunspots are depicted with *black* markings. And astronomers describe them as "black."

On the other hand, sunspots are intrinsically bright. If a sunspot could be somehow transferred from the surface of the Sun, it would shine as brightly as a star in the night sky. Sunspots are dark simply in comparison to their surroundings. The umbra of a sunspot is about

2,200 degrees centigrade, the penumbra (which looks gray) is about 3,000 degrees, and the surrounding area is about 5,500 degrees. The "penumbra" of a sunspot looks gray rather than black because it is brighter than the umbra but not as bright as the surrounding area.

Westphal's account inadvertently raises the possibility that sunspots are black (because they lower the average level of illumination) without being dark (because they are intrinsically illuminating):

> The real difference be tween black and darkness is that a black area *changes* an already present illumination, and it is surrounded by coloured things bathed in the same illumination. Darkness, on the other hand, is the *absence* of any illumination, or the lowering of an existing illumination, when it is blocked off and prevented from illuminating. Rooms in a house can be dark even though nothing in them is black or blackish, and certainly the illumination is not blackish, for the reasons already given. What is important for black is the failure of reflection of the illumination. What is important for darkness is the absence of the illumination. (1991, 83)

Sunspots do not subtract the absolute amount of illumination. Sunspots *add* light. Sunspots look dark because they add too little light. (Most psychologists agree that the norm is set by the lightest constituent of the scene—though a few think the norm is set by the average light).

Sunspots are brighter than the earthly norm but darker than the solar norm. We are ambivalent about whether sunspots are dark when we do not settle on how to set the norm. Given that we are trying to figure out how things look from a normal observation point, the solar norm is the appropriate norm. That is why astronomers describe sunspots as dark and only make side remarks about the intrinsic brightness of sunspots. These digressions correct an overgeneralization from terrestrial viewing conditions—that darkness precludes light emission.

There are darkening illusions. In many photographs of sunspots you can see an effect called "limb darkening" around the edge of the solar disk. The surface of the Sun is uniformly bright but the parts comprising the edge, "the limb," are seen through a steep angle. So the edge looks darker than it is. We are seeing more of the Sun's atmosphere (the photosphere) along the edges. A similar sort of darkening occurs at sunset. The setting sun seems less intense than the Sun at noon because we are looking through more of Earth's atmosphere at sunset.

A good test for an illusion of darkness is to switch perspectives. Thanks to refraction, a diver who looks up at the surface sees a circle of light, "Snell's window," through which he can peer at objects above the water (although the scene is compressed). This optical manhole seems surrounded by darkness. But as the diver swims into this darkness, his window moves with him. What appeared to be a dark area is now illuminated, and the region, which formerly appeared illuminated, now appears dark. Actually, all the surrounding water is illuminated. (Light from those areas just fails to reach the diver's eyes.)

Sunspots really are less illuminated than their surroundings— regardless of the angle from which they are viewed. Observers of sunspots are accurately tracking the fact that the umbra is less intense than the penumbra and the penumbra is less intense than the surrounding area.

Black holes

The existence of black holes was first predicted by the English geologist John Michell. In a paper presented to the Royal Society of London in 1783, Michell calculated that if a star were 500 times bigger than the Sun, light could not achieve the escape velocity needed to be visible to distant observers.

Like sunspots, Michell's star would be producing light. Unlike sunspots, distant observers could not receive the light. Michell's star (pictured in fig. 1.3) would satisfy Westphal's definition of "black." But the surface properties of the star are irrelevant. For instance, the surface of Michell's star would be smoother than a billiard ball. But this would not make it shiny. All that matters is the gravity. The surface color of Michell's star does not depend on its surface.

Einstein's physics builds a stronger expectation of black holes and characterizes them in a more counterintuitive fashion. Most contemporary depictions of black holes feature a black disk in a swirl of bright stellar material. This material is being taken from a star that has suffered the misfortune of having the black hole as a neighbor. These pictures seldom do justice to the spectacular gravitational lens effects. The tremendous mass of the black hole distorts surrounding light.

An astronaut who somehow survived being drawn into a black hole would be able to see. There is light inside the hole. It just cannot get out. The light also becomes bent and focused, resembling the compression of Snell's window.

Astronomers are now confident that there are millions of black holes in our galaxy alone. Since black holes capture light perfectly, they ought to be the blackest things there are.

Narrowly speaking, a black hole is a small but massive object—and so not a hole at all. Normally we cannot see objects that are as small as atoms because their effects are so weak. But a black hole the size of an atom, perhaps even just a point, can have big effects. The smallest things that can be seen are black holes. And they can be seen without a microscope.

Light traps

If you seal a white Styrofoam cup with black paper and then punch a hole in the paper, the hole will be blacker than the paper. The interior of the cup is white. White Styrofoam is a poor absorber of light. Light is reflected but has trouble escaping the enclosure.

The eyeball is a natural light trap. Its interior is pink—as disclosed by "red-eye" photographs. Red-eye photographs are accurate, but we prefer to see the black pupil, not pink eyeball linings. We doctor the photographs with black pigment to match the color of pupils.

The blackness of the hole in the Styrofoam cup is caused by something white. The blackness of shadows is also parasitic. The color of the shadow caster is not causally relevant. Black cats cast black shadows but not because the cats are black.

All surface colors are parasitic in the sense that they are altered by their surroundings. Brown is very parasitic. The blackness of a shadow is an extreme case of parasitism. The shadow contributes nothing positive to its own color.

Does blackness depend on light?

Reluctance to attribute blackness to shadows is also motivated by connections between color and light. If light is the bearer of color, then shadows cannot be black. A shadow is an absence of light and so should be colorless. If this idea is carried to its logical conclusion, then "nothing is really black, neither objects nor night skies nor light, even when they appear black" (Sinnott-Armstrong and Sparrow 2002, 280).

According to Berlin and Kay (1991), every language has between two and twelve basic color terms. Languages with at least two terms have words for black and white. Languages with three color terms almost always add a term for red, and then comes green or blue. The priority and universality of "black" make it especially surprising to hear that, since only light is colored, nothing is black even though some things are red, green, and blue.

A related objection to classifying black as a color is that color perception requires light *stimulation*. Westphal unexpectedly replies that black *does* require light stimulation. He cites an experiment described by C. L. Hardin:

> Equip yourself with a lamp that is controlled by a dimmer. Go into a darkened room, slowly turn up the dimmer, and look at the contents. Notice that when you look at them under conditions of very dim light, the gray range is tightly compressed, with little visible lightness difference between the darkest and the lightest objects. But as the light increases, the gray range expands in both directions; not only do the

whites look whiter, the blacks look blacker. An increase in the total amount of light has increased blackness. (1990, 559)

This experiment only shows that the *deepest* blacks require contrast with light. Showing that light is needed for the deepest black is compatible with black existing without light. Fat men look most fat when in the presence of thin men. But their fatness does not disappear when the thin men leave the scene.

Many factors other than illumination can make a surface look blacker. Figure 11.2 shows how lightening the background "blackens" a dark gray square. This simultaneous contrast effect is even more surprising when juxtaposed with the opposite "assimilation effect" in which a darker background makes the surface look darker. In figure 11.3, light gray stripes look *darker* against a black background.

Size matters. A black figure on a light gray background can be made to look blacker by increasing the size of the gray background. The visual system interprets wider expanses as lighter (Gilchrist 2006, 237).

Depth perception also affects blackness attributions. Consider Mach's folded card illusion. Stand a white folded card upright on a table illuminated from one direction. You will undergo a gestalt

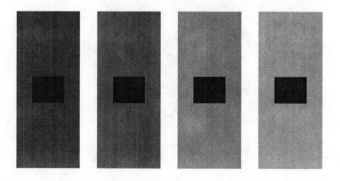

Figure 11.2 Simultaneous contrast

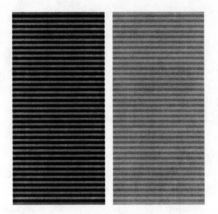

Figure 11.3 Anchoring effect

switch in which the convex corner is reinterpreted as being concave. The side in the shadow now looks to be painted a deeper black. Your visual system can no longer attribute the low luminance to shadowing and so mistakenly attributes it to a lower reflectance. Even invisible contours can create a "blacker than black" effect, as in figure 11.4. The center square framed by the white three-quarter circles looks

Figure 11.4 Blacker than black square

blacker than the larger square. The depth of blackness can vary over a surface that does not vary in how completely it absorbs light.

The lesson is not peculiar to black. Typically, there are many factors that affect the apparent intensity of a property—none of which are necessary conditions for that property.

Some contrast effects are temporal rather than spatial. The color you see now is affected by the colors you have recently seen. This phenomenon of successive contrast makes it possible to see black without light. Suppose you are in a black room with one pinhole of light. The room is very black. After the pinhole of light is eliminated, more of the room is black, not less.

Eventually, the absence of light induces "brain gray." You may experience other imagery effects such as light swirls. These effects contrast with the accurate perception of the blackness of night.

Black afterimages in the night

Westphal agrees that some afterimages are black. To experience one, stare at the picture of the black light bulb in figure 11.5 for thirty

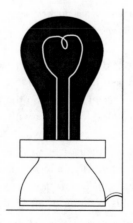

Figure 11.5 Negative afterimage light bulb

seconds. Shift your gaze to the adjoining white region. Behold, a white bulb with a black filament! Paul Hewitt's *Conceptual Physics Lab Manual* (1993) describes how to produce afterimage "photographs." Dark adapt your eyes for at least ten minutes to store up rhodopsin ("visual purple"). Take a brief look at a well-lit scene (just enough to focus), and then close your eyes again. You will see a detailed "snapshot" of the scene in purple and black. After a while, the color scheme reverses. Black afterimages are a precedent for black shadows, for they show that we do not require all that is black to absorb light.

The physicalist J. J. C. Smart denies that afterimages have color. He paraphrases "I am having a yellow orange afterimage" as "What is going on in me is like what is going on in me when my eyes are open, the lighting is normal, etc., etc., and there really is a yellowish orange patch on the wall" (Smart 1963, 94). Westphal criticizes this paraphrase. The color of the patch on the wall greatly differs from the color of the afterimage:

> Here are some of the differences: (1) The colour of the patch is in the surface mode. (2) The afterimage colour lacks texture and grain. (3) Afterimages are relatively unstable and change in colour. (4) Afterimages lack sharp outlines. (5) Afterimages move with the eye. (6) Afterimages are in some sense self-illuminating, and they can be seen in the dark. But the patch is not self-illuminating. (1991, 109)

Westphal goes on to note that afterimages can also be seen with closed eyes. This further dampens his inclination to compare the afterimage with the experience of seeing a patch on the wall. Westphal grants that we occasionally confuse afterimages with objective patches. But this is explained by the one respect in which the afterimage and the patch are genuinely alike—their sameness of color!

Why is it difficult to see black afterimages in complete darkness (or to see them in a shadow)? The natural answer is that we have trouble distinguishing the blackness of the afterimage from the blackness of the night. But Westphal cannot answer in this way. He denies the possibility of a black night. He cannot say that we confuse a shadow and a black mark on the sundial because they are genuinely alike in color. But this is what Westphal ought to say.

Methodological diagnosis

"Black" is a privational term in the same family as *dry* (absence of water), *sober* (absence of inebriation), and *healthy* (absence of disease). We are metaphysically uncomfortable with absences, so positive substitutes are offered. Mental states and dispositions are the favorite substitutes. For instance, in his *Tractatus Theologico-Politicus*, Baruch Spinoza writes, "Peace is not a mere absence of war, but is a virtue that springs from force of character: for obedience is the constant will to execute what, by the general decree of the commonwealth, ought to be done" (1677/1951, 314). Similarly, a subjectivist will deny that black is a mere absence of light and chromaticity; he suggests something is black by virtue of being judged black by normal observers in normal conditions.

Absences have heterogeneous origins because the corresponding positive state can be forestalled in many ways. We can intercept a process yielding light and chromaticity anywhere along a variegated causal chain.

There are many more ways for something not to happen than to happen. Consequently, it is simpler (both numerically and qualitatively) to focus on the positive. How do physicians promote health? By studying disease. How do diplomats cultivate peace? By studying war. This suggests that color scientists will make the most progress on studying black by studying light and chromaticity. In practice, that is where they have made notable progress.

A few physicians deny that health is the absence of disease and commence a search for wellness. More than a few color scientists deny that black is just an absence of light and chromaticity and commence a search for blackness as a positive property. Unlike the physicians, the color scientists have found an interesting candidate: indiscriminate light absorption. They have become slaves to their success.

Discomfort with absences extends to semantics, so some philosophers who agree that "black" is a negative term might assimilate it to the best understood types of negative terms. René Descartes believed that vacuums (absences of matter in a region of space) are impossible. He explained "empty" as a relative, negative quantifier. He agreed that there are empty bottles in the sense that there are some bottles empty *of liquid*. Pockets can be empty *of coins*. Streams can be empty *of fish*.

John Stuart Mill refuses to use the word "absolute" because

> It resembles the word *civil* in the language of jurisprudence, which stands for the opposite of criminal, the opposite of ecclesiastical, the opposite of military, the opposite of political—in short, the opposite of any positive word which wants a negative. (1904/1941, 27)

Roland Hall (1963) regards "civil" as a paradigm case of an "excluder term," an attributive term that serves to rule out something (highly dependent on context) rather than add anything positive. His examples of excluders include "real," "ordinary," "bare," "accidental," and "base."

Although "red" excludes green and blue, it also adds something. So it is not an excluder. Hall also denies that simple negative terms are excluders.

I side with John Locke in believing there is a sensation of blackness (and against Nassau's opinion that blackness is an absence of sensation). This sensation marks an absence of light by its absence of chromaticity. The sensation is an appropriate response to the absence of light in the visual field. Absences of light such as shadows are themselves black. But so are things that cause absences of light such as indiscriminate light absorbers and lights traps that work by enclosure or gravity. Since absences are relative to an illumination norm, sunspots can be black by virtue of their much brighter surroundings. The same applies to portions of an active television screen (even the portions that are just a dull gray when the television is inactive).

Absence of light plays an obvious role in blackness. Less obvious is the role played by absence of hues. In chapter 12, I develop the privational account of blackness by focusing on this absence of chromaticity.

12

Seeing in Black and White

Do people who see in black and white see black and white? Most people assume that totally "color-blind" people see the whiteness of their shirts, the grayness of their trousers, and the blackness of their shoes. I argue that only those who see in color see black and white.

Color vision without colors

You are viewing a single black-and-white chessboard by means of two televisions (fig. 12.1). The television images look the same to the unaided eye. (The light coming from each television has different properties, but these can only be differentiated with devices such as a prism.) Despite the indistinguishability, the color television is more informative because it is sensitive to hues. Unlike the black-and-white television, the color television gives you an opportunity to discern any hue that an object might have. When the object lacks a hue, the color television accurately conveys that absence of hue.

Ironically, part of the explanation of why we have color vision is to better discern things that are achromatic. A shadow cast across a

220

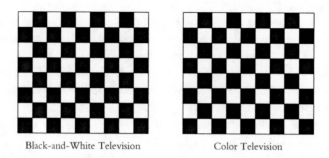

Black-and-White Television   Color Television

Figure 12.1 Televised chessboards

grass/pavement border is easier to discern in a color photograph than in a black-and-white photograph.

> The shadow is primarily a change in luminance (bright to dark) whereas the grass/pavement border is a change in both colour (green to grey) and luminance (dark to light). Colour is therefore a potential cue for helping disambiguate shadows from reflectance changes via the following rule: luminance variations that are accompanied by colour variations are variations in illumination. (Kingdom et al. 2004, 907)

Computers have particular difficulty drawing the line between objects and their shadows. Developers of machine vision have made progress by exploiting *color* television.

Seeing black is a matter of seeing the absence of light by seeing the consequent absence of color. One can see an absence of light in other ways. Seeing darkness does not entail seeing blackness. Monochromats have no color vision at all. They can see an absence of light without seeing blackness.

Color deficiency

In the headless woman illusion, a magician puts a black hood over a woman sitting in front of a black background (Armstrong 1968b).

The lady looks like she has no head! Gullible members of the audience mistake the absence of a representation of a head as a representation of the absence of a head. Similarly, when someone looks at the black-and-white television and infers that the chessboard is black and white, he mistakes the absence of a representation of hues with a representation of an absence of hue.

In the chessboard scenario, you are not given the clue that one of the televisions is a color television. When I ask whether you are seeing in color, I mean *nonepistemic* seeing. This sense of "see" does not entail that any particular belief is acquired by seeing. It is the kind of seeing easily attributed to the animals upon which color scientists experiment.

Eye doctors assume the nonepistemic sense of "see" when testing people for color deficiency. A motorist who cannot see red can see *that* a traffic light is red, for he can rely on a principle he learned from normal observers: the bottom light of a traffic box is a *red* light.

One cannot cure color deficiency by teaching the sufferers how to *infer* the colors of object. Hue differences positively correlate with differences in brightness and texture. Color-deficient people can improve their perception of these correlated differences by varying illumination conditions and by use of colored filters. For instance, James Clerk Maxwell (1855) proposed the construction of a pair of spectacles with one red glass and one green glass. Once a red-green blind person is informed which eyepiece is red and which is green, she can improve her color discriminations. But she still does not see red or green. (Such spectacles have been manufactured commercially, but they reduce the amount of light available to the viewer.)

When we describe a color-deficient motorist as seeing that the traffic light is red, we are using "see" in the epistemic sense. This epistemic sense entails characteristic beliefs. The man sees *that* the light is red only if he believes that it is red.

John Dalton's (1798) own difficulties in discerning red from blue led to his discovery of "color blindness." In recognition, Dalton was to be presented to the king in 1832. However, as a Quaker, Dalton could not wear the mandatory formal dress. One solution was to have

Dalton wear doctoral robes. These were acceptable to Quakers and were formal enough for court presentation. The hitch was that the doctoral robes were scarlet. Quakers prohibit scarlet clothing. Dalton's optical research came to the rescue. Organizers realized that Dalton would be oblivious to the infraction, so they proceeded with the plan, and Dalton received regal recognition for his research.

Often this anecdote is embellished with the claim that robe looked gray to Dalton. That exaggerates his color deficiency. Like most color-deficient people, Dalton could see several hues.

Dalton was fascinated by the fact that his inner experience differed from the vast majority of people. But his concern about the phenomenal aspect of experience never played any role in the subsequent testing for color deficiency. Nor does it play any essential role in the nature of color deficiency. Scientists who think of animals as robots still attribute color vision to them. What matters is the perceiver's responsiveness to hues. This functionalism extends to human beings.

Since sensitivity to hues does not require triggering, you are getting more information from a color television than from a black-and-white television even if the color television registers no hues. The advantage of having a chromatic receiver for achromatic stimuli is that one gets the information that the stimuli are achromatic. There is information about what is *not* there.

Two representations are informationally equivalent if and only if they are positively and negatively equivalent. They are positively equivalent if and only if they provide the same information about what is the case. They are negatively equivalent if and only if they provide the same information about what is not the case. The two television images of the chessboard show that positive equivalence does not entail negative equivalence.

The presence–absence search asymmetry

People spot the presence of a feature more quickly than the absence of a feature (Treisman and Souther 1985). For instance, experimental subjects spot a Q in a field of Os quicker than they can discover an O in a field of Qs (fig. 12.2). People more easily find a moving figure in a field of stationary figures than a stationary figure in a field of moving figures. (A figure is stationary if it has an absence of movement.) Silhouettes of bumps are easier to spot in a field of black ellipses than is an ellipse in a field of bumps. (Bumps have three-dimensional curvature; black ellipses have an absence of three dimensionality.) People search for an orange figure in a field of red figures more efficiently than they search for a red figure in a field of orange figures. (Relative to red, orange involves the presence of yellow. Relative to orange, red involves the absence of yellow.) (Wolfe 2001)

One explanation of these asymmetries is that the presence of a feature allows us to do a parallel search instead of examining the items one by one. A Q is an O with a line added. We just look for the presence of that line in the scene as a whole. The target just pops out of a homogeneous field. Therefore, adding extra Os has little influence on the search. In contrast, a search for an absence is always a search for something relative to a figure. There are no autonomous absences. We are forced to engage in a serial search. Consequently, adding extra Qs increases search time.

There is an asymmetry in checking whether a patch is dark blue rather than black. Finding *some* blueness is enough to show the patch

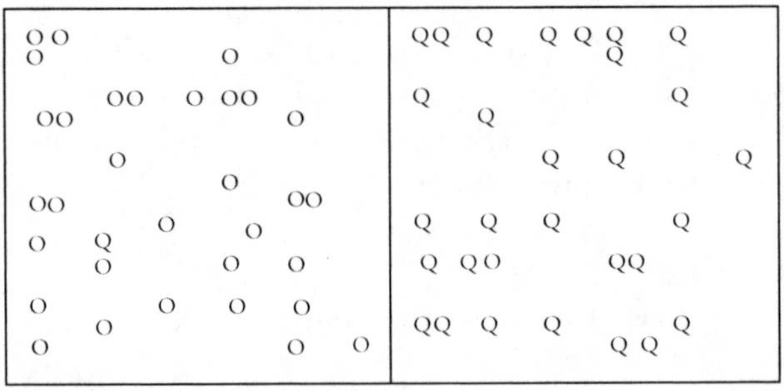

Figure 12.2 Presence–absence search asymmetry

is blue. Confirming that the patch is black requires "proving the negative," that there is *no* blueness. You need to do an exhaustive elimination of candidates for blueness.

Confirming achromaticity is harder than confirming chromaticity.
There is no extra difficulty in *dis*confirming achromaticity; verifying
the presence of any hue refutes the chromatic hypothesis. The asymmetry of confirmation and disconfirmation also affects absences of
light. So blackness requires confirmation of a double absence.

Human beings have excellent color vision. They look for an absence of light by searching for hues. Hence, blackness is detected as
much by our *cones* as by our rods.

Proofs of absences are subject to vagueness despite the aura of
absoluteness suggested by the language of privation. As the day pro-
gresses, the sky gradually changes from blue to gray and gradually
changes from gray to black. There is no definite first moment at which
the sky becomes achromatic. There is no definite first moment at
which the sky becomes lightless.

Attributions of blackness are also affected by the relativity of
"black." The moon's sky is blacker than the Earth's night sky because
Earth has an atmosphere. Air in the upper atmosphere scatters starlight,
creating a faint airglow. This permanent low-grade aurora annoys
some astronomers. They will deny the night sky is really black. Even
if the atmosphere were removed, perfectionists would complain about
the sunlight reflected off of interplanetary dust (zodiacal light). If the
dust were removed, they would complain about the background light
from faint, unresolved stars and nebula.

The only as/as only fallacy

Christopher Boorse (1994) warns against the syntactic slide from
"only as" to "as only."

Golf Illustrated treats Annika Sorenstam only as a golfer. But *Golf
Illustrated* does not treat her as only a golfer—that would be demean-
ing. Exclusively focusing on the golfing aspects of Sorenstam does not

carry the message that this is an exhaustive treatment of her—that Annika Sorenstam is nothing more than a golfer.

Boorse's distinction helps us distinguish only representing in black and white from representing as only in black and white. In the 1950s television series *Father Knows Best*, the characters are portrayed only in black and white. They are not portrayed as being only black and white. This contrasts with the 1998 movie *Pleasantville*. The main character is David, a 1990s teenager addicted to the 1950s situation comedy *Pleasantville*. With the help of a mysterious television repairman, David and his unaddicted twin sister, Jennifer, enter Pleasantville. Everybody in this 1950s utopia is white, employed, and clean-cut. The weather is always nice. When a basketball player makes a shot, it always goes in. There are no toilets in the restrooms. And everything and everyone is in black and white. Things begin to change as Jennifer and David begin to make people act out of character. In particular, some people begin to acquire hues—to the consternation of the community.

The director/screenwriter Gary Ross depicts the town of Pleasantville by shooting scenes with black-and-white film. (More precisely, the scenes were filmed in color and then the hues were subtracted so that Ross could selectively reintroduce hues as the plot developed.) We would miss the point of Ross's depiction if the movie were interpreted as merely involving a switch to a less sensitive medium. We are supposed to pretend that we are seeing in color and infer that there are just no colors to see.

Irreducibility of information about absences

Negative information is trickier than positive information. If it could be reduced to positive information, philosophical difficulties would be bypassed.

The history of logical atomism suggests that this cannot be done. Bertrand Russell initially assumed he could paraphrase negative true statements as being indirectly about positive facts. But eventually he gave up and admitted that there are negative facts.

The basic problem is that negative statements are more power- ful than positive statements. Knowing how things are not gives you knowledge of exhaustiveness. If there is any reduction to be achieved, it runs from positive statements to negative facts. For instance, one reductive strategy is to exploit a kind of double negation; to say that the cat is on the mat is to say that there is no negative fact of the cat not being on the mat.

Absences of absences are part of the political ontology of negative campaigning. In 1959 the Democratic Party candidate for president, John F. Kennedy, alleged that the Republican Eisenhower administra- tion had permitted the growth of a missile gap between the United States and the Soviet Union. After his narrow electoral victory over Vice President Richard Nixon, Kennedy acquired overwhelming evidence from aerial surveillance and a spy that his allegation was false. Although Kennedy conceded the absence of a missile gap to his secretary of defense, he continued to rely on the fear of a missile gap to support an American buildup of missiles—thereby fueling the arms race.

Negative facts are repugnant to human philosophers. People have a strong intuition that reality is fundamentally positive. But from a logi- cal point of view, negative facts provide a more powerful reductive base than do positive facts. Negative metaphysics may be as effective as it is repugnant.

Seeing and conceiving colors

Black-and-white televisions do not enable the viewer to distinguish between black and dark red or between white and light yellow. A red- and-yellow chessboard is indistinguishable from a black-and-white chessboard. When a black-and-white chessboard is seen through a black-and-white television, the viewer cannot see the blackness of the black squares. To see the blackness, he would have to be sensitive to the absence of hue. Only the color television gives him this sensitivity. The viewer of the color television of the chessboard sees the blackness of the black squares even if he does not realize that he is watching color television. He does not see *that* the squares are black but he will see the blackness of the squares.

In dim lighting, I cannot tell whether I am holding my gray tie or my green tie. The tie in my hands *looks* gray. But my green tie would also look gray in such low lighting. I gradually increase the illumination. The tie continues to look gray. Eventually I see that the tie in my hands is indeed gray. But I only saw the grayness of the tie after the light was increased.

Seeing the grayness of the tie is more than a matter of it looking gray. Nor is it good enough that the grayness of the tie causes me to experience the tie as gray. To see the grayness of the tie, I must see an absence of hue. "Gray" is a privational concept like "colorless" and "sober." Monochromats are insensitive to hues. Therefore, they cannot see the grayness of my tie. Nor can they see any other achromatic color such as black and white. Consequently, people who see in black and white cannot see black and white.

Some monochromats make remarks that I construe as acknowledging this inability to see gray. In "The Case of the Colorblind Painter," Oliver Sachs describes an artist, Jonathan I., who became completely monochromatic at age sixty-five. Jonathan probably had a stroke that disabled the V-4 area of his visual cortex. Although his cones continued to signal, Jonathan could no longer synthesize the information into hues. This meant that he could not dream in color or hallucinate in color or have colored afterimages. Nor could he visualize colors in imagination. Jonathan initially compared what he experienced with what we see when watching a black-and-white television:

> Subsequently, he said neither "grey" nor "leaden" could convey what his world was actually like. It was not "grey" that he experienced, he said, but perceptual qualities for which ordinary experience, ordinary language, had no equivalent. (Sachs 1995, 11)

Nevertheless, Jonathan I. tried to convey what the world looked to him by painting fruit gray. He felt most comfortable in a room he decorated in black and white.

Loss of color vision plunged Jonathan into months of depression. Frances Futterman, who was born monochromatic, wrote Sachs after reading his account of Jonathan:

> I was struck by how different that kind of experience must be, compared to my own experience of never having seen color before, thus never having lost it—and also never having been depressed about my colorless world. . . . The way I see in and of itself is not depressing. In fact, I am frequently overwhelmed by the beauty of the natural world. . . . People say I must see in shades of gray or in "black and white," but I don't think so. The word gray has no more meaning for me than the word red or blue—in fact, even less meaning, because I have developed inner concepts of color words like red and blue; but, for the life of me, I can't conceive of gray. (1995, 33 fn. 24)

Talk of what we can and cannot conceive is tricky. If Futterman had no clue at all as to what "gray" means, she would not be able to comment on gray. Even if she cannot conceive of grayness, she can conceive others conceiving the grayness.

Meta-conception is enough for linguistic competence when the speaker can rely on linguistic division of labor. Futterman became a member of a linguistic community dominated by color-normal people, some of whom taught her "gray." She in turn could teach "gray" to children. Indeed, Futterman could impart the grammar of color terms to children along with her ample encyclopedic knowledge about colors: stop signs are red, violets are blue, pink resembles red more than green, and so on.

One of the standard tests for color deficiency is the ability to identify colors. But unless the tests are administered carefully, color-deficient people can pass by employing their background knowledge and by exploiting indirect visual clues. For instance, monochromats can tell whether a photograph is in color by looking at it edgewise, thereby spotting the layers of pigment. They also exploit the fact that color photographs lack the sharp contours of black-and-white film.

Color-deficient pedestrians can see that the traffic light is green by its location. They can see that a sign is red by its hexagonal shape and the word "stop." People with normal color vision do not need to rely on these clues. Since nonepistemic seeing does not involve inferences, the deficit constituted by color deficiency is clearer when we stick to nonepistemic seeing.

Futterman can also conceive of grayness in the way she can conceive of the fourth dimension. Topologists can imagine the fourth dimension discursively with the help of algebra. From high school, Futterman knows Cartesian geometry in which shapes are described in terms of two variables along the x- and y-axes. From there she can proceed to projective geometry by adding a third variable. Algebraically, it is now a trivial step from the third dimension to the fourth dimension. Color mixing is also governed by an algebra. Once one learns the rules for adding light and subtracting light by means of pigments, one's conception of color is deepened. Even if one cannot visualize hues, one can appreciate how they constitute an extra dimension to vision.

Both of these alternative ways of understanding grayness require a language community containing people with color vision. In the past, there may have been isolated populations that have been entirely monochromatic (Sachs 1997). On the island of Pinglap in the South Pacific, more than 5% of the population are genetic achromats. Heavy inbreeding caused this after one of the island's periodic floods. In 1775, typhoon Lengkieki reduced the population of this remote island from roughly a thousand to about twenty. One of the survivors must have carried the recessive gene for monochromaticity. In four generations, achromatic children were born. Since genetic achromats are often segregated, another flood could leave a population composed solely of achromats. These survivors would breed true. Memories of hues would die out over the generations. In this purely achromatic population, no one could conceive of grayness by using linguistic division of labor.

In recent history, educational institutions enable monochromats to acquire a detailed understanding of color. One of the foremost experts on color deficiency, Knut Norby, was born monochromatic:

> Although I have acquired a thorough theoretical knowledge of the physics of colours and the physiology of the colour receptor mechanisms, nothing of this can help me to understand the true nature of colours. From the history of art I have also learned about the meanings often attributed to colours and how colours have been used at different times, but this too does not give me an understanding of the essential character or quality of colours. (1990, 305)

But Norby competed for his post at the University of Oslo on the strength of subtle insights into the nature of color and color deficiency. Why would Norby ask color-normal people about how azure relates to blue if he could not understand the answer?

Sampling and simulating color deficiency

When Thomas Nagel asked, "What is it like to be a bat?" he chose a creature that is very alien to us. But color-deficient people are our neighbors and colleagues (and some of my readers).

The "best" way to learn what it is like to be color deficient is to become color deficient. Many drugs and diseases disable elements of color vision. There are also ways of becoming temporarily color deficient. Staring at a bright light through a colored filter can induce a type of partial color deficiency resembling anomalous trichromatism. The V-4 section of your visual cortex can be disabled by magnetic stimulation. You can sample the perspective of Jonathan I.

Some people have one color-deficient eye and one normal eye (Graham and Hsia 1958). These people can experience color deficiency by simply closing the normal eye. One such unilaterally color-deficient woman helped researchers construct a room that gives normal occupants a good idea how things look to a person who is insensitive to red and green (Kalmus 1965, 12–13). She was normal in her right eye but dichromatic in her left eye. Specifically, she was deuteranope. When using both eyes, her vision was normal. But when she used only her left eye, she was limited to three kinds of color sensations in her dichromatic eye: gray, yellow, and blue. She lacked any green or red sensations. The experimenters then furnished a room exclusively from gray, yellow, and blue materials. The woman verified that the room looked the same to each eye.

Those who cannot visit the dichromatic room can see color photographs of it. This is not as effective as an environmental simulation. The photograph of the deuteropic room is surrounded by a normally colored background. A better approximation is a slide presented in darkness. Better yet is a movie. Dean Farnsworth made a documentary movie, *Color Vision Deficiencies*, that shows, among other things, the color world of this woman.

Environmental and photographic simulations are helpful in showing the limitations of what a dichromat sees. Designers of traffic lights make important safety improvements by examining dichromatically doctored videotapes of traffic lights. The 8% of Western men who are color deficient now face fresh difficulties navigating the World Wide Web. As becomes evident to those who employ a monochrome monitor, Web pages are heavily color coded. There are now Web sites (based on Brettel et al. 1997; Viénot et al. 1999) that help by allowing color-normal people to see what their Web pages look like to color-deficient people. You insert the HTML code and enter the type of color deficiency you wish to simulate. Out comes your Web site in not so glorious color. Other Web sites let you enter digital photographs to see how they look like to color-deficient viewers.

These simulations are highly instructive. However, they tempt us to overestimate how much color-deficient people see. Although the monocularly dichromatic consultant helping in Dean Farnsworth's film could not distinguish what she was seeing from her dichromatic left eye and normal right eye, I say she was seeing more through her normal eye, for only her normal eye was enabling her to see *absences* of green and red. There is positive equivalence without negative equivalence.

A homuncular fallacy

When we try to imagine what it is like to see in black and white, we have trouble subtracting our color vision. A photographer who wants to convey a dog's perspective will focus on something of interest to a dog from a low angle and use black-and-white film. (The effectiveness of this technique survives the debunking of the myth that dogs see only in black and white.) We take ourselves to be seeing through the dog's eyes because we see blacks, whites, and shades of gray. True, the surface of the photograph has achromatic color patches, and we are seeing their blackness, whiteness, and grayness. But we ought not to infer from this perception of the photograph's surface that a monochromatic dog is also seeing the blackness, whiteness, and shades of gray. Features of the surface of the photograph need not be features of what the photograph depicts. A black-and-white photograph depicts only differences in brightness.

When I try to "get into the head" of a monochromat, I tend to picture his eyes as delivering black-and-white images. It is as if I were a little man lodged in his head watching black-and-white television. From my internal vantage point, I see the blackness and whiteness and grayness of portions of the image. This tempts me to infer that the color-deficient person also sees the blackness and whiteness and grayness of his internal image. I have been warned of similar fallacies. Yet I keep committing these "Cartesian theater" mistakes. I note the source of temptation for the edification of my fellow recidivists.

The closest approximation we color-normal people have to monochromaticity is night vision. At night, trichromats see in black and white. But this environmental color deficiency is not as restrictive as monochromatism. Our cones are not turned off in dim conditions. Just the reverse: dark-adapted cones are at their peak sensitivity. When Sachs (1997, 55) accompanied night fishermen, he could see the yellowish light of bioluminescent protozoa *Noctiluca*. They light up when the water is disturbed. Their flash of light marks the lift-off of a flying fish and then its splashdown.

The ability to see colors varies with external conditions. At night, the environment offers too little light for us to see the colors of objects. The objects are still colored at night. Our *physiological* ability to discriminate colors is highest at night. But it is not enough to compensate for the light shortage. We are blind to the colors of objects in dim conditions. We see only in black and white. This is environmental color deficiency.

The phenomenal view

According to the phenomenal analysis of seeing in color, one sees in color if and only if one has colored experiences ("qualia"). If a sufferer of jaundice is watching the black-and-white television broadcasting a black-and-white chessboard, then he sees the white squares as light yellows. On a simple phenomenal view, sufferers of jaundice see in color in virtue of this yellowish illusion. Under this view, seeing in color does not entail accurately seeing in color. Nor does it entail that anything is colored or that anything exists besides the perceiver. If color experiences suffice for seeing in color, then a brain in a vat can see in color.

Of course, one could combine the sensitivity analysis with the phenomenal view by demanding that both conditions be satisfied for color vision. Given this double requirement, you see in color when your colored experiences reliably track chromatic stimuli.

The combined view has trouble with mixed viewing conditions. Do you see the whole scene in color only when every bit of it is colored? If so, I can end your color vision by showing you this in black and white.

Is it good enough for there to be some color—like a red cherry in a field of snow? If so, I can take away your color vision by snatching away the cherry. Or suppose the scene alternates between having a green dot and gray dot. Is your color vision going in and out with the dot?

Concepts from experiences of privations

In Frank Jackson's (1986) thought experiment, Mary grows up in a black-and-white room, reading black-and-white books and watching black-and-white television. Although there are no hues in Mary's environment, she has access to physics textbooks and becomes an expert on color. She knows all there is to know about the physics of color. Even so, Mary learns something when she is released from her room and sees a ripe tomato. Now she knows what red looks like. Since the facts about color cannot be reduced to physics, Jackson concludes that physicalism is false.

Since Jackson is assuming that Mary has normal sensitivity to hues, Mary sees more than does a totally color-deficient person. Mary is seeing absences of hues (whether she realizes it or not). Unlike the monochromat, Mary sees the blackness of her telephone, the whiteness of her chalk, and the grayness of her couch.

Since Mary is seeing an absence of red, she must have the concept of red. Mary should be understood as a counterexample to concept empiricism. According to concept empiricism, we acquire all of our concepts through experience of their positive instances. We start life as blank slates and acquire basic concepts by perceiving things that correspond to those concepts. From this stock of basic concepts, we derive complex concepts. For instance, we have the concept of a unicorn by conjoining the concept of a horse with the concept of a horn. Unlike basic concepts, derivative concepts need not have positive instances.

"Red" is generally taken to be a simple concept. So Mary should first acquire the concept of red only upon first contact with something red. But I say Mary had the concept of red before she saw any red thing. She has it independently of her expertise in physics. If Mary had been untrained in physics, she would still have the concept of red in virtue of her color vision. The same is true if the people on the outside of her room were monochromats with no concept of hues.

Concept empiricism antecedently faces David Hume's famous counterexample of the missing shade of blue. Although Hume is a concept empiricist, he concedes that if one has never experienced a certain shade of blue, one could still have the concept of that shade of blue by virtue of experiencing the shades leading up to that shade of blue. We acquire some concepts by experiencing near misses of instances.

Mary is a different kind of counterexample. She has the concept of red even though she is entirely bereft of positive colored experience. So we cannot say Mary learns a new fact in virtue of having newly acquired the concept of red. If concept empiricism were true, then depriving the subject of instances can limit her conceptual range. But concept empiricism is false. Mary has the concept of red by virtue her disposition to recognize red things when they are presented to her.

Step-downs

Lastly, consider the case of "Colored Colleen." Her environment is censored so that she has never seen achromatic colors (black, white, shades of gray). When she is presented for the first time with a black telephone, she is excited: "That is what black looks like!"

Is Mary any more of a counterexample to physicalism than Colleen? Mary is stepping *up* to a new dimension of experience. Colleen is stepping *down*. The step-down does not threaten physicalism because Jackson is complaining that physicalism leaves something positive out.

Step-downs generally count as novel experiences. People are aesthetically stimulated by restrictive color schemes. Consider Dartmouth College alumni who decorate their kitchens in the school colors of green and white. The absence of nongreen hues leaps out at you. (And also simulates the rare color deficiency of a tritanope—they lack the yellow/blue sense.)

Chapter 13 focuses on the limit case of a step-down: total darkness.

13

We See in the Dark

In 1969, Rod Serling followed his television series *The Twilight Zone* with *The Night Gallery*. The second episode, "Eyes," was Steven Spielberg's directorial debut. Joan Crawford starred as Claudia Menlo, a ruthless fifty-four-year-old New York dowager—blind from birth. Claudia has learned of an optic nerve transplant that would enable her to see for eleven hours. She locates a desperate bookie who agrees to sell his sight for $9,000 (to avoid being murdered the next day by his underworld creditor). Claudia's eye doctor, Dr. Frank Heatherton, refuses to perform the transplant. She blackmails him. After operating, Dr. Heatherton warns Claudia not to remove the bandages prematurely. Claudia Menlo has prepared for her precious eleven hours of sight by filling her Fifth Avenue penthouse with artwork and scheduling a tour of the city's finest sights. She dismisses her servants. Alone in her apartment, Claudia is impatient. She unwraps the bandages. Claudia catches a glimpse of a crystal chandelier. But then everything goes black. The enraged Claudia rampages through her suite throwing statuary, the telephone, and anything else in her path. She collapses in tears—unaware that the whole city has suffered a power outage. At dawn she sees the rising sun. Her vision dims. Claudia Menlo rushes to grasp this vanishing bauble—and crashes through a window to her death.

How many things did Claudia Menlo see? Most people say she saw only the chandelier and the sun (and possibly the pavement on the way down). But I say Claudia saw something in between seeing the crystal chandelier and seeing the rising sun: the darkness of her blacked-out apartment. Claudia had never seen darkness before and mistook this visual experience for an absence of visual experience.

Seeing nothing

We are naturally inclined to deny that we see anything in complete darkness. To see, we need light. In the dark, there is no light; therefore, we do not see.

"We cannot see" is usually restricted to what we are looking for and the manner in which we wish view to it. A lady who has lost her spectacles says, "I cannot see" even though she is *looking* for her spectacles. A sailor in a thick fog correctly reports that he cannot see anything even though he sees the shipmate he is addressing. Reports of not being able to see in the dark are continuous with these domain-restricted remarks. We see in the dark but not what we generally wish to see or in the manner we generally wish to see.

Commonly, the thing we see in the dark is the dark. Darkness is a puzzling "thing." Thanks to the optical research of Isaac Newton, we know that darkness is the mere absence of light. The privational nature of darkness deepens reluctance to say we see in the dark, for if we are seeing total darkness, we are seeing an absence. Many philosophers say we see a positive state of affairs and then *infer* an absence. Few think we *directly* perceive absences. But I think we directly perceive darkness just as we directly perceive shadows. Shadows are somewhat less puzzling because there is typically a combination of light and dark. But I argue that complete darkness is merely shadow unbounded by light.

Philosophers followed Newton's lead in emphasizing the critical role of light in vision. Thomas Reid writes, "We see no object, unless rays of light come from it to the eye" (1814–15/1969, essay 2, chap. 1, 80). This tight connection between sight and light penetrates well into the twentieth century (Chisholm 1957, 144–49). According to John Hyman, "One does not possess the concept of vision until one can deduce the proposition that S cannot see x from the proposition that x is in darkness" (1993, 214)

However, some later philosophers objected that the light ray requirement implies that we do not see shadows, crows, and the black letters on a page (Hall 1979). As I argue in chapter 1, we see some objects by virtue of the contrast they make with their illuminated environment. But seeing in complete darkness cannot involve spatial contrasts with objects that transmit light.

David Lewis is ambivalent about seeing total darkness. On the one hand, there is some theoretical support. According to Lewis's own analysis of seeing, I see if and only if "the scene before my eyes causes matching visual experience as part of a suitable pattern of counter-factual dependence" (1986, 285). In the dark, "the scene before our eyes causes matching visual experience as part of a suitable pattern of counterfactual dependence" (283). Thus, Lewis's unamended analysis of vision implies that we see in the dark.

On the other hand, seeing in the dark seems occult. The ancient Egyptians justified their reverence toward cats by citing the cat's divine ability to see in the dark. A sober analysis of vision avoids attributing supernatural powers. Accordingly, Lewis contemplates adding the condition that the sort of visual experience would not match a wide range of scenes equally well. The visual content of a perceiver in the dark lacks this rich content. With his signature restraint, Lewis leaves the business of revision unconcluded. He says we are of two minds:

> We think we do not see in the dark; but also we think we find things out by sight only when we see; and in the pitch dark, we find out by sight that it is dark. How else—by smell? By the very fact that we do not see?—No, for we also do not see in dazzling light or thick fog, and it is by sight that we distinguish various situations in which we do not see.
>
> In a sense, we do see in the dark when we see that it is dark. In a more common sense, we never see in the dark. There is an ambiguity in our concept of seeing, and the condition of rich content is often

but not always required. When it is, it admits of degree and thus permits still another sort of borderline case of seeing. (1986, 283)

I deny there is any such ambiguity. We see in the dark under all senses of "see."

I am not sated by the reason Lewis dishes out in favor of "We see in the dark." Upon waking, I check whether my contact lenses are still in my eyes by looking about the room. If I see clearly, then I have perceptual knowledge that my contact lenses are in my eyes. But I only see my contact lenses when they are out of my eyes. I see *through* perfectly transparent objects without seeing them. I learn that they are perfectly transparent by my inability to see them and by my ability to see through them. Visual detection is not sufficient for seeing.

An object must look a certain way to be seen. When a dark object looks black to normal subjects in normal conditions, that object is itself black. Under laboratory conditions, a black disk can be made to look white by focusing intense light upon it and concealing the source of illumination from the subject. This does not refute John Locke's example of a self-evident truth "That White is not Black" (1690, bk. 1, chap. 2, 18). Just as a green object can be made to look blue in abnormal conditions, a black disk can be made to look white.

Instead of following Lewis's focus on perceptual knowledge, I concentrate on a more basic form of seeing. I contend that we sometimes see in the dark even when we fail to see *that* it is dark. The darkness stops us from seeing most of what we want to see, but not everything. If there is enough contrast over time, we even see objects in the dark.

In pitch darkness, we at least see the darkness. We distinguish between black experiences that lock onto darkness and illusory black experiences. For instance, if a cave explorer is in a completely dark cave dreaming that he is in a completely dark cave, then he does not see the darkness of the cave—or the darkness of anything else. To see the darkness of the cave, the explorer must wake up and look around. The newly awake explorer makes a fresh connection with the darkness of the cave even if there is no discontinuity in his black experience.

Imagine yourself surrounded by darkening purple light. Eventually, you cannot see whether there is any hue left, but you know you are seeing either purple or total blackness.

Divided darkness

If a flashbulb goes off in the cave explorer's face, he will have an afterimage that lingers after the resumption of total darkness. Like other afterimages, this "blob of light" is at the foreground of a black background. That black background is not part of the afterimage; it is a perception of the darkness. A similar figure/ground point holds for hallucinations. If the explorer in total darkness stands up suddenly from a prolonged crouch, the blood rushes from his head and he "sees stars." These white dots swirl against an accurately perceived background.

A standard procedure for experiments with hallucinogens is to have subjects narrate their experiences from within a dark room. The darkness controls for a nuisance variable: if there is any light, subjects might perceive movements of their eyelids or internal structures of their own eyes. The depressant phenobarbital produces black and white random forms moving about aimlessly. Mescaline causes subjects to hallucinate in color. Powerful hallucinogens may lead to involvement of the whole visual field. But there are intermediate cases in which the subject is partly seeing the dark and partly having a visual experience unrelated to the environment.

To see a lightning bug *flashing* in the dark, we need to see the absences of light between the light flashes. Mere alternation between seeing the light emission and failing to see does not suffice for the perception of flashing. Consider an electrical device that cyclically blinds a subject. If the subject is viewing a steadily glowing light and the cyclical blinder is present, the light may appear to be flashing. The blinder can be synchronized with a flashing light, so that when the blinder is on the blinker is off and vice versa. Now the light is flashing and looks like it is flashing. But the subject still does not see the light *flashing*.

Our two eyes are normally focused on the same scene. But they can be artificially segregated. Suppose each of your eyes is covered with a blackened cup. Inside the cups are flashlight bulbs. While the bulbs are off, each cup is dark. Although you may think you are seeing only one dark scene, you are really seeing two dark scenes. This becomes evident when one light bulb is turned on. You are now seeing one illuminated cup interior and one unilluminated cup interior.

When the light goes out, only one of the scenes changes. Thus, the unchanged scene is distinct from the changed scene even though the visual experience seems monolithic.

The entrances of some caves are so small that if you stick your head inside, your body blocks all the light. This illustrates the possibility of seeing the darkness without being in the dark. The next section demonstrates the converse.

Seeing in the dark without seeing the darkness

If your only light source for this page is a fluorescent light bulb, then you are now seeing in the dark. The bulb illuminates the room intermittently. If the on–off alternation were slow, the room would look like a stroboscopic dance hall. But the frequency of the alternation is so high that you fuse the illuminated scenes together. Movie theaters exploit the same phenomenon. To see the film properly, the illuminated scenes must alternate with darkness. Thus, the audience is in the dark for half the duration of the movie. Because the audience sees the movie continuously and their illumination is intermittent, they must be seeing in dark.

Seeing by the light of a slow stroboscope is staccato seeing: an alternation between seeing the dancer and not seeing the dancer. Each flash of light lasts long enough for a sighting. These perceptual gaps may stimulate musings about whether one knows what is transpiring during the dark intervals. The musings are vindicated when the stroboscope is aimed at periodic phenomena. For instance, if the flashes of the stroboscope are synchronized with the dripping of a faucet, the intermittent lighting makes it seem as if a single drop of water is suspended in midair. Actually, you are seeing many homogeneous drops in sequence.

The period of illumination for fluorescent lighting is too brief to permit microseeings. The perceiver can see the scenes collectively. This is because the excitation of the retina outlasts the stimulus. The retina is like a bell that rings steadily by being struck intermittently. This uniform excitation of the retina by intermittent stimuli fuses the scenes together.

The darker the environment gets, the longer the excitation. To see at night when light is scarce, one must either prolong the photoreceptor's exposure or widen the receptor. Accordingly, the pupil expands, and the retina follows the prolongation strategy. In darkness, the retina takes a long time to calm down. That's why a movie looks most vivid when the theater is nearly lightless.

Visual persistence also shows that healthy people sometimes *fail* to see the darkness in the dark. The dark alternations are entirely missed. Moviegoers do not fuse the dark bits together. They fail to see them.

Moviegoers are blind to the darkness in the same way we are blind to speedy shadows. The shadow of a fishing pole seems to lose its tip when rapidly jiggled. But high-speed photography reveals that the shadow is just moving too quickly to be seen.

The speed of darkness is the speed of light. Suppose our nearest star, Proxima Centauri, goes dark. In about a month, the starlight from Alpha Centauri A and B ceases. After 1.7 years elapses, Barnard's star can no longer be seen. What is going on? Some astronomers would grimly conjecture that 4.2 years before Proxima Centauri became invisible, all the stars outside the solar system simultaneously vanished. They would say that the appearance of a sequential darkening of the night sky is a time lag effect. Their "lights out" hypothesis predicts that in 1.7 years, the next closest star, Wolf 359, will also become invisible. The darkness we see between the stars is old darkness. As time passes, we would see more and more of the darkness. But we will never see it all.

The dark ganzfeld

Psychologists studying ganzfelds would resist the rich content condition contemplated by Lewis. A ganzfeld is a structureless visual field. Pilots experience a ganzfeld when flying in a homogeneously blue sky. A simple way psychologists create a ganzfeld in the laboratory is through the use of split Ping-Pong balls. The psychologists stick half the ball over one eye and the other half over the other eye. The subjects sit still under the constant illumination of a light bulb. The subjects initially see the innards of the Ping-Pong balls (contrary to Lewis's rich content condition). Admittedly, their visual field *eventually* fades out. Indeed, some subjects suspect that the experimenter has gradually turned down the lights. The speed with which the light appears to dim varies with the color of light. When a red light is used, subjects "black out" in about ten seconds. These subjects are suffering an illusion because they have a black experience even though they are being stimulated by ample red light.

The subjects will begin to see if an object passes in front of them, thereby creating a shadow. But as long as the stimulation is constant, they fail to see anything. Their visual experience is the default state of "brain gray."

Given that we see in the dark, we should agree with Irvin Rock (1975, 503) that there is an even simpler way to create a ganzfeld: put the subjects in complete darkness. Most specialists characterize the ganzfeld in terms of homogeneous *stimulation* of the retina. However, this must be a mistake because a ganzfeld can be produced by visual persistence. Experimenters have probably done this inadvertently by illuminating their Ping-Pong ball subjects with fluorescent bulbs.

The phenomenal character of the ganzfeld applies to darkness. Many subjects report at times seeing something vaguely surfacelike in front of the face (Gibson and Waddell 1952). Many observers also describe the field as "close at hand." When prompted, subjects estimate the distance at no farther than six inches.

Psychologists have a second reason to resist Lewis's rich content condition. If we require that the visual experience fit a fairly specific range of scenes, we preclude rudimentary vision. That would implausibly limit the number of nonhuman perceivers and implausibly shorten the history of vision. In explanations of the evolution of sight, the most primitive form of vision consists of a light sensitive patch that allows the organism to distinguish light from dark. The content gets richer after that: movement, inference of shapes from shadows, and so on. The primitive organism is seeing—and seeing the darkness. Just as rudimentary digestion is digestion, rudimentary seeing is seeing.

The rich content condition also has the reverse problem of being too quick to judge that vision has ended. Eye disease diminishes sight bit by bit. Before becoming totally blind, James Thurber had a little residual vision even though he did not satisfy Lewis's rich content requirement.

The evolutionary path to blindness works the same way. Just as the atrophied hearing of human beings is still hearing, the atrophied vision of bats is still vision.

Nonepistemic seeing

Seeing *that p* entails believing that *p*. Seeing in this epistemic sense always requires belief about what is seen. But there is also an important kind of seeing that does not entail belief (Dretske 1969, 88). Nonepistemic seeing is compatible with belief but is also compatible with the absence of belief or even disbelief. Do we nonepistemically see in the dark?

Claudia Menlo is an example. She sees the darkness but believes she is not seeing at all. Inconveniently, Miss Menlo is a medical impossibility. Even if the donor's optic nerve could somehow be spliced in, Claudia lacks the cortical infrastructure to immediately see crystal chandeliers. Congenitally blind animals miss a developmental opportunity to consolidate the neural groundwork for normal vision.

One may also doubt whether Claudia would infer blindness from her experience of blackness. Sighted people tend to conceive of blindness as a steady experience of blackness. But blind people deny that they see blackness (Magee and Milligan 1995, 11). Blindness is an absence of experience rather than an experience of absence. It is like the "experience" you have behind your head where you have no eyes.

When a sighted woman is in complete darkness, she experiences only the darkness in front of her face. She does not experience darkness behind her head. To check whether it is dark behind her head, she must turn and take a look.

A man with blind-sight may be able to visually sense an absence of light stimulation in a room. However, the blind-sighted man does not have a black visual experience. Sensing the darkness with one's eyes is not sufficient for seeing the darkness.

The distinction between visually sensing darkness and seeing darkness raises a skeptical doubt about animal vision. In 1794, Lazzaro Spallanzani was studying the ability of nocturnal animals to navigate under conditions of low illumination. When an owl's beating wings extinguished the small candle that provided the sole source of light, the owl became helpless. Owls cannot see objects in complete darkness. We know they sense the darkness with their eyes because only sighted owls become suddenly cautious when all light is eliminated. But do owls *see* the darkness? Although I am inclined to believe that owls do see the darkness, there is a possibility that they do not. Perhaps owls are like blind-sighted people who can visually sense the darkness but cannot see the darkness.

Spallanzani's more spectacular discovery was that bats can navigate in complete darkness. Even blinded bats performed well. In 1795, a Swiss surgeon, Charles Jurine, conjectured that bats navigate by ear. When he plugged the ears of bars, they could not navigate. Jurine (and later Spallanzani) concluded that the bats navigate by hearing sounds that are inaudible to human beings. The scientific community rejected their empirically well-documented hypothesis in favor of Baron Georges Cuvier's less grounded contention that bats navigate by *feeling* sound waves. Opinion changed only in 1938 after Donald Griffin recorded ultrasonic bat calls.

We can overcome the technical glitches of Rod Serling's "Eyes." Subjects in sensory deprivation experiments frequently worry that they have become blind (Vernon 1963, 168–69). They could easily be supplied with evidence to strengthen this fear. Suppose kidnappers announce that they will blind their two hostages, Mrs. Atheist and

Mr. Agnostic, with a laser blast to their retinas. Each of the hostages sees a flash of red light and then blackness. Mrs. Atheist infers that she is blind. Actually, kidnappers merely turned out the light after the red flash. Mrs. Atheist believes she is not seeing anything, but she is really seeing the darkness of the room.

Mrs. Atheist closely parallels Claudia Menlo. A more revealing case is her co-hostage, Mr. Agnostic. He is more circumspect than Mrs. Atheist. Mr. Agnostic neither believes nor disbelieves that he is blind. He thinks he does not have enough evidence to settle the issue and so is neutral about whether he sees anything.

The patently nonepistemic nature of Mr. Agnostic's seeing makes him a good candidate for being a seer of negative facts (in particular, the fact that there is no light in the room). The case of Mr. Agnostic is an improvement over Richard Taylor's (1952, 444–45) classic illustration of seeing an absence (fig. 13.1). Taylor claims that we directly perceive the dot in the left circle and directly perceive the absence of a dot in the right circle. Critics note that the right circle is also empty of dashes, strokes, squares, triangles, and crosses. We do not see the absence of these alternatives. Taylor's critics insist that we can only perceive the absence of an *F* if we are looking for an *F*. Thus, "there *is* something from which we can infer the circle's being empty of dots, other than the fact itself, namely, the perception of the circle and failure to perceive the dot" (Molnar 2000, 80).

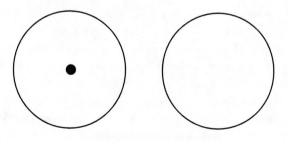

Figure 13.1 Taylor's missing dot

There is wide agreement that there is no *direct* perception of negative things. Jean-Paul Sartre has a famous illustration of perceiving an absence. He has an appointment to meet his punctual friend Pierre at a café. When Sartre arrives fifteen minutes late, he sees that Pierre is not there. Sartre contends he has witnessed a genuine absence and lengthily affirms the reality of nothingness. Yet he carefully emphasizes, "It is evident that non-being always appears within the limits of human expectation" (1969, 38).

"Expectation" wrongly suggests that Sartre must believe that Pierre might be at the café. Sartre would see the absence of Pierre even if he believed that Pierre would definitely not wait for fifteen minutes. Sartre need only be psychologically primed. Sartre does not see the absence of the Duke of Wellington at the café because Wellington's presence never became a live issue for Sartre.

Neuroscientists find Sartrean subjectivism congenial. They have measured neurons firing in recognition of pauses and gaps in tone sequences (Hughes et al. 2000). The scientists deny that there is any direct perception of absences. They emphasize that the brain has been forming expectations by listening to other tones that lead up to the missing tone.

We should be suspicious of Sartre and his fellow travelers. Who made human beings the arbiters of nonbeing? When a bear follows you into a cave, he sees the same darkness as you. This darkness existed long before anyone saw it and would have existed even if no creature ever beheld it.

Nonbeing is as objective as being. When Mr. Agnostic sees the darkness without believing that it is dark, he is not making an inference that it is dark. He does not employ the premise "I am not seeing anything." He is not drawing any conclusions. Therefore, Mr. Agnostic's expectations are not playing any role. He sees the darkness of the room just as a scuba diver sees the blueness of the water (even if the scuba diver worries that she is merely hallucinating the blueness).

According to Sartre, "In perception there is always the construction of a figure on a ground" (1969, 41). As Sartre surveys each face in the café ("Could this be Pierre?"), its candidacy for being at the forefront of attention is defeated. This first wave of negations forms the ground. If Pierre were spotted, he would pop out from the crowd.

> But now Pierre is not here. This does not mean that I discover his absence in some precise spot in the establishment. In fact Pierre is absent from the whole cafe; his absence fixes the cafe in its evanescence; the cafe remains ground; it persists in offering itself as an undifferentiated totality to my only marginal attention; it slips into the background; it pursues its nihilation. Only it makes itself ground for a determined figure; it carries the figure everywhere in front of it, presents the figure everywhere to me. This figure which slips constantly between my look and the solid, real objects of the cafe is precisely a perpetual disappearance; it is Pierre raising himself as a nothingness on the ground of the nihilation of the cafe. So that what is offered to intuition is a flickering of nothingness; it is nothingness of the ground, the nihilation of which summons and demands the appearance of the figure—the nothingness which slips as a *nothing* to the surface for the ground. It serves as foundation for the judgment—"Pierre is not here." (1969, 42)

I do not know what Sartre would say about the perception of utter darkness. A uniform black experience does not have a figure–ground structure. Nor need there be any judgment that it is dark.

The case of Mr. Agnostic has advantage of homogeneity. True, total blackness echoes the phenomenal curiosities of ganzfelds. In a cave, the darkness seems vaguely surfacelike and close to one's face. But these impressions are not constitutive of the black experience. Since darkness is merely the absence of light, we should expect the black experience of darkness to echo this simplicity.

Black illusions

In psychology, the reigning account of vision is the opponent process theory. The basic principle is that healthy human beings have three antagonistic pairs of photoreceptors: red-green, yellow-blue, and white-black. Blackness is the appropriate visual response to the absence of light.

One of the roles of the "appropriate" qualification is to exclude visual experiences that are independent of seeing. Colors can be experienced by pressing your eyeballs, imbibing hallucinogens, or receiving a blow to the head. Newton excluded such experiences when trying to explain color in his *Opticks* (1704/1952, bk. 1, pt. 2, prop. 7, 443). Contemporary color scientists extend this tradition. For instance, Leo Hurvich's classic *Color Vision* orients the reader by segregating color experiences that help us see from nonfunctional visual experiences:

> These forms of stimulation are, of course, inappropriate for vision, and although the phenomena emphasize the role of the nervous system in light and color perception, they are of interest mainly to the visual scientist. Ordinarily, we see objects and colors only when our eyes are open and light enters them. (1981, 26)

Hurvich goes on to explain how particular color responses are produced by direct light stimulation on a given retinal locus. The single exception is the blackness response. Blackness must be elicited by either a simultaneous or successive contrast:

> Blackness is not evoked by the direct action of light from any particular portion of the spectrum; blackness does result indirectly from the contrast between stimuli (one of which is "white") presented side by side to different places on the retina. It also results at the same place on the retina when "white" stimulation is terminated. (1981, 61)

Blackness is a functional visual response to darkness. In this unique case, we see by virtue of an absence of light.

Absence of light stimulation differs from absence of light. An astronaut with his back to the sun would see space as black even though she is bathed in much light. Unless light energy is directed right into the eye, it is invisible. That is why photographs of light beams must use smoke or some other medium that scatters or reflects or refracts or diffracts the light. Because darkness is the absence of light, the astronaut's black experience is a *false* representation of darkness. The darkness is pictured as filling the conical region emanating from his eyes (not just the region immediately in front of his eyes). The astronaut is experiencing an illusion because he is in an usual situation in which the ambient light fails to make its way into his eyes.

There are other ways of having black experiences in illuminated environments. To film the blackout scene of "Eyes," Joan Crawford performed within a limbo set. She was surrounded by black drapes and illuminated from above. Since Crawford was dazzled by the lights, acting like a blind woman was not a stretch. She could not see the camera or any other familiar object. She saw only the bright light. What would happen if Crawford were instead illuminated from behind and clothed head to toe in a black gown? Since material such as black velvet absorbs almost all light, Crawford would have an experience comparable to the black illusion of the astronaut.

Temporally contrastive seeing

In Robert Redford's 1998 movie *The Horse Whisperer*, there is a kissing scene that makes a sophisticated use of silhouettes. The movie delicately develops a romance between a Montana horse trainer and a New York magazine editor. The relationship climaxes with the pair kissing in silhouette. As the camera advances toward the couple, cinematic voyeurism becomes self-defeating: the couple's heads block out all the light. As their heads move slightly away from the camera, the outlines of their heads reappear. The head outlines again disappear as the pair move slightly closely to the camera. Thus, their privacy is protected by the *intimacy* of the close-up. The philosophical question raised by the romantic scene is almost anatomical: are we seeing the lovers' heads even while the whole scene goes black? I answer that we continuously see the lovers' heads.

Well, it is just a movie. Many insist we are seeing only images of heads, not heads. This objection could be circumvented by reenacting the scene on stage. Drawing inspiration from René Magritte's painting "The Lovers," we put black hoods on the lovers' heads. A member of the audience moves up to the kissing pair of actors until their heads overflow his visual field.

It is simpler to instead use a black balloon that will be viewed through an aperture (e.g., a blackened paper towel roll). The outline of the balloon is initially visible. When the balloon is inflated, the outline expands beyond the range set by the diameter of the tube. Thus, the scene through the tube is black. When the balloon is deflated a bit, the outline again becomes discernible. The black balloon oscillates quickly back and forth in this manner.

If the balloon were fluorescent green, then one would see the balloon even when it overflowed the optical boundary. One does not need to see the spatial outline of an object to see the object. Obviously, the outline of an object is very useful for *recognition* of the object. But the issue is nonepistemic seeing. The only hitch introduced by making the balloon black is that the overflowed optical field is black instead of fluorescent green.

This hitch is not enough to prevent the tube viewer from seeing the black balloon, for the rapidly oscillating balloon gives the observer sufficient contrast over time. In the case of spatially contrastive seeing, we see by virtue of what is illuminated and unilluminated at one moment. Temporally contrastive seeing also involves an interplay of illumination of nonillumination but over the dimension of time. There is no reason to treat time differently than space. This impartiality is encouraged by physics. Given a static, block universe in which time is treated as a fourth dimension, we should be indifferent between temporal and spatial contrasts.

I do not see the black balloon if it remains permanently inflated. If I am in a room that is completely darkened by the closing of a door, then I see the darkness of the room, but I do not see the door. If the door is rapidly opened and closed, then I do see the door even during the intervals it is briefly closed. As the openings and closings slow down, it becomes increasingly doubtful whether I am seeing the door in the dark. We are unable to ascertain how quickly the door must move to be seen. This is a benign manifestation of the vagueness of "see."

How much do we see in the dark?

Visual persistence aside, we see little of practical value in a complete absence of light. That is why darkness is alarming to human beings. We are highly visual animals who are greatly disadvantaged when the lights go out:

> For in utter darkness, it is impossible to know in what degree of safety we stand; we are ignorant of the objects that surround us; we may every moment strike against some dangerous obstruction; we may fall down a precipice the first step we take; and if an enemy approach, we know not in what quarter to defend ourselves; in such a case strength is no sure protection; wisdom can only act by guess; the boldest are staggered, and he who would pray for nothing else towards his defence, is forced to pray for light. (Burke 1757, chap. 4, sec. 14)

Edmund Burke is rebutting John Locke's *An Essay Concerning Human Understanding* (1690, bk. 2, chap. 7, 4) contention that darkness is not naturally feared. Locke suggests that the ghost stories told to children lead them to associate supernatural threats with darkness (bk. 2, chap. 33, 10). For many, the superstition persists into adulthood. Locke advises parents to keep their children away from the purveyors of superstition. Children will then never fear the dark. Burke objects to this nurture theory:

> Surely it is more natural to think that darkness being originally an idea of terror, was chosen as a fit scene for such terrible representations, than that such representations have made darkness terrible. The mind of man very easily slides into an error of the former sort; but is very hard to imagine, that the effect of an idea so universally terrible

in all times, and in all countries, as darkness, could possibly have been owing to a set of idle stories, or to any cause of a nature so trivial, and of an operation so precarious. (1757, chap. 4, sec. 14)

The belief that darkness is dangerous is a promising counterexample to Locke's thesis that there is no innate knowledge. Protohuman beings who did not fear the dark were not as reproductively successful as those who did have the fear. Thus, the generate-and-eliminate mechanism of natural selection is a plausible explanation of the reliability of our belief that darkness is dangerous. Under the innateness hypothesis, frightened toddlers are not even vicariously relying on the experience of nonancestors who were injured by darkness. Children know without relying on anyone's experience that dark places are dangerous.

The possibility that children are merely *learning* that the dark is dangerous can be excluded by the developmental regularity with which the fear matures (Valentine 1930). Children begin to manifest fear of the dark at about age two, and the fear intensifies until about age five. When the fear persists into adulthood, it counts as a phobia. Surprisingly, the brave Augustus Caesar had achluophobia.

Because human beings are menaced by darkness and aided by light, it is little wonder that evil is symbolized by darkness and that goodness is symbolized by light.

Still, I am not willing to go as far as Burke. He mistakenly believed that the darkness is actually painful to our eyes (1757, chap. 4, sec. 17). In fact, it is sudden bright light that is painful. Bony fish are even more prone to dazzlement than we are. Fish kept in a darkened tank are wide-eyed because they lack eyelids and have their iris and pupil fixed in an open position. If suddenly exposed to bright light, they fall to the bottom, stunned and blinded.

All mammals are descended from nocturnal ancestors that took refuge in the dark in the days of the dinosaurs. Being warm-blooded, they could be active when the cold-blooded dinosaurs were torpid. Under the cover of darkness, these early mammals evolved good night vision and felt safest at night. If they used the light/dark continuum to symbolize good and evil, they would choose daylight as evil and dark gray as good.

Prehistoric human beings prized caves as dwellings. Thus, they must have tolerated darkness in the way they also tolerated heights and crowding and fire. Greater toleration of darkness proved an asset to a chimpanzee named Austin (Jolly 1988). Another chimp, Sherman, dominated him. Sherman was so afraid of the dark that he would not leave their joint cage at night. Austin would go out at night and make strange noises (tapping pipes, windows, etc.) and then come rushing inside again, hair bristling. Instead of bossing Austin, the frightened Sherman would seek a hug of reassurance.

Fear of the dark accounts for the thrill obtained from safe exposures to darkness (or, more accurately, those that we *believe* to be safe). Unlike a roller coaster ride and bungee jumping (which involve artificially safe accelerations), the adrenaline rush from extreme light deprivation occurs in quiet, immobile circumstances. Consequently, our emotional state is more apt to cross the Burkean threshold from fear to awe. Little wonder that caves are popular religious sites.

A lowly glowworm can disrupt the darkness. Michelangelo extols the fragile beauty of total darkness:

> *Any place covered, any sheltered room,*
> *Whatever any solid circumscribes,*
> *Preserves the night as long as day's alive,*
> *Against the sun playing its glittering game.*
>
> *And if she's overmatched by fire or flame,*
> *By the sun she'll be ravished and deprived*
> *Of her divine look, baser things besides*
> *Can break her more or less, even any worm* (1623/1963, sonnet 101)

This aesthetic reaction is evidence that darkness has a characteristic appearance. As John Locke points out,

> The idea of black is no less positive to [one's] Mind, than that of
> White, however the cause of that Colour in the external Object,
> may be only a privation. . . . And thus one may truly be said to see
> Darkness. For supposing a hole perfectly black, from whence no light
> is reflect, 'tis certain one may see the Figure of it, or it may be painted.
> (1690, bk. 2, chap. 8, sec. 3, 6)

Locke had in mind paintings that show a mixture of light and darkness. Could there be a picture of total darkness? The paintings of Ad
Reinhardt (1970) became more minimal as his career progressed.
Eventually, he painted nothing but five foot by five foot black squares.
Reinhardt took special care to eradicate any sign of brushstrokes
and to have a matte finish to minimize the reflectivity of the surface.
Although unsure whether Reinhardt intended it as a representation
of darkness, I think his imposing paintings would make it a better
depiction of darkness than my miniature reproduction in figure 13.2.

Size matters. The darkness of a cave *envelops* the observer; a big
painting conveys this completeness better than a small one. The symmetry conveyed by a square shape is also appropriate (though a circle
might have been even better).

Figure 13.2 Reinhardt's black square painting

Light deprivation has always been a common punishment. English prisoners were jailed in darkness at Peveril Castle. This is a Norman Castle in the Peak District in Derbyshire. Peveril Castle stands above a dark stream. The stream emerges from a large cave system underneath. The locals call this cave system the "Devil's Arse." Prisoners were thrown into the Devil's Arse by jailers, who claimed that "if the fall doesn't kill them then the darkness will drive them mad."

When tourists sample the darkness of the Devil's Arse, how much do they see? Some quantitatively minded people answer that the amount of information presented by pitch blackness is a single bit, in particular, that there is no light as opposed to some light. This is a big underestimation. Consider a ten by ten matrix of light bulbs. Each of the hundred light bulbs can be on or off. Thus, there are 2^{100} possibilities. Any on–off listing of all 100 bulbs carries 100 bits of information. That includes the report that lists each bulb as being off. The report that all the light bulbs are off is easier to remember than any other report (except for the one which lists each bulbs as being on). Most of the reports are equivalent to random sequences and so cannot be compressed into a short summary. But this lack of memorability does not mean they carry more information; the report merely requires more information to express.

In a thin sense, the Rand Corporation's tome *A Million Random Digits* (1955/2001) contains as much information as books of equal heft on the library shelf (actually more information because there is no redundancy). I am claiming that the complete blackness experienced by a sighted person is informative in a thicker sense: the blackness indicates facts about the environment. There is a reliable connection between each black portion of one's visual field being black and there being an absence of light in the corresponding region of the environment. The above remarks imply that a high-resolution photograph of an utterly black tunnel is more informative than a low-resolution photograph.

My analogy with the ten by ten matrix of light bulbs is also oversimplified in its failure to reflect depth. If a person in complete darkness suddenly sees the light of a candle, he can judge how far away that light source is. If the candle is not lit, then the observer's black experience accurately reflects an absence of a light at that distance. Despite the feeling that you are seeing a black surface close to one's eyes, you are actually seeing three dimensionally in the dark.

You are also seeing right side up. George Stratton (1896) wore spectacles that inverted the image on his retina. Because the image is normally "upside down," Stratton is sometimes hailed as the first man to see the world right side up. In any case, the spectacles made the world *look* upside down. He wanted to see how well he would adapt to transposed vision. To protect the adaptation process, Stratton would take the spectacles off at night in a totally dark room. I maintain that as Stratton removed his spectacles, he switched from seeing upside down to seeing right-side up.

Using two eyes increases the amount of light available to the brain. The increase is not as dramatic as with hearing. Under almost any circumstances, we hear noticeably less by covering an ear. Covering an eye in daylight yields little or no noticeable increase in brightness. But the increase is noticeable when we are watching very dim things. Because two eyes can discern more dim things, our failure to see even a very dim object is more instructive when the search has been conducted with two eyes. Therefore, we see more in complete darkness with two eyes than with one eye.

In his *Science of Logic*, Georg Hegel says,

> In absolute clearness there is seen just as much, and as little, as in absolute darkness, that the one seeing is as good as the other, that pure seeing is a seeing of nothing. Pure light and pure darkness are two voids, which are the same thing. Something can be distinguished only in determinate light or darkness (light is determined by darkness and so is darkened light, and darkness is determined by light, is illuminated darkness), and for this reason, that it is only darkened light and illuminated darkness which have within themselves the moment of difference and are, therefore, *determinate* being. (1812/1989, 93)

However, Hegel presupposes that we cannot see in the dark in his famous quip against romantic monists such as Frederich Schelling:

To pit this single insight, that in the Absolute everything is the same, against the full body of articulated cognition, which at least seeks and demands such fulfilment, to palm off its Absolute as the insight in which, as the saying goes, all cows are black—this is cognition naively reduced to vacuity. (1807/1977, 9)

The correct answer to "Do we get as much information in total darkness as we get in daylight?" is a qualified no. We get less information because our cones perform only a negative service.

We have two visual systems, one suited for day and the other for night. Our night vision relies on our rods. Rods only let us represent scenes in black, white, and shades of gray. As is well known among astronomers, our night vision has its best resolution when we view objects a little off-center. The center of the eye is dominated by cones (which require much more light to perform a positive service). The richest distribution of rods lies outside this region. Thus, the region that gives us the most information in daylight becomes subordinated at night.

In "the dim," night vision is enough to maneuver about, hunt, flee, and find your way home. Monochromats, who are truly color blind, are handicapped but are far from blind. So it is still striking that the amount of raw information conveyed by total blackness is equal to the information used in achromatic vision.

There is a tendency to think that we see no more than a monochromat at night. But a trichromat, a person with normal color vision, sees more. If a green glowworm were to shine in the dark, a person with normal color vision would see the greenness. The monochromat would not.

The trichromat's intrinsic ability to see hues *increases* in dim conditions; his cones are at peak sensitivity when dark adapted. What decreases is the trichromat's opportunity to exercise that ability in a positive fashion. Relative to dim lighting conditions, the trichromat is insensitive to the hues of almost all objects. He cannot tell whether a shirt is red or blue. More profoundly, he cannot tell whether the shirt is red or gray; that is, he cannot discriminate between things that have hues and those that have an absence of hues. If the shirt is gray, then he does not see the grayness even though the shirt looks gray.

The hues of luminescent objects and unusually reflective objects can be seen when there is no general illumination. At night, an Alaskan trichromat can see a *green* aurora, a *blue* moon, and *red* brake lights. When marine biologists descend to great ocean depths in a diving bell, they experience utter blackness until "the stars come out" in the form of bioluminescent fish. The scientists are seeing in color even though they are being careful to preserve their night vision (by keeping the illumination low in the diving bell).

Less obviously, the trichromat sees more than the monochromat even when nothing in the scene has a hue, for the trichromat is seeing an absence of hues. Our cones still operate in complete darkness. There is a difference between being turned off and registering an absence.

Human color vision is concentrated at the center of the visual field. At the periphery of the visual field, a healthy human being can only see in black and white. Farther out in the periphery, one sees only *moving* objects (just as a frog sees only *mobile* flies). Yet farther to the periphery, all that is discernible is that *something* moved. And at the extreme periphery, a moving object does not cause any visual experience but does cause the head to turn toward the object.

Suppose a person is in a room that is completely dark except for one stationary spot of light at the periphery of his vision. Since that portion of the eye is only sensitive to moving things, the spot would be invisible except when it moved. If the spot were made more peripheral, the black experience would be uninterrupted even though the man sensed movement. Messages could be sent to the viewer by Morse code via the "invisible" light.

When a man is unsure whether he is in complete darkness, he puts a hand in front of his face. If nothing is seen, he makes the further test of waving his hand. Our sensitivity to motion suggests that the man's supplemental test is not redundant.

If the observer himself moves through the darkness, he will see more than if stationary. Interestingly, the moving observer has an impression that the blackness is itself moving. This cannot be entirely due to tactile sensations. For the experience of moving blackness can be experienced at the movie theater. The three-dimensional movie *Aliens* contains roller coaster scenes in which one rides through several tunnels. The blackness of the tunnels seems to accelerate as one hears the quickening sound of the roller coaster tracks.

Aristotle's waterfall illusion also involves an impression of movement in a static visual field. Staring at a waterfall fatigues motion detectors. When one then gazes at neighboring rocks, they seem to move in the direction opposite of the waterfall's. If the rushing blackness were a species of the waterfall illusion, then one should have the impression of moving *backward*. But one's apparent movement through the tunnel is forward. This suggests that hearing and expectation play a role in how things look—even when they look totally black.

Individuating privations by origin

Tourists pay to experience the total blackness of the Devil's Arse. Visitors to this cave cannot experience this particular blackness by staying home and turning out the lights in their cellar at midnight. Although the experiences are indistinguishable, they differ by virtue of their distinct origins.

Objects have hues in virtue of their causal powers. The same is true for objects that have achromatic colors. Enclosures can cause a black experience by blocking light.

Suppose that you are in a light-tight container that is itself suspended within a larger light-tight container (fig. 13.3). If the interior of the larger container is illuminated, the darkness you see is the darkness of the small container. But what happens when the light bulb of the big container is turned off?

Do you still see the darkness of the small container or do you see the darkness of the big container? Most people say that you see the darkness of the small container. All agree that you would not see the darkness of the small container if it were riddled with holes, for then the container would not be blocking light. But actually the container is just as causally

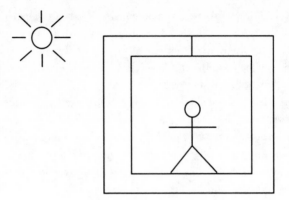

Figure 13.3 Observer in a light-tight box

idle when there are no holes. Only the big container is blocking light. Hence, you see the darkness of the big container.

It does not follow that one is seeing through the walls of the small container. You are seeing in the dark but not seeing any farther than the walls of the small container, for the walls of the small container prevent you from seeing any light that might be beyond the inner walls. You cannot see the walls of the small container. The walls constitute a limit to your field of vision. If the walls were removed, you would see farther into the darkness. In sum, you see the darkness of the big container but only that part of the big container's darkness that lies within the small container.

By metonymy, the locution "the darkness of x" can be read as an absence of light associated with x. The value of x can be temporal as in "the darkness of night." The value of x can also be a place. Consider a region of the universe that has no light sources. There are no shadows in this region, yet it is dark. I speak of this extended usage only to prevent confusion.

In its primary causal sense, "the darkness of x" works like "the shadow of x." As one closes the door to a light-tight room, the shadow of the door grows until the room is completely enveloped in darkness. We then speak of the darkness of the room rather than the shadow of the door because we can no longer differentiate the shadow of the door from the shadows cast by the walls. But the darkness of the room is just a seamless composite of shadows. Those who deny that a completely dark room has shadows are letting the epistemology of shadows distort the metaphysics of shadows.

The darkness at night is Earth's shadow. Since transparent substances are not perfectly transparent, they can cast shadows when thick enough. The darkness of the ocean is a shadow casts by the top layer of water. At night, the ocean is still dark even though the top layer of ocean is no longer blocking light. Here we are talking about the darkness of the region bounded by the ocean. In this extended use of "darkness," the man in the box can see the darkness in the region bounded by the small enclosure. Similarly, if the universe goes dark, the observer sees the darkness of the universe. He does not see all of the darkness because his range of vision is limited. The limit is not imposed by an obstruction. The observer just has limited acuity, like a man amid the vast expanse of the ocean.

Resemblance theories of vision falsely imply I see the same thing when I have indistinguishable experiences. If an experimenter places Ping-Pong ball halves over my eyes, my left eye sees a different ball innard than my right eye. There are also counterexamples involving duplicates that each contains much detail. When I see the pristine interior of the new McDonald's restaurant in Scranton, Pennsylvania, I see that interior rather than its identical twin in Rutland, Vermont, for it is the Scranton interior that is the appropriate cause of my experience.

Just as origins individuate positive experiences, origins individuate privational experiences. If blacked-out tourists in the Devil's Arse were merely having the absence of an experience, origin would be irrelevant. The blindness that arises from a stroke and the blindness that arises from eye damage are not distinct kinds of experience.

I am free to grant that the tourists in the Devil's Arse see the blackness only for a while. Maybe their visual systems soon revert to the default state of brain gray. Although brain gray is still very dark, it may not count as a black experience. (On the other hand, it might; if you are in a scarlet room, the redness eventually becomes less dark.) In any case, few tourists notice the transition from black to brain gray. May be the tourists are not getting as much black experience as they paid for. But they are still getting some black experience.

There are acceptable impurities in the initial black experience. When the lights first go out, you may experience afterimages and other residues of recent viewing. It takes about ten minutes for your eyes to reach the baseline state psychologists call "dark adaptation." Failure to be dark adapted in the first ten minutes is compatible with seeing. Your vision does not need to be perfect to see. I still see without my contact lenses. Pilots still see when they experience tunnel vision. Of course, they do not see in the region of the "tunnel wall." In this area, they are blind.

Normal generalizations about improving vision extend for the condition of complete darkness. Near-sighted people see better in the dark if they are wearing their corrective lenses. In complete darkness, partially blind people see only where they are not blind.

Dark-adapted eyes are affected by retinal noise. They are straining to see just as an amplifier strains to pick up a faint signal. Under these circumstances, there will be the hum of random fluctuations and even the occasional false alarm. You can experience retinal noise by sitting in the dark after you wake up in a dark room. You will begin to "see" shifting clouds of floating light spots (Hurvich and Jameson 1966, 20). Some observers describe them as curved bands with dark intervals between them. Some describe them as cloudlike streamers and ribbons. The effects have attracted many labels: light chaos, light dust, self-light, intrinsic light, idioretinal light. If you try to move about in the room, the retinal light swirls may be confused with real objects in the room. The visual experience is not one of blackness. Only with increased illumination do we experience the deep black of a black telephone.

Sight without light

If I am seeing without any current light, does it follow that I have been exposed to light earlier or later? No. Babies are born seeing. They have trouble focusing, and their vision is undeveloped in several respects, but they see well enough to distinguish light from dark. Consequently, if a girl is born into an utterly dark room, the infant sees the darkness even though she has never seen the light. If she dies soon after birth, then she will have seen without ever having been exposed to light.

The conditions I have described have probably transpired with sad frequency. So I think that there have been actual cases of sight without light. Sight only requires sensitivity to light.

Sight is historically connected to light in the sense that eyes would not have evolved had there not been light. Animals that become permanent cave dwellers eventually bear descendants with atrophied eyes and, in some cases, no eyes at all. Eyes are metabolically expensive and so begin to disappear when there is no longer any pressure to have them.

Extension to other senses

Visual persistence is a portable gift from science. When people learn of the role of visual persistence in perceiving movies, they sometimes are grateful for our ability to synthesize static images into moving images. But this gratitude wrongly construes visual persistence as a positive phenomenon. It is actually an engineering limit. To perceive when there is little information, one must either increase the amount of gathering time or spatially widen the field from which one gathers. Bats do both. They have evolved big ears and adjust the excitability of their eardrums to the availability of sounds. Thus, a bat will form a continuous sonar image even for intermittent stimuli.

We can be grateful for the *low threshold* for visual persistence. If we had the higher threshold of a bee, the movie would look like a slide show. To adjust, we would have to use more film and faster motors. But we ought not to be grateful that there is some threshold or other. That's inevitable. And it is inevitable for all the senses—even the exotic senses of other organisms. In principle, bats could have sonar movies. Star-nosed moles could have olfactory movies. And sharks could have magnetic movies for their magnetic sense.

We should not stop at the boundaries of *our* planet. Biologically literate astronomers have mounted a compelling case for the existence of extraterrestrial perceivers. The persistence effect almost certainly applies to aliens.

Such confidence would be rash if it rested on the postulation of a special perceptual mechanism that positively enables fusion. However, the generality of perceptual persistence springs from its negative nature as an engineering limit. Persistence is a side effect of a limited budget for building a perceiver. Limited budgets are pervasive. Therefore, we can soberly generalize: the "feat" of perceiving in the midst of privation is achieved by extraterrestrials throughout the universe.

In addition to concluding that visual persistence provides a loophole by which we see normally in complete darkness, I also answered yes to a string of more specific questions: Do we see darkness? Are there illusory black experiences? Can signals be visually detected when one experiences only blackness? Are there circumstances in which some ordinary objects can be seen in the dark? Is there a difference between seeing the darkness of the Devil's Arse and the darkness of one's cellar? Does the perception of absences go beyond vision?

I have concentrated on vision because it is our master sense. But even profounder lessons about the perception of absences can be learned by turning attention to our second most important sense: hearing.

14

Hearing Silence

In the course of demarcating the senses, Aristotle defined sound as the proper object of hearing: "Sight has color, hearing sound, and taste flavor" (*De anima*, bk. 2, chapter 6, page 418a, line 13). Sound cannot be seen, tasted, smelled, or felt. And nothing other than sound can be directly heard. (Objects are heard indirectly by virtue of the sounds they produce.) All subsequent commentators agree, often characterizing the principle as an analytic truth. For instance, Geoffrey Warnock (1953/1983, 36) says "sound" is the tautological accusative of the verb "hear."

I argue that there is a single exception. We hear silence, which is the absence of sounds. Silence cannot be seen, tasted, smelled, or felt—only heard.

How does hearing silence differ from not hearing?

Hearing silence is successful perception of an absence of sound. It is not a failure to hear sound. A deaf person cannot hear silence.

In chapter 13, I made a parallel comparison for seeing darkness. A blind man cannot see the darkness of a cave. His sighted companion can. Darkness *conforms* to Aristotle's principle that color is the proper object of sight. Aristotle (correctly) regarded black as a color. Indeed, he thought the chromatic colors were derived from the achromatic colors of black and white. Contemporary color scientists treat blackness as the appropriate color response to the absence of light (Hurvich 1981, 61).

Is hearing silence just a matter of inferring an absence of sound from one's failure to hear? No, a wounded soldier who wonders whether he has gone deaf can hear silence while being neutral about whether he is hearing silence. He hopes he is hearing silence but neither believes nor disbelieves that he is hearing silence.

Some eccentrics make the wrong inference from silence. They think that when they appear to hear silence, they are actually hearing the music of the spheres. They believe that this sound is always present. The eccentrics' belief that there is no silence does not prevent them from hearing silence. In the terminology refined by Fred Dretske (1969, 88), people can "nonepistemically" hear silence. Hearing in the epistemic sense requires belief. Hearing in the nonepistemic sense is compatible with belief but is also compatible with the absence of belief about what is being perceived. That is why we can be surprised by what we hear and even the very fact that we are hearing it. On August 27, 1883, people on the island of Rodriques heard the explosion of Krakatoa 4,800 kilometers away. They only later believed that the sound was that of Krakatoa exploding. The grammatical mark of the epistemic sense is the propositional attitude construction "hears that p." The radar operator hears that a sonic boom is approaching by hearing a beep from equipment monitoring an incoming jet. He hears the beep, not the boom.

Hearing silence does not depend on reflective awareness of the silence. Sometimes we become aware of a lengthy silence only after it has been broken. A marginal kind of sensitivity suffices for hearing silence. Turning off a radio awakens listeners who have fallen into a dreamless sleep.

One may dream a silence that is unreal. Even a match between a real moment of silence and dreamed silence is not sufficient for hearing that silence. There can be veridical hallucinations of silence.

Consider a man who experiences auditory hallucinations as he drifts off to sleep. He "hears" his mother call out his name, then wait for a response, and then call again. The cycle of calls and silence repeats eerily. As it turns out, his mother has unexpectedly paid a late-night visit and is indeed calling out in a manner that coincidentally matches the spooky hallucination. The hallucinator is not hearing the calls and silence of his mother.

Is hearing silence detecting silence by ear?

Like other animals, human beings evolved to detect sounds *and* to detect the absence of sound. However, detection of silence is not enough for hearing silence.

You can *detect* the electric charge of a nine-volt battery with your tongue. But an electric eel can *sense* the electric charge (Keeley 1999). The eel has an organ dedicated to this form of energy.

Human beings have ears that are dedicated to sounds. The nose is devoted to odors, the tongue to flavors. Ordinary people spontaneously demarcate the senses by their corresponding sense organs.

Is using your ears to detect a sound sufficient for hearing it? No. When my neighbor blows a dog whistle, I infer by ear (from the puffing noise) that there is an ultrasonic sound. But I do not hear the ultrasonic sound.

Are your ears necessary for hearing sound? Hearing aids show that people hear with defective ears thanks to mechanical assistance. As the substitute components improve, the entire ear may become dispensable. Technological progress suggests that, in principle, ears are not needed to hear.

This extrapolation carries over to hearing silence. The hearer of silence can rely on a hearing aid or a stethoscope. When an unconscious pilot leaves his microphone on, flight controllers can hear silence in the cockpit.

The perception of silence must be direct in other respects. For instance, one cannot hear silence by listening to a remote sound meter that sounds an alarm when there is silence at a monitored location. You can hear *that* it is silent by means of a sound. But you cannot hear silence by means of a sound. There is a difference between hearing silence and hearing the effects of silence.

Does silence sound like anything?

Are you *seeing* this sentence or are you *hearing* it? You can easily answer without checking whether you are using your eyes rather than your ears. You can tell by introspection. This suggests a second strategy for demarcating the senses: appeal to the characteristic experiences of the senses (Smith 1990, 239).

The appeal to characteristic experiences explains why future people may see and hear with prostheses. It also handles the perception of darkness. There is a color experience dedicated to darkness. Black is commensurable with other colors. For instance, black (visually) resembles purple more than pink.

Sense datum theorists were naturally attracted to this mode of demarcating the senses. In the original edition of *Perception* owned by Dartmouth College, H. H. Price (1933, 39) proceeds to its logical conclusion: "We are never destitute of tactual data; and very rarely (if at all) of auditory ones, for what we call 'silence' can be heard." "What?" has been scribbled in the margin. The reader's puzzlement was not quieted by Price's footnote: "When I say, 'There was silence' I mean something like 'My auditory data were of faint intensity and none of them differed greatly from any other.'" The reader balked because silence does not *auditorily* resemble any sound. Silence has no loudness, timbre, or pitch.

Westerners are amused by *shiiin*, the Japanese onomatopoeia for silence. But English has "shush," "hush," and "shhhhhhh." Perhaps we are imitating white noise in lieu of a sound of silence.

Silence does *acoustically* resemble white noise; there is an absence of discriminable tones. When you turn on a hotel fan to mask the conversation in the next room, you mix sounds. Just as white light combines all of the frequencies of visible light, white noise combines all the frequencies of sound. Hearing white noise is hearing all sounds; hearing silence is hearing no sound.

White noise varies in loudness. Silence is invariant. White noise sounds different from silence. When you eventually halt the hotel fan, you are relieved by the silence. You can hear the difference between white noise and silence.

The experience of silence has a qualitative aspect. A hypothetical scenario featuring an acoustic scientist Audrey can bring this out. She lives in a noisy environment and so has never experienced silence. Audrey knows the physical aspects of silence. But she wants to experience silence and so constructs a soundproof chamber. When she enters the chamber, Audrey learns something: what it is like to hear silence. She closes her eyes to listen more intently. She enjoys the silence as others might enjoy the burble of a brook or the jug-o-rum of bullfrogs.

Audrey is introspecting an absence of auditory sensations while perceiving an absence of sound. A patient with an ear problem can introspect gaps in his auditory sensation of a rising tone. Audrey wanted more than the gap in her sensations. She wanted an auditory gap that originates through healthy hearing of an external state of soundlessness.

Austen Clark prefaces *A Theory of Sentience* (2000) with a thought experiment. Suppose your senses are discreetly incapacitated, step by step, so as not to disturb your meditation on an abstract issue (which you are conducting with closed eyes to avoid the distraction of the senses). At the end of the subtractions, you are conscious but sense nothing. Clark draws the lesson that consciousness without sentience is conceivable. But his thought experiment can be diverted to make a different point. When you become aware that you are blind, deaf, and generally senseless, you are *introspecting* an absence of sensations. For you no longer perceive anything. Introspection is your only remaining means of detecting the absence.

Perhaps we approximate Clark's scenario during sleep. If there is a stage of sleep in which there are no sensations, we might introspect this absence. The introspection of absences is continuous in Clark's scenario. But in a "dead sleep," introspection also stops. The gap in consciousness could still be sensed after the fact. This awareness may be what we are appealing to when we compare death to sleep. If experience requires sensations, then one cannot know what death is like (at least from a first-person perspective). However, if there is a qualitative aspect of experiencing absences, then we do have an inkling of what it is like to be dead. Our experience with intermittent losses of consciousness gives us a basis to extrapolate to the permanent loss of consciousness.

It does seem overly modest to say that a man knows nothing more of death than a toddler or a turtle or a termite. The man has a better understanding of what it is like to be dead because he has more experience of mental gaps and better means to learn from those experiences.

Parmenides characterized death as the brother of sleep. A man's thought is a ratio of light and night in his body. With sleep as in death (and aging), that ratio changes in direction of night.

> For according as the hot or the cold predominates, the understanding varies, that being better and purer which derives from the hot. . . . But that he [Parmenides] also attributes sensation to the opposite element in its own right is clear from his saying that a dead man will not perceive light and heat and sound because of the loss of fire, but that he will perceive cold and silence and the other opposites. And in general, all being has some share of thought. (Theophrastus, *De Sensu* 3–4, in Robinson 1968, 124)

I have three disagreements with Parmenides' development of the analogy between sleep and death. First, the dead do not continue to have experience (even at a low order). Second, the perception of the dark, the cold, and silence is perception of what is not rather than what is. (Absences are not at the low end of a hierarchy of being.) Third, Parmenides fails to privilege silence. Hearing silence is the most negative of perceptions: there is nothing positive being sensed *and* no positive sensation representing that absence.

Clark's scenario has a haunting resemblance to death. The introspected absence of sensation is global. Audrey's scenario is the more typical introspection of a local absence of sensation.

Audrey might want to share her chamber's silence with her husband. Audrey's husband could get the same type of experience from another soundproof chamber. But his attachment to Audrey makes him want to hear the silence she arranged and to jointly experience the same particular silence she is hearing. Audrey's silence differs from the silence of others because it is caused differently. The darkness of caves varies the same way.

When you see the darkness of a cave, you can introspect the visual sensation of darkness. When you feel the cold (which is the absence of heat), there is a different sensation to introspect. The qualitative aspect of the cold sensation explains our surprise at the burning sensation of dry ice.

Introspection may help us correct confusions between absences. Many people believe that it is darkest before the dawn. But they are actually experiencing the extremity of another privation. The landscape cools off all night, making it *coldest* just before dawn. (It is darkest at midnight when the sun is farthest from sunrise and sunset.)

Synesthetes have experiences that trespass between sense modalities. They "see" sounds and "hear" colors. Possibly there is synthesia for the perception of absences. A synesthete who can "see" coldness might have a special impetus for asserting that "it is darkest before the dawn."

When you hear the silence of Audrey's chamber, there is no sensation of silence to introspect. You instead introspect the absence of auditory sensations. Just as you can perceive the blanks between the words of this sentence, you can introspect gaps between sensations. Just as blanks can sometimes be organized into a gestalt pattern, gaps can form patterns that can be introspected holistically.

Pauses are used to chunk speech into perceptual units. But pauses themselves can be unified within sounds. Musicians exploit these higher order forms of silence perception.

In addition to having neurons that fire in recognition of tones, we have neurons that fire in recognition of pauses and gaps in tone sequences (Hughes et al. 2000). Perhaps this is the neurological basis for the introspection of missing sensations.

One can say pauses sound like something in the guarded way one can say that blanks look like something. You can show someone a blank by pointing at one on a page. You can exhibit a pause by having the learner listen to a specimen. The difference between seeing a blank and hearing a pause is psychological. We are primed to see letters and so see the absence of letters. We are primed to hear sounds and so hear the absence of sounds. Absences are relative. They draw their identity from their relata.

The differences between absences are nonetheless objective. Members of the British National Antarctic Expedition were killed in 1912 by the cold. They were not killed by silence or the dark.

Empiricists trace all of our knowledge of the world through the senses. Sensationalists further say that sensations are the basic elements of experience. But there is no auditory sensation of silence.

Sensationalists overestimated the role of introspection. We hear mostly without introspection. That includes hearing silence. There may be creatures that hear silence despite their total inability to introspect. Audrey can savor silence because she can attend to the workings of her own mind.

How long can silence last?

Pauses depend on sounds just as the hole of a doughnut depends on the doughnut. If the sound does not return, then the pause does not last indefinitely.

Sounds are generally short-lived, and this makes pauses even briefer. There are exceptions. J. O. Urmson claims, "The sound of Niagara Falls outdates our most cherished antiquities" (1968, 119).

One complication is that the roar of Niagara Falls has not been continuous. On March 30, 1848, the flow was stopped for more than twenty-four hours by an ice jam upstream. Those who believe that sounds cannot survive interruption will date the present roar to

no earlier than 1848. Surely there have been longer pauses in the
12,000-year history of Niagara Falls. Silence can have an impressive
duration.

Indeed, there is no upper bound on how long silence can last.
Imagine Seshat, the Egyptian goddess of mathematics, is counting
one number per second. She utters the prime numbers out loud but
silently counts the composite numbers. Thus, there are moments of
silence in Seshat's oral recitation:

$$2, 3, \ldots, 5, \ldots, 7, \ldots, \ldots, \ldots, 11, \ldots, 13, \ldots, \ldots, \ldots, 17, \ldots$$

There are infinitely many prime numbers, but they become sparser
and sparser down the number line. Thus, the stretches of silence
become longer and longer without limit.

Can silence be infinitely long? First let us consider whether a
sound can be infinitely long. Aristotle believes that infinity is always
potential, never actual, so he would reject an example of Apollo
continuously playing his lyre. At any point in the future, the im-
mortal Apollo is finitely old, and so his music is always finitely
long.

However, Aristotle appears to have believed that species have an
infinite past. So consider the murmur of a hive of bees. The murmur
is the collective effect of many bees. None of these sources is essential; a bee can leave while the murmur continues. Indeed, the murmur can continue through the gradual replacement of all the bees.
Since we are imagining the species has an infinite past, the murmur
could be infinitely old while each bee is only finitely old.

The murmur of the innumerable bees illuminates the metaphysics
of sound. If sounds are dependent on a particular source (O'Callaghan
2007, chapter 5), then no sound is older than its source. Yet the murmur is older than any bee.

Given the Big Bang theory of the origin of the universe, no sound
is infinitely old. It could still be the case that there are sounds older
than any source. And there could be silences older than any sound.
A pause can take place between distinct sounds.

Is silence a proper object of hearing?

The third method of demarcating the senses is by what they sense. Common sensibles (number, shape, magnitude, motion, etc.) are available to more than one sense. Proper objects (flavor, odor, sound, color, tactile qualities) can only be directly accessed by a single sense.

Contemporary defenders of this demarcation strategy face two problems. First, proper objects seem like an obsolete, arbitrary grouping. They fail to mesh with the natural kinds that have come to light through modern physics and chemistry.

A second classic problem is specifying the proper objects for sight and touch. Theorists have trouble coping with the sheer variety of what we see and feel (Sanford 1976).

In contrast, the specification of the proper object for hearing seems straightforward. That is why proponents of the proper object strategy, such as George Berkeley, model sight on sound. They are drawn more strongly to sound than to odor and flavor because sound better approximates the spatiality and informativeness of what we see.

However, silence shows that the proper object of hearing is, in one respect, trickier to specify than the object of vision. There is a color corresponding to the privation of light. But there is no sound corresponding to the privation of sound. Silence presents a new anomaly for those who wish to demarcate the senses by their proper objects.

Does the same apply to odorlessness?

We detect that a rhododendron flower is odorless by smelling it. But do we smell its odorlessness? We detect that tofu is flavorless by tasting it. But do we taste its flavorlessness?

These perceptions of absences are less clearly sensings than is seeing darkness or hearing silence. The reason is that odorlessness and flavorlessness are of only marginal significance to human beings.

Obviously, odors and flavors are important to us. Loss of the sense of smell or taste merits medical attention. But our encounters with odorlessness and flavorlessness are dispassionate. We do not savor the flavorlessness of tofu. We do not stop to smell the odorlessness of the rhododendrons.

There are characteristic emotions (e.g., disgust) and behaviors (e.g., nose wrinkling) associated with odors. Odors also interact with other sense modalities. Much of what is ascribed to taste is actually odor.

The emotional significance of odors is a legacy of our hunter-gatherer past. Odors provide clues to food, sex, and health. Odorlessness did not betoken opportunity or danger. That makes odorlessness emotionally flat.

Contemporary people make use of unprecedented substances that are dangerous because they are odorless. Natural gas must be adulterated with mercaptan (which stinks like sulfur) to make leaks noticeable to homeowners. If odorlessness, in the Paleolithic Era, had been an exploitable sign of danger or opportunity, we would have evolved behavioral responses to odorlessness and emotions that organize those behaviors. As it stands, odorlessness scores low on criteria we use to distinguish between sensing and detecting.

Silence scores much higher. There are characteristic behaviors to generate and detect silence. There are also characteristic emotional reactions to silence. Moreover, the perception of silence is integrated with the rest of the perceptual and cognitive systems.

Does silence interact with sound?

Primitive predators quiet down to listen. Their prey freeze to avoid making a sound. Sophisticated animals find silence instructive at a meta-level. Hush is a sign that conspecifics have acquired information. Just as animals stop and orient to an unexpected sound, they stop and orient to an unexpected silence. When a group is wary of predators or other enemies, silence may serve as an alarm.

What begins as a natural sign can develop into a conventional sign. Pauses punctuate conversation, playing a variety of grammatical roles. "Signs of omission" are easier to see in written language (Sorensen

1999). We can afford to demarcate written words with blanks. Inscriptions last for a while. Spoken words linger only in working memory. To get the message across quickly, the speaker runs his words together. He merges some of the phonetic components of a word into a single sound. Hearers are equipped with a module that unpacks these coarticulated phonemes.

Small silences have a phonetic effect (Dorman et al. 1979). For instance, insertion of a gap makes the difference between hearing a sound as "split" as opposed to "spit."

I conjecture that silence also has intermodal effects. Studies that show how sound affects vision generally feature a baseline condition of silence. I interpret some of these studies, such as the motion bounce illusion (Sekuler et al. 1997), as evidence that *silence* affects vision. In the silent condition two moving dots pass through each other in an X pattern. When a "ping" sound is inserted at the point of intersection, subjects instead see the dots as bouncing off of each other. The usual interpretation is that the intermodal effect is restricted to the sound condition. My speculation is that the silence condition also features an intermodal effect. The silence encourages us to interpret the dots as shadows.

Our emotional reactions to silence are shaped by what silence signified to our hunter-gatherer ancestors. Silence is a sign of abandonment or ostracism. This may be at the root of our fear of silence. In his *Pensees*, Blaise Pascal writes, "The eternal silence of these infinite spaces frightens me" (1670/2003, 61). Why be afraid of nothing? Because silence is associated with shunning.

Since silence conveys nothing on its own, it is usually sensitive to context. Depending on the circumstances, silence can convey assent, dissent, or uncertainty. Its message is heavily context dependent. Silence can be an expression of respect. One of the rituals of Armistice Day is a two-minute silence held at 11 A.M., "the eleventh hour of the eleventh day of the eleventh month" (the time at which the 1918 armistice went into effect, bringing World War I to a close).

The gesture of silence can be amplified by darkness. In Poland, the death of Pope John Paul II was commemorated on the *evening* of

April 8, 2005. The lights were switched off in homes throughout the nation to reinforce five minutes of silence.

Signs for silence are conventional. Egyptian statues represent the child Horus as a naked boy with his finger on his mouth. This incarnates the hieroglyph for "child." However, the Greeks and Romans misinterpreted the finger placement as a gesture for silence. Thus, was born Harpocrates, the god of silence and secrecy.

The meaning of silence is also colored by its physiological effects. Silence is welcome when it betokens the resolution of a crisis: blood pressure ebbs, heart rate declines, muscles relax. Silence is conducive to concentration. Seneca trained himself to philosophize amidst the hubbub of ancient Rome. But most thinkers require a refuge from noise.

Does silence have a location?

Peter Strawson (1959, 65–66) denies that sounds have an intrinsic location. We can correlate sounds with various locations. For instance, I was taught to calculate my distance from the source of thunder by counting the seconds between the lightning strike and the thunder. I was told that one second equals one mile. (Much later I got the bad news that this rule involves a fivefold underestimate of the proximity of the electrical discharge.) Strawson concedes there are *contingent* connections between sound and locations. He denies there is an auditory field comparable to the visual field. A purely visual concept of space is possible (even if impoverished). A purely auditory concept of space is impossible.

Matthew Nudds suggests that Strawson's point is that we can see a portion of space as empty. When you look at a ring, you are aware of the hole. Your awareness does not depend on seeing anything in the hole.

It is this visual awareness of places where there is nothing which has no auditory equivalent. We are simply not auditorily aware of empty places—there's no difference between not experiencing a sound at some place, and experiencing no sound there. One may hear nothing

at some place, but in doing so one never comes to be aware of a place
at which there is no sound—one is simply unaware. (2001, 213)

But a teacher can hear the silence of her classroom while also hearing a lawnmower outside. She thinks "It is silent in here but noisy out
there." A conductor can hear silence from the left half of the choir
while hearing the right half singing.

To develop the import of these counterexamples, I rely on the
principle that the location of silence is parasitic on the location of
sound. Just as a shadow borrows the shape and volume of a material
object that might have filled its space, silence borrows the direction
and location of a possible filler sound. This draws me into controversy about the location of sounds.

Most sounds have a location and a direction. Hearing a sound
in your right ear and silence in your left ear can help you pinpoint
the location of faint noise. This is just a limiting case of exploiting
the sound shadow formed by your head. Your head blocks incoming
sound waves like an island blocks ocean waves. If the waves are strong
enough to make it around the head, there will be an informative time
delay and an informative change in amplitude.

The location of a sound does not have the same qualitative status
as loudness, pitch, and timbre. We postulate the property of timbre
because sounds that have the same pitch and loudness can sound different. For instance, a cello is mellower than a flute even when the two
have the same pitch and loudness. Two sounds from different locations can sound alike (Clark 2000, 60). If identical watches are placed
on either side your ears, the tick-tock of one watch will be heard as
coming from the left and the tick-tock of the other watch from will be
heard as coming from the right. But it will be the same type of sound.
The same goes for a gap in the tick-tock. You will simultaneously hear
a brief silence on the left and a brief silence on the right.

Just as there is nothing intrinsic to a tone to indicate its location,
there is nothing intrinsic to a silence. Yet we can locate silence. After
a building collapse, rescuers sometimes only hear silence from the
rubble (Clark 2000, 61).

Chapters on sound location are standard fare in textbooks on hearing. Robert Pasnau (1999) says these chapters conflict with the chapters identifying sound with waves in a medium. If sounds are in the medium (typically, for human beings, the air), then they are all around us. Sounds would lack the specific, differential locations we commonly attribute to them. The sound waves are actually moving *away* from the source. So Pasnau thinks that those who identify the sound with sound waves must say hearers are overly narrow when locating sounds. The sound waves caused by a loon are not just at the loon; the sound waves are all around you.

To avoid postulating an illusion, Pasnau denies that sounds are sound waves. He argues that sounds are vibrations of the source (or, more cautiously, that sounds supervene on these vibrations). Objects have sounds in the way they have colors. The sound of a tuning fork is more intense as you approach it. But this is no more a change in the sound than a change of its look as you approach it. The tuning fork's image size increases but it does not really look bigger. A tuning fork sounds better in a concert hall than in a meadow in the same way it looks better in daylight than twilight. In the dark, we cannot see the color of the tuning fork but its color still exist. In a vacuum, we cannot hear the sound of the vibrating tuning fork but it still has a sound. The conditions are just bad for hearing the sound.

Casey O'Callaghan (2007) agrees that Pasnau has shown incoherence in the acoustic textbooks and in common sense. However, he tries to preserve insights from the wave theory of sound by characterizing sounds relationally as events in which a source disturbs a medium. Since there is no medium to disturb in a vacuum, O'Callaghan denies that a vibrating tuning fork makes a sound in a vacuum.

Whereas Pasnau thinks each sound is a property of the source (e.g., the redness of a rose), O'Callaghan agrees with the wave theorist that sound is a particular. O'Callaghan believes that sounds depend on their sources; each sound must have a source, is always located at its source, and can never switch sources. The wave theorist acknowledges that sounds have sources but grants autonomy to sounds. The wave theorist is impressed by the linearity of sounds. Instead of rebounding, our voices pass right through each other.

Pasnau and O'Callaghan grant that the wave theory of sound is endorsed by both science and common sense. However, they are so impressed by the problem of locating sound that they are willing to take on both of these authorities.

Since the critics of the wave theory concede its positive merits, my defense of the wave theory is restricted to defusing the appearance of locational inconsistency. I rely on the traditional method of semantic ascent. Instead of immediately discussing the location of sound, I discuss how we answer "Where is it?" questions.

Many things are located by their edges. But we also locate by centers. American football players tackle a deceptive runner by concentrating on his center of gravity (or a salient spot that tends to project from that location such as the runner's navel). When edges are indiscernible, we have no choice but to use interior features (the eye of a hurricane, the foci of an elliptical orbit, the solar system's center of mass). Authors of acoustics textbooks describe sound as a train of waves emanating from a source in all directions. In a uniform medium, the shape of the sound will therefore be a sphere. Discussants of a sound are talking about a big, rapidly expanding phenomenon that envelops them. Since the edges of the sound are unknown, orientation by the boundary is forbidden by H. P. Grice's (1975) maxim of quality ("Do not say what is false"). Grice's conversational maxim, "Be informative," rules out the true but trivial remark that the sound is in the air. So if anything is to be said about the location of sound, it must be in terms of its source. The speed and invisibility of the sound prevent us from experiencing the sound like an approaching water wave. Any attribution of movement to the sound will be based on movements of the source.

The linguistic aspects of locatedness are more pronounced in an example that is free of the phenomenology of locatedness. Seismology textbooks have a chapter that defines an earthquake as a series of shock waves caused by failure of brittle rocks in Earth's crust. The same textbook will have a chapter explaining how to locate an earthquake by triangulating to the hypocenter of the failure. The hypocenter (also called the focus) is below ground and so is not readily recognized by us surface dwellers. Therefore, seismologists refer to the point on Earth's surface directly above the hypocenter: the epicenter.

Are the seismologist's assertions jointly consistent? The earthquake cannot be located at just the epicenter *and* just at the hypocenter. If the earthquake is the train of seismic waves emanating from the hypocenter, then the quake is in its medium and so encompasses a wide area. These waves are moving *away* from the hypocenter. One wave front briefly heads *toward* the epicenter but then spreads out from there.

One might try to avoid seismic incompatibilism by claiming that "earthquake" is ambiguous. Disputes over "Where is New York located?" are dissolved by noting that 'New York' is ambiguous between Manhattan, the City of New York (which includes Manhattan as a borough), and New York State. However, disputes over "Where was the earthquake?" cannot be dissolved in the same way. For all seismologists agree that there is no sense in which the earthquake is its epicenter. The epicenter is a physically insignificant point. Despite the belief that the earthquake is not its epicenter, seismologists truthfully answer "Where was the earthquake?" by locating its epicenter. (An earthquake without an epicenter is geometrically possible. Suppose the hypocenter is at the center of Earth or, far more plausibly, near one of the bulges of Earth—at the poles or along the equator. In these cases, there is no unique point closest to the surface.)

Seismic incompatibilism is less attractive than acoustic incompatibilism. First, we have no seismic phenomenology of locatedness that orients our perception to a central source. Second, the effects of pragmatics are salient for earthquake location. The term "epicenter" was obviously introduced in the same instrumental spirit as "arctic circle." Answers to "Where was the earthquake?" will vary with our purposes. The feeling of inconsistency is being generated by our failure to relativize to these interests.

We need a uniform treatment of the acoustic and seismic cases because their phenomena overlap. If the primary wave of an earthquake refracts out of the rock surface with a frequency of more than twenty hertz, human beings will hear the earthquake as a low rumble. Seismologists search for a mechanism to explain how acoustic sand dunes manage to boom (Nori et al. 1997). Blind mole rats communicate by thumping their heads on tunnel walls (Nevo et al. 1991). The seismic waves are conducted through their bones and processed by their auditory system. (Deafened mole rats stop thumping.)

If we had a phenomenology of earthquake location, it would resemble our phenomenology of sound location. We would feel the earthquake as being at a central point, for the phenomenology of locatedness is governed by perceptual counterparts of Grice's maxims of quality and informativeness. It is true but trivial to say the quake is inside Earth. The edges of the quake were never accessible during the evolution of our perceptual systems. So we would have no choice but to orient toward the center.

Since silence is an absence of a sound, it has a location where the sound would have been. Pragmatic factors will dictate whether we locate in accordance with the absent sound waves or the inactive source.

Since I identify sound with acoustic waves, I think silence is the absence of acoustic waves. Waves are positive phenomena that depend on a medium. Silence is equally dependent but negative.

When silence is a missing sound, it will be at the place normal for sound. Consequently, the location of silence is as predictable as the location of sound. Even so there are surprises. On May 18, 1980, there was silence around the sixty-mile blast zone of Mount Saint Helens. Since sound waves travel faster in warmer air, they bend toward cooler air. The volcano's sound was bent up to the higher altitudes. About fifteen miles up it was refracted down again. Thus, the sound had the shape of an expanding doughnut. The silence was the hole of the doughnut.

The dramatic, deceptive effects of refraction, wind, and temperature move some scientists to speak of sound mirages. In the early twentieth century, physicists interested in foghorn design became alarmed by how sound can skip over areas near the coast and land at amazing distances from the foghorn. More ominous than these "false alarms" was the inaudibility of the foghorn at the zone targeted for warning. Physicists carefully plotted the boundaries of this dangerous area of silence (Mallock 1914, 73–74).

Are there silence mirages? Given that all mirages work by refraction, silence mirages are impossible because silence cannot refract. Given that all echoes work by reflection, silence cannot echo. However, silence does obey almost all the laws of refraction and reflection. In chapters 6 and 7, I called this parasitic behavior "para-refraction" and "para-reflection." Although there cannot be silence mirages or silence echoes, silence may have para-mirages and para-echoes.

Transmission devices enhance our ability to hear silence at a distance. One of Jack Benny's radio skits was designed to underscore his miserliness. A mugger confronts Benny: "Your money or your life!" After a prolonged pause, members of the audience begin to laugh. They realize that Benny must be thinking it over. To get the joke, the audience must not interpret the absence of noise as a failure of transmission. They must interpret the absence as being conveyed from the radio station.

One cannot hear the difference between silence from a source and silence from an absent source. This indeterminacy is explored in Harold Pinter's 1959 radio play *A Slight Ache*. The play appears to have three characters: Edward, Flora, and a match-seller invited into their home. Edward and Flora confide much to the match-seller. But he never speaks. Eventually the audience begins to wonder whether Edward and Flora have just invented the match-seller. The play is propelled by the unresolved question of whether the silence is coming from anyone. That is why the play is difficult to televise and very difficult to stage.

The composer Leopold Stokowski once reprimanded a noisy audience: "A painter paints his pictures on canvas. But musicians paint their pictures on silence. We provide the music, and you provide the silence" (Applewhite et al. 2003, 284). The silence of the audience does not mean that the auditorium is silent. The whole point of refraining from making sounds is so that the musicians can fill the hall with music.

Is silence a limiting case of sound?

One might protect the generalization that we directly hear only sounds by characterizing silence as a zero-value sound. There are determinables such as temperature that have zero-value determinates. Temperature is defined as a measure of the average amount of molecular motion. The absence of all motion is not an absence of temperature. It is a temperature of zero degrees on the Kelvin scale. Yuri Balashov (1999) argues that some key physical properties conform better to a zero-value hypothesis than to an absence hypothesis: spin, electric charge, and perhaps mass (to cover photons).

If silence is a zero-value sound, then what does it have zero of? We cannot answer that it has zero decibels because zero decibels is the softest sound audible to average, young human beings. This is about the softest sound that any creature perceives. The vibrational amplitude of the air at zero decibels is only about the diameter of a hydrogen atom. It is counterproductive to make the ear more sensitive than this. Creatures hear by virtue of *systematic* variations in air pressure. Variations below zero decibels become random because of the thermal agitation of molecules (Brownian motion). If the sensitivity were set too low, the hearer would be distracted by a meaningless, ambient hiss.

Some speculate that young children can hear the hiss. If so, they might lose this useless capacity in the way they lose the capacity discern phonemes that are not used in their language.

But let us suppose that we can make sense of zero loudness in some other way. Does silence have a zero-value pitch? Is silence very low or very high? Can two silences of equal loudness and pitch differ in timbre? Unlike loudness and pitch, timbre cannot be scaled from high to low.

Two sounds can cancel out because of destructive interference. But the interpenetrating sound waves still exist. They are superimposed at the "dead spot" and will become audible as they move beyond this area. If the destructive interference is perfect, then the hearer will report hearing nothing. Orhe might take himself to be hearing silence. But he is actually hearing two sounds that sum to zero. The listener can be shown that he is not hearing silence by deactivating one of the sources of the sound waves. He will then hear one sound that has always been there.

A loud sound differs from silence by its magnitude. Lowering the sound decreases this difference. However, a quiet sound still differs from silence in the way a slightly dirty sheet differs from a clean sheet. To be clean is to have no dirt, so it is not a kind of dirtiness.

Is silence impossible?

What counts as "no dirt" depends on the domain of discourse. The knife emerging from your dishwasher is clean but not by surgical standards. What counts as silence in a classroom does not count as silence in a recording studio.

Restricted quantification is common. Silent movies have no sounds from the recorded events but do have accompanying music.

"Silence" is an absolute term like "flat" and "certain." There is a tendency to privilege the strictest standard—to let the quantifiers be "wide open." One is then apt to conclude that there is very little silence.

The impossibility of silence is a popular thesis in literary philosophy. Maurice Blanchot writes, "Silence is impossible. That is why we desire it" (1986, 11). Georges Bataille characterizes "silence" as a "slipping" word because it is "the abolition of the sound which the word is; among all words it is the most perverse, or the most poetic: it is the token of its own death" (1988, 16).

The impossibility of silence is most methodically championed by philosophical commentators on music, especially since John Cage's 4′33″ (Davies 2003, chap. 1). The first performance was at the Maverick Concert Hall in 1952. The pianist opened and closed the piano at the end of each movement but did nothing else. The performance lasted four minutes and thirty-three seconds. Most of the audience interpreted the performance as a period of silence—or perhaps three periods to correspond to the three movements in Cage's

program notes. Of course, there was the usual coughing and shuf-
fling plus noises that wafted in from outside. But the audience did
not count these sounds as part of the performance just as they do not
count as part of the performance in the case of conventional music.
According to Cage, the original audience

> missed the point. There's no such thing as silence. What they
> thought was silence, because they didn't know how to listen, was
> full of accidental sounds. You could hear the wind stirring outside
> during the first movement. During the second, raindrops began pat-
> tering the roof, and during the third the people themselves made all
> kinds of interesting sounds as they talked or walked out. (quoted in
> Kostelanetz 1988, 65)

Cage reports that 4′33″ was inspired by a trip to the soundproof
anechoic chamber at Harvard University. Although he expected
silence, he heard a high noise and low noise. The engineer explained
that the high noise was the sound of his nervous system in operation,
and the low noise was the blood in circulation.

More precisely, the high noise is tinnitus—"ringing in your ears."
Prolonged exposure to loud noise (greater than ninety decibels)
accelerates the degradation of hearing associated with aging. Students
are rightly alarmed by how much hearing damage is revealed by their
visit to an anechoic chamber.

Just as the skeptic lowers the standards of doubt to show that cer-
tainty is impossible, Cage lowers the standards of sound to show that
silence is impossible. He does this quantitatively by letting very faint
sounds count as sounds. He does this qualitatively by letting a wide
variety of phenomena count as sound (even the auditory sensations
that are not due to sound waves).

"Silence" echoes the semantic unclarities of "sound." Is sound
the vibration of an object? Or does it consist of the waves produced
by the object? Or is it the auditory sensation produced by those
waves?

The skeptic is notoriously difficult to refute. Cage is more vulnerable. The sounds he mentions are observer dependent. An anechoic chamber is silent when unoccupied.

But can silence be heard? Yes, because we can overcome observer effects. A microphone can be installed in the chamber, and we can listen from outside. The sounds we make in the listening booth are not in the empty anechoic chamber.

Can silence be *directly* heard? Yes, engineers could drill an ear-sized hole into the anechoic chamber so that only Cage's pinna fits. Cage's head and torso would still be outside the chamber.

In any case, tinnitus and the sound of circulating blood are logically contingent aspects of human observers. There could be less intrusive observers.

Mark Nyman summarizes Cage's project:

It is a well-known fact that the silences of 4′33″ were not, after all, silences, since silence is a state which it is physically impossible to achieve. . . . 4′33″ is a demonstration of the non-existence of silence, of the permanent presence of sounds around us, of the fact that they are worthy of attention, and that for Cage environmental sounds and noises are more useful aesthetically than the sounds produced by the world's musical cultures. 4′33″ is not a negation of music but an affirmation of its omnipresence. (1974, 22)

4′33″ fails to prove any of these theses. True, if we set standards high, silence is hard to achieve—as is flatness, straightness, and cleanliness. But there is no reason to privilege high standards. A high standard is appropriate for special purposes (surveying, pharmaceutical production, etc.). But normally a high standard conflicts with our master goal of being informative. Engineers raise standards only when new technology makes it feasible to meet them.

When Cage sets a high standard for silence, we are naturally inclined to set a high standard for other absolute terms. Cage says that sound is omnipresent. Given unrestricted quantification, "omnipresent" means *everywhere* in the universe. The vast majority of the universe is empty. And empty space is silent. As Cage grew older, he expressed optimism about the future of music. He took solace in the conviction that there will always be sound. But given high standards, "always" means *every time*. The laws of thermodynamics doom the universe to heat death. Everything, everywhere, will end in silence.

References

Abbott, Edwin. 1884. *Flatland: A romance of many dimensions*. London: Seely & Co.

Airy, George B. 1970. On the total solar eclipse of 1851, July 28. In *Astronomy*, vol. 1. The Royal Institution Library of Science. Barking, Essex: Elsevier Publishing (speech originally presented on May 2, 1851).

Anderson, C. E., and Hamelin, Joseph P. 1990. *To fly and fight: Memoirs of a triple ace*. New York: St. Martin's.

Antis, S. M., and Loizos, C. M. 1967. Cross-modal judgments of small holes. *American Journal of Psychology* 80/1: 51–58.

Applewhite, Ashton, Evans, William R., and Frothingham, Andrew. 2003. *And I quote*. New York: St. Martin's.

Armstrong, David. 1961. *Perception and the physical world*. London: Routledge & Kegan Paul.

———. 1962. *Bodily sensations*. London: Routledge & Kegan Paul.

———. 1968a. *A materialist theory of mind*. London: Routledge & Kegan Paul.

———. 1968b. The headless woman illusion and the defence of materialism. *Analysis* 29/2: 48–49.

Balashov, Yuri. 1999. Zero-value physical quantities. *Synthese* 119: 253–86.

Bataille, Georges. 1988. *Inner experience*, trans. Leslie Ann Boldt. Albany: State University of New York Press (originally published in *L'experience interieure*, Paris: Gallimard, 1954).

Baxandall, Michael. 1995. *Shadows and enlightenment*. New Haven, Conn.: Yale University Press.

Bean, Homer. 1938. The blind have "optical illusions." *Journal of Experimental Psychology* 22: 283–89.

Beck, Jacob. 1971. Surface lightness and cues for illumination. *American Journal of Psychology* 84/1: 1–11.

Bergstrom, S. 1994. Color constancy: Arguments for a vector model for the perception of illumination, color, and three-dimensional form. In *Lightness, brightness, and transparency*, ed. A. Gilchrist, 257–86. Hillsdale, N.J.: Erlbaum.

Berkeley, George. 1901. *The works of George Berkeley*. Oxford: Clarendon Press.

Berlin, B., and Kay, P. 1991. *Basic color terms: Their universality and evolution*. Berkeley: University of California Press.

Bevis, J. 1769. Observations of the last transit of Venus, and of the eclipse of the Sun the next day, made at the house of Joshua Kirby, Esq. at Kew. *Philosophical Transactions* lix: 189–91.

Blanchot, Maurice. 1986. *The writing of the disaster*, trans. Anne Smock. Lincoln: University of Nebraska Press (originally published as *L'ecritirure du desastre*, Paris: Gallimard, 1980).

Boorse, Christopher. 1994. Two only as/as only fallacies. Unpublished manuscript.

Boyer, Carl. 1959. *The rainbow: From myth to mathematics*. New York: Thomas Yoseloff.

Braasch, Gary. 1990. *Photographing the patterns of nature*. New York: Amphoto.

Brain, R. 1965. The neurological approach. In *Perception and the physical world*, ed. R. J. Hirst. New York: Macmillan.

Brettel H., Viénot, F., and Mollon, J. D. 1997. Computerized simulation of color appearance for dichromats. *Journal of the Optical Society of America* 14: 2647–55.

Broackes, Justin. 2007. Black and white and the inverted spectrum. *Philosophical Quarterly* 57: 161–75.

Burgess, Colin, Doolan, Kate, and Vis, Bert. 2003. *Fallen astronaut heroes who died reaching for the moon*. Lincoln: University of Nebraska Press.

Burke, Edmund. 1757. *The sublime and beautiful*. London: J. Dogsley.

Burke, Michael B. 1992. Copper statues and pieces of copper: A challenge to the standard account. *Analysis* 52: 12–17.

Butler, Samuel. 1917. *The note-books of Samuel Butler*, ed. Henry Festing Jones. New York: E. P. Dutton.

Byhill, A. Terry, Baldwin, David G., and Venkateswaran, Jayendran. 2005. Predicting a baseball's path. *American Scientist* 93: 218–225.

Cajori, Florian. 1898. *A history of physics in its elementary branches, including the evolution of physical laboratories*. New York: Macmillan.

Casati, Roberto. 2003. *The shadow club*, trans. Abigail Asher. New York: Knopf.

Casati, Roberto, and Varzi, Achille. 1994. *Holes and other superficialities.* Cambridge, Mass.: MIT Press.

Chisholm, Roderick. 1957. *Perceiving: A philosophical study.* Ithaca, N.Y.: Cornell University Press.

Clark, Austen. 2000. *A theory of sentience.* Oxford: Oxford University Press.

Dalton, John. 1798. Extraordinary facts relating to the vision of colours; with observations (read in October 1794). *Memoirs of the Literary and Philosophical Society of Manchester* 5: 28–45.

Dante. 1957. *Divine comedy,* trans. Henry Francis Cary. Oxford: Oxford University Press (originally published 1321).

Davidenko, Nicolas. 2007. Silhouetted face profiles: A new methodology for face perception research. *Journal of Vision* 7/4: 1–17.

Davies, Paul. 2003. *Themes in the philosophy of music.* New York: Oxford University Press.

De Poncins, Gontran, in collaboration with Lewis Galantiere. 1988. *Kabloona.* New York: Carroll & Graff (originally published 1941).

Dorman, M., Raphael, L., and Liberman, A. 1979. Some experiments on the sound of silence in phonetic perception. *Journal of the Acoustical Society of America* 65: 1518–32.

Dretske, Fred. 1969. *Seeing and knowing.* Chicago: University of Chicago Press.

Falconer, Kenneth. 1990. *Fractal geometry.* New York: John Wiley & Sons.

Fechner, G. T. 1838. Ueber eine Scheibe zur Erzeugung Subjectiver Farben. *Poggendorfs Annalen der Physik und Chemie* 45/121: 227–32.

Firth, Roderick. 1966. The men themselves; or the role of causation in our concept of seeing. In *Intentionality, minds, and perception,* 357–82. Detroit, Mich.: Wayne State University Press.

Forrest, Peter. 1984. Is motion change of location? *Analysis* 84: 177–78.

Frankfurt, Harry. 1969. Alternate possibilities and moral responsibility. *Journal of Philosophy* 66: 829–39.

Gale, Richard M. 1976. Negation and non-being. *American Philosophical Quarterly,* Monograph 10. London: William Clowes & Sons.

Gibbard, Allan. 1975. Contingent identity. *Journal of Philosophical Logic* 4: 187–221.

Gibson, J. J. 1979. *The ecological approach to visual perception.* Boston: Houghton Mifflin.

Gibson, J. J., and Waddell, D. 1952. Homogenous retinal stimulation and visual perception. *American Journal of Psychology* 62: 63–270.

Gibson, J. J, and Walk, R. D. 1960. The visual cliff. *Scientific American* 202: 64–71.

Gibson, James. 1976. Three kinds of distance that can be seen, or how Bishop Berkeley went wrong. In *Studies in perception: Festschrift for Fabio Metelli,* ed. G. D'Arcais. Milan: Martelli-Giunti.

Gilchrist, Alan. 2006. *Seeing black and white*. New York: Oxford University Press.

Giralt, N., and Bloom, P. 2000. How special are objects? Children's reasoning about objects, parts, and holes. *Psychological Science* 11: 503–7.

Goethe, J. W. 1970. *Theory of colors*, trans. C. L. Eastlake. Cambridge, Mass.: MIT Press (originally published 1840).

Goldman, Alvin. 1976. Discrimination and perceptual knowledge. *Journal of Philosophy* 73/20: 771–91.

——. 1977. Perceptual objects. *Synthese* 35: 257–84.

Gombrich, E. H. 1995. *Shadows: The depiction of cast shadows in Western art*. London: National Gallery Publications.

Goodman, Nelson. 1978. Review of *Remarks on colour*. *Journal of Philosophy* 75: 503–4.

Gordon, Jan E., and Cooper, Colin. 1975. Improving one's touch. *Nature* 256: 203–4.

Graham, C. H., and Hsia, Y. 1958. Color defect and color theory. *Science* 127/3300: 675–82.

Grandin, Temple, and Johnson, Catherine. 2005. *Animals in translation: Using the mysteries of autism to decode animal behavior*. New York: Scribner.

Gray, Jeremy. 1993. Mobius's geometrical mechanics. In *Mobius and his band*, 79–103. Oxford: Oxford University Press.

Grice, H. P. 1961. The causal theory of perception. *Proceedings of the Aristotelian Society* 35(suppl): 121–68.

——. 1975. Logic and conversation. In *The logic of grammar*, ed. Donald Davidson and Gilbert Harman, 64–75. Encino, Calif.: Dickenson.

Grusser, O. J., and Hagner, M. 1990. On the history of deformation phosphenes and the idea of internal light generated in the eye for the purpose of vision. *Documenta Opthalmologica* 74: 57–85.

Hacking, Ian. 1983. *Representing and intervening*. Cambridge: Cambridge University Press.

Hall, Richard J. 1979. Seeing perfectly dark things and the causal conditions of seeing. *Theoria* 3: 127–34.

Hall, Roland. 1963. Excluders. In *Philosophy and ordinary language*, ed. Charles E. Caton, 66–73. Urbana: University of Illinois Press.

Hardin, C. L. 1990. Color and illusion. In *Mind and cognition: A reader*, ed. William G. Lycan, 555–67. Oxford: Blackwell.

Harrison, Edward R. 1987. *Darkness at night: A riddle of the universe*. Cambridge, Mass.: Harvard University Press.

Hastings, J. W., and Mitchell, George. 1971. Endosymbiotic bioluminescent bacteria from the light organ of pony fish. *Biological Bulletin* 141: 261–68.

Hayward, W. G. 1998. Effects of outline shape in object recognition. *Journal of Experimental Psychology: Human Perception and Performance* 24: 427–40.

Hegel, Georg. 1977. *Phenomenology of spirit*, trans. A. V. Miller. Oxford: Clarendon Press (originally published 1807).

——. 1989. *Hegel's science of logic*, trans. A. V. Miller. Atlantic Highlands, NJ : Humanities Press International (originally published 1812).

Helmholtz, Hermann von. 1962. *Treatise on physiological optics*, 2nd ed., trans. J. P. C. Southall. New York: Dover (originally published 1866).

Hering, E. 1964. *Outlines of a theory of the light sense*, trans. L. M. Hurvich and D. Jameson. Cambridge, Mass.: Harvard University Press (originally published 1874).

Hewitt, Paul. 1993. *Conceptual physics lab manual*. New York: HarperCollins.

Hinde, Robert A. 1954. Factors governing the changes in strength of a partially inborn response as shown by the mobbing behaviour of the chaffinch (*Fringilla coelebs*). I. The nature of the response and an examination of its course. *Proceedings of the Royal Society of London* (Series B) 142: 306–21.

Hooke, Robert. 1894. *Micrographia*. Edinburgh: Alembic Club (originally published 1665).

Hughes, H. C., et al. 2001. Responses of human auditory association cortex to the omission of an expected acoustic event. *Neuroimage* 13: 1073–89.

Humphrey, W. J. 1964. *Physics of the air*. New York: Dover.

Hurvich, Leo M. 1981. *Color vision*. Sunderland, Mass.: Sinauer.

Hurvich, Leo M., and Jameson, Dorothea. 1966. *The perception of brightness and darkness*. Boston: Allyn & Bacon.

Hyman, John. 1993. Vision, causation, and occlusion. *Philosophical Quarterly* 43: 210–14.

Jackson, Frank. 1977. *Perception—A representative theory*. Cambridge: Cambridge University Press.

——. 1982. Epiphenomenal qualia. *Philosophical Quarterly* 32: 127–36.

——. 1986. What Mary didn't know. *Journal of Philosophy* 83: 291–95.

Johansson, G. 1973. Visual perception of biological motion and a model for its analysis. *Perception and Psychophysics* 14: 201–11.

Jolly, A. 1988. The evolution of purpose. In *Machiavellian intelligence*, ed. R. Byrne and A. Whiten. Oxford: Oxford University Press.

Kalmus, H. 1965. *Diagnosis and genetics of defective colour vision*. New York: Pergamon Press.

Karmo, Toomas. 1977. Disturbances. *Analysis* 37: 147–48.

Katz, David. 1989. *The world of touch*, trans. Lester E. Krueger. Hillsdale, N.J.: Erlbaum.

Keeley, Brian L. 1999. Fixing content and function in neurobiological systems: The neuroethology of electroreception. *Biology and Philosophy* 14: 395–430.

Kersten, D., Mamassian, P., and Knill, D. 1997. Moving cast shadows induce apparent motion in depth. *Perception* 26: 171–92.

Kingdom, Frederick A., Beauce, Catherine, and Hunter, Lyndsay. 2004. Colour vision brings clarity to shadows. *Perception* 33: 907–14.

Kostelanetz, Richard. 1988. *Conversing with Cage*. New York: Limelight.

Kukso, Boris. 2006. The reality of absences. *Australasian Journal of Philosophy* 84/1: 21–37.

Land, E. H. 1959. Experiments in color vision. *Scientific American* 200/5: 84–99.

———. 1977. The retinex theory of color vision. *Scientific American* 237/6: 108–28.

Land, Michael F., and Nilsson, Dan-Eric. 2002. *Animal eyes*. Oxford: Clarendon Press.

Lauxtermann, P. F. H. 1990. Hegel and Schopenhauer as partisans of Goethe's theory of color. *History of Ideas* 51: 599–624.

Le Catt, Bruce. 1982. Censored vision. *Australasian Journal of Philosophy* 60: 158–62.

Lederman, S. J. 1982. The perception of texture by touch. In *Tactual perception: A sourcebook*, ed. W. Schiff and E. Foulke, 130–67. New York: Cambridge University Press.

Le Grand, Yves. 1967. *Form and space vision*. Bloomington: Indiana University Press.

Leibniz, Gottfried. 1981. *New essays on human understanding*, trans. Peter Remnant and Jonathan Bennett. Cambridge: Cambridge University Press (originally published 1765).

Lewis, David. 1979. Scorekeeping in a language game. *Journal of Philosophical Logic* 8: 339–59.

———. 1986. Veridical hallucination and prosthetic vision. *Philosophical Papers* 2, vol. 2: 273–86. New York: Oxford University Press (originally published in *Australasian Journal of Philosophy* 58: 239–49, 1980).

———. 2004. Void and object. In *Causation and conditionals*, ed. John Collins, Ned Hall, and L. A. Paul. Cambridge, Mass.: MIT Press.

Lewis, David, and Lewis, Stephanie R. 1970. Holes. *Australasian Journal of Philosophy* 48: 206–12.

Lin, Shih-Schon, Yemelyanov, K. M., Pugh, E. N., Jr., and Engheta, N. 2006. Separation and contrast enhancement of overlapping cast shadow components using polarization. *Optics Express* 14: 7099–108.

Locke, John. 1690. *An essay concerning human understanding*. New York: Dover.

Luce, A. A. 1949. *The life of George Berkeley, bishop of Cloyne*. New York: Thomas Nelson & Sons.

Lynch, David K., and Livingston, William. 2001. *Color and light in nature*, 2nd ed. Cambridge: Cambridge University Press.

Mach, Ernst. 1897. *Contributions to the analysis of sensations*, trans. Cora May Williams. Chicago: Open Court Publishing Company.

——. 1953. *The principles of physical optics*, trans. John S. Anderson and A. F. A. Young. New York: Dover (original work published 1926).

——. 1986. *Principles of the theory of heat*, trans. Philip E. B. Jourdain. Dordrecht: D. Reidel (original work published 1886).

Magee, Bryan, and Milligan, Martin. 1995. *On blindness*. Oxford: Oxford University Press.

Mallock, A. 1914. Fog signals—Areas of silence and greatest range of sound. *Proceedings of the Royal Society of London* (Series A) 91/623: 71–75.

Marr, David. 1982. *Vision*. San Francisco: W. H. Freeman.

Martin, C. B. 1996. How it is: Entities, absences, and voids. *Australasian Journal of Philosophy* 74/1: 57–65.

Martin, Michael. 1992. Sight and touch. In *The contents of experience*, ed. Tim Crane, 196–215. Cambridge: Cambridge University Press.

Maxwell, Grover. 1962. The ontological status of theoretical entities. *Minnesota Studies in the Philosophy of Science* 3: 3–27.

Maxwell, James Clerk. 1855. Experiment on colour, as perceived by the eye, with remarks on colour-blindness. *Transactions of the Royal Society of Edinburgh* 21: 275–98.

McLaughlin, Brian. 1984. Perception, causation, and supervenience. *Midwest Studies in Philosophy* 9: 569–92.

——. 1996. Lewis on what distinguishes perception from hallucination. In *Perception*, ed. Kathleen Akins. New York: Oxford University Press.

Michelangelo. 1963. *Complete poems and selected letters of Michelangelo*, trans. Creighton Gilber and ed. Robert N. Linscott. New York: Random House (originally published 1623).

Mill, John Stuart. 1941. *A system of logic*. London: Longmans, Green and Co. (originally published 1904).

——. 1973. Bailey on Berkeley's theory of vision. In *Dissertations and Discussions*, vol. 2. New York: Haskell House.

Molnar, George. 2000. Truthmakers for negative truths. *Australasian Journal of Philosophy* 78/1: 72–86.

Moore, C., and P. Cavanagh. 1998. Recovery of 3D volume from 2-tone images of Novel objects. *Cognition* 67: 45–71.

Moore, G. E. 1939. A proof of the external world. *Proceedings of the British Academy* 25: 273–300.

——. 1962. *The commonplace book, 1919–1953*. London: Allen & Unwin.

Morgan, M. J. 1977. *Molyneux's question: Vision, touch and the philosophy of perception.* Cambridge: Cambridge University Press.

Nassau, Kurt. 2001. *The physics and chemistry of color: The fifteen causes of color,* 2nd ed. New York: John Wiley & Sons.

Nelson, Ralph, and Kolb, Helga. 2004. ON and OFF pathways in the vertebrate retina and visual system. In *the Visual Neurosciences,* vol. 1, ed. Leo M. Chalupa and John S. Werner, 260–78. Cambridge, Mass.: MIT Press.

Nevo, E., Heth, G., and Pratt, H. 1991. Seismic communication in a blind subterranean mammal: A major somatosensory mechanism in adaptive evolution underground. *Proceedings of the National Academy of Sciences of the U. S. A.* 88/4: 1256–60.

Newton, Isaac. 1952. *Opticks.* New York: Dover (originally published 1704).

Noe, Alva. 2004. *Action in perception.* Cambridge, Mass.: MIT Press.

Norby, Knut. 1990. Vision in a complete achromat: A personal account. In *Night vision: Basic, clinical, and applied aspects,* ed. R. Hess, F. L. T. Sharper, and K. Nordby, 290–315. Cambridge: Cambridge University Press.

Nori, Franco, Sholtz, Paul, and Bretz, Michael. 1997. Booming sands. *Scientific American* 277/3: 84–89.

Norman, J. F., Dawson, T. E., and Raines, S. R. 2000. The perception and recognition of natural object shape from deforming and static shadows. *Perception* 29/2: 135–48.

Nudds, Matthew. 2001. Experiencing the production of sounds. *European Journal of Philosophy* 9: 210–99.

Nyman, Michael. 1974. *Experimental music: Cage and beyond.* New York: Schirmer Press.

O'Callaghan, Casey. 2007. *Sounds: A philosophical theory.* New York: Oxford University Press.

O'Shaughnessy, Brian. 1989. The sense of touch. *Australasian Journal of Philosophy* 67/1: 37–58.

Parsons, L. M. 1995. Inability to reason about an object's orientation using an axis and angle of rotation. *Journal of Experimental Psychology: Human Perception and Performance* 21/6: 1259–77.

Pascal, Blaise. 2003. *Pensees,* trans. W. F. Trotter. New York: Dover (originally published 1670).

Pasnau, Robert. 1999. What is sound? *Philosophical Quarterly* 49: 309–24.

Price, H. H. 1933. *Perception.* New York: Robert M. McBride and Co.

Price, Theodore J., O'Toole, Alice J., and Dambach, Kimberly C. 1998. A moving shadow diminishes the Pulfrich phenomenon. *Perception* 27: 591–93.

Quine, W. V. 1969. Natural kinds. In his *Ontological relativity and other essays,* 114–38. New York: Columbia University Press.

Ramachandran, V. S. 1990. Perceiving shape from shading. In *The perceptual world: Readings from "Scientific American" magazine*, ed. I. Rock, 127–38. New York: W. H. Freeman.

Rand Corporation. 2001. *A million random digits with 100,000 normal deviates*. Santa Monica, Calif.: RAND (originally published 1955).

Ratliff, Floyd. 1965. *Mach bands: Quantitative studies on neural networks in the retina*. San Francisco: Holden-Day.

Reid, Thomas. 1969. *Essays on the intellectual powers of man*. Cambridge, Mass.: MIT Press (originally published 1814–15).

Reinhardt, Adolf. 1970. *Ad Reinhardt: Black paintings, 1951–1967*. New York: Marlborough Gallery.

Rensink, Ronald A., and Cavanagh, Patrick. 2004. The influence of cast shadows on visual search. *Perception* 33: 1339–58.

Robinson, John Mansley. 1968. *An introduction to early Greek philosophy*. Boston: Houghton Mifflin.

Rock, Irvin. 1975. *An introduction to perception*. London: Macmillan.

———. 1966. *The nature of perceptual adaptation*. New York: Basic Books.

Rock, I., and Victor, J. 1964. Vision and touch: An experimentally created conflict between the two senses. *Science* 143: 594–96.

Rolf, N., and Palmer, S. E. 2001. Of holes and wholes: The perception of surrounded regions. *Perception* 30: 1213–26.

Rothman, Milton A. 1960. Things that go faster than light. *Scientific American* 203/1: 142–52.

Rundle, Bede. 1972. *Perception, sensation, and verification*. Oxford: Clarendon Press.

Ruskin, John. 1906. *Modern painters*. Vol. 1. London: George Allen.

Russell, Bertrand. 1921. *The analysis of mind*. London: Unwin.

———. 1937. *The principles of mathematics*, 2nd ed. London: Allen & Unwin.

Sachs, Oliver. 1995. The case of the colorblind painter. In his *An anthropologist on Mars*, 3–41. New York: Random House.

———. 1997. The island of the colorblind. In his *The island of the colorblind*, 28–57. New York: Alfred A. Knopf.

Sällström, P. (ed). 1979. *Goethes färglära*, trans. Bo Dahlin. Järna: Kosmos förlag.

Salmon, Wesley. 1984. *Scientific explanation and the causal structure of the world*. Princeton, N.J.: Princeton University Press.

Sanford, David. 1967. Volume and solidity. *Australasian Journal of Philosophy* 45: 329–40.

———. 1976. The primary objects of perception. *Mind* 85: 189–208.

Sartre, Jean Paul. 1969. *Being and nothingness*, trans. H. E. Barnes. New York: Washington Square Press.

Sayan, Erdinç. 1996. A mereological look at motion. *Philosophical Studies* 84/1: 75–89.

Schaefer, Bradley E. 2001. The transit of Venus and the notorious black drop effect. *Journal for the History of Astronomy* 32 (pt. 4)/109: 325–36.

Schöne, Hermann. 1984. *Spatial orientation*, trans. Camilla Strausfeld. Princeton, N.J.: Princeton University Press.

Schwartz, Robert. 1994. *Vision: Some Berkeleian themes*. Cambridge: Blackwell.

Schwayder, D. S. 1961. The varieties and the objects of visual phenomena. *Mind* 70/279: 307–30.

Sekuler, R., Sekuler, A., and Lau, B. R. 1997. Sound alters visual motion perception. *Nature* 385: 308.

Sepper, Dennis L. 1988. *Goethe contra Newton*. Cambridge: Cambridge University Press.

Settles, G. S. 2001. *Schlieren and shadowgraph techniques: Visualizing phenomena in transparent media*. Berlin: Springer-Verlag.

Shapley, Robert, and Man-Kit Lam, Dominic. 1993. *Contrast sensitivity*. Cambridge, Mass.: MIT Press.

Shiga, David. 2004. Where was the black drop? *Sky and Telescope*, July 12.

Siegel, Susanna. 2006. How does visual phenomenology constrain object-seeing? *Australasian Journal of Philosophy* 84/3: 429–41.

Sinnott-Armstrong, Walter, and Sparrow, David. 2002. A light theory of color. *Philosophical Studies* 110/3: 267–84.

Slote, Michael. 1979. Causality and the concept of a "thing." *Midwest Studies in Philosophy* 4: 387–400.

Smart, J. J. C. 1963. *Philosophy and scientific realism*. London: Routledge.

Smith, A. D. 1990. Of primary and secondary qualities. *Philosophical Review* 100: 221–54.

Sober, Elliott. 1985. A plea for pseudo-processes. *Pacific Philosophical Quarterly* 66: 303–9.

Sorensen, Roy. 1999. Blanks: Signs of omission. *American Philosophical Quarterly* 36/4: 309–21.

Spinoza, Baruch. 1951. *A theologico-political treatis and a political treatise*, trans. R. H. M. Elwes. New York: Dover (originally published 1677).

Stewart, Ian. 1991. What in heaven is a digital sundial? *Scientific American* 265/2: 104–6.

Stratton, George. 1896. Some preliminary experiments on vision without inversion of the retinal image. *Psychological Review* 3: 611–17.

Strawson, Peter. 1959. *Individuals*. London: Methuen.

Stroll, Avrum. 1988. *Surfaces*. Minneapolis: University of Minnesota Press.

Taylor, James. 1962. *The behavioral basis of perception*. New Haven, Conn.: Yale University Press.

Taylor, Richard. 1952. Negative things. *Journal of Philosophy* 19/13: 433–49.

Tinbergen, Niko. 1951. *The study of instinct*. Oxford: Clarendon Press.

Todd, Mabel Loomis. 1900. *Total eclipses of the sun*, rev. ed. Boston: Little, Brown.

Todes, Samuel. 1975. Shadows in knowledge. *Selected Studies in Phenomenology and Existential Philosophy* 5: 95–113.

Todes, Samuel, and Daniels, Charles B. 1975. Beyond the doubt of a shadow: A phenomenological and linguistic analysis of shadows. *Selected Studies in Phenomenology and Existential Philosophy* 5:203–16.

Tooley, Michael. 1988. In defense of the existence of states of motion. *Philosophical Topics* 16/1: 225–53.

Treisman, A., and Souther, J. 1985. Search asymmetry: A diagnostic for preattentive processing of separable features. *Journal of Experimental Psychology: General* 114: 285–310.

Tye, M. 1982. A causal analysis of seeing. *Philosophy and Phenomenological Research* 42: 311–25.

———. 2002. *Consciousness, color, and content*. Cambridge, Mass.: MIT Press.

Unger, Peter. 1975. *Ignorance: A case for scepticism*. Oxford: Clarendon Press.

Urmson, J. O. 1968. The objects of the five senses. *Proceedings of the British Academy* 54: 117–31.

Valentine, C. W. 1930. The innate bases of fear. *Journal of Genetic Psychology* 37: 394–419.

Van Fraassen, Bas. 1989. *Laws and symmetry*. Oxford: Clarendon Press.

Vernon, Jack A. 1963. *Inside the black room*. New York: Clarkson N. Potter.

Viénot, Françoise, Brettel, Hans, and Mollon, John D. 1999. Digital video colourmaps for checking the legibility of displays by dichromats. *Color Research and Application* 24: 243–52.

Vision, Gerald. 1997. *Problems with vision*. Oxford: Oxford University Press.

Wallach, H., and O'Connell, D. N. 1953. The kinetic depth effect. *Journal of Experimental Psychology* 45: 205–17.

Warnock, G. J. 1983. *Berkeley*. Notre Dame, Ind.: University of Notre Dame (originally published 1953).

Warrington, E. K. 1982. Neuropsychological studies of object recognition. *Philosophical Transactions of the Royal Society of London* (Series B) 298: 15–33.

Weinberg, F. J. 1963. *Optics of flames: Including methods for the study of refractive index fields in combustion and aerodynamics*. London: Butterworths.

Westphal, Jonathan. 1991. *Colour: Some philosophical problems from Wittgenstein*, 2nd ed. Aristotelian Society Series, vol. 7. Oxford: Basil Blackwell.

Wittgenstein, Ludwig. 1977. *Remarks on color*, ed. G. E. M. Anscombe. Berkeley: University of California Press (originally published 1951).

Wolfe, Jeremy M. 1979. The computer paper illusion. *Perception* 8/3: 347–48.

———. 2001. Asymmetries in visual search. *Perception and Psychophysics* 63/3: 381–89.

Zimmerman, Dean. 1998. Temporal parts and supervenient causation: The incompatibility of two Humean doctrines. *Australasian Journal of Philosophy* 76: 265–88.

Index

subjectivity, 16
sundial, 76, 79–80, 132, 197–98
supervenience, 192
Stalin, Joseph, 154
Stratton, George, 258
Strawson, Peter, 125, 279
stroboscope, 242–43
Stroll, Avrum, 44–47
subjective color, 162–63
sunspots, 55–56, 208–9
surface
    absorption, 44–48
    abstract, 45, 68–69, 73
    backs, 44–54
    color, 205, 212
    immaterial, 45, 68–69
    spinning, 47
synthesia, 273

tactile field, 107–8
tactile illusion, 123–24
Taylor, Richard, 247–48
temperature, 118, 286
temporally contrastive seeing, 251–53
texture, 10
Thales, 11
Theon of Alexandria, 157
Theophrastus, 272
thermal sensing, 117–18
thermodynamics, 290
Thomason, Richmond, 53
Thorstensen, John, 64
Thurber, James, 4–5, 245
time travel, 192
Tinbergen, Niko, 34–35
tinnitus, 288
Todd, Mabel Loomis, 80, 149
Todes, Samuel, 30, 98
Tooley, Michael 87–88
touch, 12, 105–35, 125–35
translucency, 26, 47–48, 51–52
transparency, 4–5, 203, 240
trigonometry, 11
tunnel, 58
twilight, 79
twilight fallacy, 172

twinkling, 148–49, 152
twins, 59
Tye, Michael, 17, 22, 199

umbra, 72, 208–9
Unger, Peter, 45
Uranus, 96
Urmson, J. O., 274

vacuums, 104, 118, 190–91
van Fraassen, Bas, 53
Varzi, Achille, 88–92, 127–29, 141, 189, 193–94
Venus, 46–47, 64, 150–51
Vision, Gerald, 6, 22
visual capture, 106
visual differentiation, 54–55, 63
visual gap, 70–71
visual persistence, 242–43, 265–66
visual phenomenology, 63
visual purple, 216
volcanoes, 96, 189
von Guericke, Otto, 145, 155
von Helmholtz, Hermann, 161–62, 202

Warnock, Geoffrey, 125, 267
wave theory of light, 172
waves, 13, 78, 282–85
Weinberg, F. J., 147–48
Westphal, Jonathan, 51–52, 159, 202–19
Wheatestone, Charles, 111
white, 29–30, 51–52, 203–5
white noise, 270–71
Wittgenstein, Ludwig, 29–30, 51–52, 161, 202–5

X-rays, 56

Yale shadow puzzle, 52–54, 98–99
Yarkovsky, Ivan, 198

Zeno, 87
zero-value determinates, 286
Zimmerman, Dean, 76